Unstuck in Time

A Memoir and Mystery on
Loss and Love

Also by
Nancy Avery Dafoe

Naimah and Ajmal on Newton's Mountain
Murder on Ponte Vecchio
Both End in Speculation
You Enter a Room
An Iceberg in Paradise: A Passage Through Alzheimer's
The House Was Quiet, But the Mind Was Anxious
Innermost Sea
Poets Diving in the Night
The Misdirection of Education Policy
Writing Creatively
Breaking Open the Box

Unstuck in Time

A Memoir and Mystery on
Loss and Love

Nancy Avery Dafoe

Pen Women Press

Cover design and illustration: Matt Cincotta

Book Editor Coordinator: Lucy Arnold

Library of Congress Cataloging-in-Publication Data
LCCN 2021909158 (print)

ISBN 978-1-950251-04-9 (print)
ISBN 978-1-950251-05-6 (electronic)

First edition
Printed in the United States of America

Published by
National League of American Pen Women, Inc.
PEN WOMEN PRESS

Founded in 1897,
National League of American Pen Women, Inc.
is a nonprofit dedicated to promoting the arts.
1300 17th Street NW
Washington, D.C. 20036-1973
www.nlapw.org

Dedication

This book is dedicated to Blaise Martin Dafoe
(1987-2019)

Acknowledgments

My son Blaise Martin is the inspiration and reason behind the writing of this memoir. I am indebted to my husband Daniel and daughters Colette and Nicole for their support and loving encouragement in the creation of this nearly impossible-to-write work. Colette and Nicole also allowed me to include in my book the speeches they gave at Blaise's funeral.

I am grateful to my writer friends and family who read early versions of my manuscript and made comments: my sister Phyllis Ann Avery, sister-in-law Marilyn Avery, and dear friends Cindy Hlywa, Karen Hempson, Judith McGinn, Bobbie Dumas Panek, and Mary Gardner. I am indebted to Blaise's many friends who shared stories with me and to Ben Connery for his words delivered at Blaise's funeral which appear in this book.

I would like to acknowledge my debt to authors Janine DeBaise, Rachel Dickinson, Judith McGinn, and Bobbie Dumas Panek who read my manuscript and provided endorsements. Acknowledgement and a most heartfelt thank you is extended to psychologist Ralph Hess who wrote the Foreword.

A most appreciative thank you is extended to Lucy Arnold and Pen Women Press; and to Evelyn B. Wofford, NLAPW President.

Lastly, I would like to deeply thank the Onondaga County medical examiner for her extraordinary kindness and patience in providing me the comprehensive knowledge that had been a secret all the years of my son's life.

Poetry Acknowledgments

All of the poems in this book are the original work of the author. A few first appeared in other publications: "Returning to That Mineral State" in *An Iceberg in Paradise: A Passage through Alzheimer's* (SUNY Press, 2015).

"Hope for Water Bears," first appeared in the author's book of poetry *Innermost Sea* (FLP, 2018).

"Sometimes Loss Weighs Lightly," was first published in *Innermost Sea* (FLP, 2018).

"After Lightning, Before Thunder," was published in *The Cortland Standard* (December 2020).

A Note About the Title

Inspiration for the title of this book, *Unstuck in Time*, came from one of Blaise's dearest friends, Alena Turturro, who alluded to Kurk Vonnegut's novel *Slaughter House-Five* in a Facebook posting she wrote about Blaise.

Praise for *Unstuck in Time*

"This is a thorough book on grief. *Unstuck in Time* evokes and alludes to a myriad of emotions, ripples, memory, poets, authors, quotes, sadness deeper than the cosmos, truer than sound. *Unstuck in Time* is so inclusive and honest and joyful. Joyful? That Dafoe can express such love for her son, that she can share her heart with so many, that she cares to bare her grief to help others. It is a work of grace."

Bobbie Dumas Panek,
Author of the memoir *Just Another Day*

"In this courageous meditation on grief, a mother sifts through broken memories in a fierce desire to understand the sudden death of her 32-year-old son Blaise. Even as she struggles to new realizations about her son's undetected disorder, Marfan syndrome, she is grounded by the lake outside their family home. We see the infant Blaise sleeping on his mother's chest as she listens to waves lapping the shore, eight-year-old Blaise in a canoe looking at turtles, adult Blaise boating with his rescue puppy Bogie, and thirty-something Blaise watching fireworks over the water with his parents. With unflinching honesty, Nancy Dafoe shares intimate details: her son's battle with addiction in his twenties, the beard he grew once he was sober and clean, the acts of kindness he kept secret. In a treatise of wisdom and anguish, Dafoe shares with us a grieving process that mimics the crash and churn of lake waves in a vast world where humans are powerless."

Janine DeBaise,
Author of *Body Language* and *Of a Feather*

Contents

Foreword

There is a remarkable relationship between emotion and time. We can relate to those experiences: for example, when frightened as we skid off any icy road, we are propelled into a reality of slowed movement; each instant amplified into a lengthened interval. Perhaps we also recognize how shock can stop time, recalling those flashbulb frozen moments of horror as we see twin towers falling or a President assassinated. And who cannot agree with the maxim "time flies" when we joyously look back at the glories of a college experience or a memorable vacation. Indeed, emotion so powerfully adjusts the arc of time that one wonders if emotion itself might be one of those "forces" or "dimensions," like gravity or energy, that physicists love to muse over when discussing the relativity of speed and mass.

But grief…grief fractures time, exploding it into pieces, creating a patchwork of memories often isolated from each other, no longer connected by linearity or development. The moment a child you deeply love dies, the future is suddenly rendered irrelevant while the present pulses in and out of clarity. It is the past that becomes everything, with each of its fragments re-lived, coming at you without necessary order and overtaking the meaningfulness of the present.

It is no small irony that Dafoe's book, on the grief of losing her son Blaise, was written during those first fearful months of the COVID-19 pandemic. This was a "time outside of time" for all of us, when clocks and calendars lost their utility and served merely as accoutrements of design and fashion. A bitterness that can often accompany grief arises from the realization that everyone else is going about their busy daily lives. They are impatient that a breakfast order is taking too long to arrive, that a commute is slowed by traffic, that a less-than-stellar coworker remains employed at their office. Who cares about trivial matters? asks the aggrieved. Why are you all so callous about my loss? Why are you engaged in the little intricacies of your lives while mine has stopped? But paradoxically, those early spring months of 2020 found almost everyone disengaged from the rhythms and routines of living, working, and playing. Might that provide some level of comfort to those paralyzed by grief?

No. There is no consolation in grief. No words or circumstances will make you love your lost one less. It is a truism we all need to be mindful of when seeking to provide solace for a wounded friend. For a wrong word, or an ill-conceived attempt at consolation, however well-meaning and innocent, can become a wound not forgotten by the recipient. Address grief simply by your presence, by listening, and by allowing the person to feel comfortable to express themselves, even if for the moment, you get silence in return.

Grief cannot be fully understood through definition and analysis. It is best revealed through storytelling. It is deeply personal and as unique as the love between the griever and the person grieved for. The most popular study on grief comes from Elizabeth Kubler-Ross's "five stages of grief," detailed in her book *On Death and Dying* (1969), an examination wholly insufficient to understand grief's depth and singularity. Some additional threads to the standard "denial, anger, bargaining, depression, and acceptance" of grieving are poignantly expressed by Dafoe in this memoir about her son Blaise. It includes the fact that grief entails periods of persistent pain; sometimes striking suddenly and sharply, and at other times descending as a heavy blanket, dulling the senses throughout the day and night. There is also an obsessional quality to grief in which every encounter with the present transports you to a memory of your lost loved one. And finally, grief takes you into a state of dissociation, whereby the depths and intensity of your loss separates you from the clarity of connecting with others.

Near the beginning of Dafoe's book, she writes that grief destroyed her optimism and severely challenged her sense of hope. It is an ironic sentiment because out of grief, musicians, artists, and writers throughout the ages have created works of immense inspiration and beauty. Dafoe's book is a gift to her son Blaise and a gift to us; and out of this, the reader is given both hope and optimism.

Ralph Hesse, psychologist

Introduction
Unstuck in Time

Blaise Martin is standing with his back to me, all six-foot, five-inches of him, lean and strong, wearing his gray, baggy sweat pants and a navy-blue sweatshirt. He is searching for something in a drawer, agitated, then he starts to turn and disappears. I do not mean he walked out of the room. He is gone. His death is sudden and unexplained. Yet, I see him again and again.

This is the book I never wanted to write. September 30, 2019. Stop. Everything stops. Blaise Martin has left us, but time does not appear to stop for everyone else. Paradigm shift in what I perceive; what I think I know. Every established foundation of order fallen into utter ruin on the day of his leaving and the days and nights that immediately followed.

Around two months subsequent to my son Blaise's death, someone asked me when he died, and I mechanically stated, "September 30," then pulled back. What had happened to all that intervening time? Everything was collapsing. Time, logic, order, fairness all fallen into a vortex.

"Time is lost," wrote philosopher Pascal Quignard in his book *The Roving Shadows*; "it's traces are disappearing at a fearful rate that takes us all with it." I read the French author's book a second time with new appreciation. The many days since my son's death had been compressed into a hard, knotted ball. What had happened to my understanding of time, of experience during the interval in which my world crashed and before realizing the ground beneath me had radically altered?

In writing a memoir about my love for my son Blaise and the devastation of his loss, about dealing with grief, in which my present implodes with experiences from my past every day, I recognized that organizing this memoir, the structure of the book would have to reflect the anachronic experience of life. Rather than indulgence, the thirty-two chapters in this work allude to my son's thirty-two years and are designed to move the narrative in a nonsequential order to more closely approximate life experience.

A second challenge for readers, but precisely the challenge I felt essential in relating this true story, is repetition in the blueprint of the manuscript. Grief washes over you. Nearly every author writing about grief uses the metaphor of being hit by waves that are at once familiar yet sudden and disorienting. They arrive over and over. To offer a proximation of the experience, I have created loops of repetitive phrases that reveal a little more with each occurrence. Anaphora's effectiveness rests with the reader but feels right to the nature of this writing about loss. Novelists use these devices—metaphors, conceits, anaphora, epistrophe, negative-positive restatement— more often than non-fiction writers, but the techniques are as useful in nonfiction as fiction. This book is as honest a representation as I could achieve about the anguish of losing my son and his bravery in the face of impossible odds. I promised to be brave enough to face it again for him and for others who may experience such devastation.

The third challenge for readers rests in uncovering the reasons behind the young man's death as it is gradually revealed, an experience that approximates the mystery genre.

Opening my Facebook page, I find an entry from a very good friend of my son's. Alena Turturro had posted a photo of herself and Blaise in which he is full of life, indomitable in his physical gifts, his vulnerability hidden. Alena appears dancing, and he is giving her the floor and all his attention. If only that photograph could be lifted back into life. Of course, in the instant I stare at that picture, everyone is in motion again. He is smiling. I smile.

Above Alena's photo is a caption: "In all these other moments you're fine. You're just unstuck in time." Instantly struck by the phrasing, I recognize Alena's use of displaced quotation from Kurt Vonnegut, Jr.'s novel *Slaughter House-Five*. Compelling and weirdly comforting, Vonnegut's quotation caused me to seek out its fullness for context.

Protagonist Billy Pilgrim "meets" aliens who offer their alternate view of death and time: "When a Tralfamadorian sees a corpse, all he thinks is that the dead person is in bad condition in that particular moment, but that the same person is just fine in plenty of other moments...All moments, past, present, and future always have existed, always will exist...It is just an illusion we have here on Earth that one moment follows another...and that once a moment is gone it is gone forever."

Identifying with the concept of illusion regarding time in lived experience, I realized I could not bear my son gone forever.

Blaise Martin was born with Marfan syndrome, a spontaneous genetic mutation that went undetected until after his death. Inside his body, tissues were coming apart even as he grew. My son was at odds with time and with his own body working against him far more quickly than normal. There was no honest way to tell a story about losing him and my love for Blaise in any kind of chronological order. I look back to find him as he appears full of life, ready to tackle anything, half smiling with an expression that says he knows, and he knew all of it, perhaps, on some subconscious level.

"Common sense tells us that our existence is but a brief crack of light between two eternities of darkness," wrote the famed Russian-American author Vladimir Nabokov in his autobiography *Speak, Memory*. But Nabokov tempers this crushing statement with these words: "How small the cosmos…in comparison to human consciousness, to a single individual recollection, and its expression in words!" My aims are to give my son's remarkable unspoken passage an expression in words and to share with others who must make a journey into grief.

I recognize I am caught between the extremes proposed by Nabokov, between alarm from my son disappearing into darkness and hope in recognizing the human ability to create and recreate: Blaise coming onto the page and into the room, not an illusion but a recollection so powerful that all else pales.

"The past lives as nervously and unpredictably as the present into which it protrudes its face," wrote Quignard in *The Roving Shadows*. Numerous writers, scientists, and philosophers have offered differing views of time from that typically presented to school children, but nearly everyone comes to understand through experience that the "past" is never really past.

In the horrific event of my son's death, I entered a strange and awful realm of dissonance. Each time the scene of his death is before me again, the moment looks somewhat different but is always annihilating. For my sanity, I needed to do something which shifted the terror that kept rising up when I felt the weight of his loss again and again. From Tralfamadorian perspective, I grasp there are a million moments, however, in which my son is just fine. I reexperience some of them every day. How to continue thinking like a Tralfamadorian, at least somewhat, I wondered? Anything to lessen the horror and panic caused by Blaise's sudden death at the age of thirty-two.

Compelled to write this narrative memoir about my son, of inexplicably losing and tremendously loving him, I had to devise a paradoxical frame and disclose the impossible. The impossible would be simultaneously expressed in terms of the painfulness of his death and my joyful experiences interacting with him, experiences which jumped around in time in the way our minds relay this arbitrary measurement of our brief existence. To order a book around Vonnegut's Tralfamadorian construct, my passages would appear and disappear, leaping between moments actuated by a familiar sound, a scent, a sight, a taste that pulled forth another exposure in this figurative camera held up to life.

Vonnegut wrote, "Blink" to indicate his sudden shifts in "time" in his novel. My sudden shifts are signaled by the words, "Deep Breath." Another scene, another moment in which he/we are perfectly fine. In that blink of an eye or intake of breath, everything changes.

Measurement in terms of the man-made device of a clock is useful in many respects for record-keeping but not reflective of lived experience. Philosophers and physicists have joined poets and fiction writers in eloquently and smartly relating the nebulous concept of time, unrelated to a timeline.

We were taught there is beginning, middle, and end. Or not. Or not in that particular order. William Faulkner famously wrote in his novel *The Sound and the Fury*, "clocks slay time." In Faulkner's experimental story, the second of the singular Compson children, Quentin, narrates the second section of the novel before committing suicide, but his chapter reveals Quentin's words as related in those last seconds of consciousness which reads as a lifetime. The passage is initially disorienting, yet mirrors life experience. Faulkner's character, a brilliant Harvard freshman, muses on the formulation of his ideas about time, first from his Grandfather and then his Father through the gift of a watch on the face of which can be read, "the mausoleum of all hope and desire; it's rather excruciatingly apt that you will use it to fit your individual needs no better than it fitted his or his father's. I give [the watch] to you not that you may remember time, but that you might forget it now and then for a moment and not spend all your breath trying to conquer it."

Faulkner had intriguing ideas about the absence of future and a continual past that are as old as the Greek philosopher Epicurus and as radical as science's string theory. A promised future is very different from a nebulous equation, but what is future if not only a promise? Standing in the middle of experience, there is no separation between past and present, but reoccurring experience or life continuously flooding back.

Our human need and emotions are more powerful than our reason and intellect, and I feel the past returning. Nabokov "reflects his hunch that there must be something beyond time in both the texture of *Speak, Memory's* individual sentences and the structure of the whole," stated literary critic Brian Boyd. Boyd, a professor of literature, wrote in the introduction to Nabokov's autobiography, "He finds ways to resist the relentless linearity of time, time as mere succession." Resistance to linearity appears to be high praise if it really is a more authentic expression of our actuality.

Contemporary physicists treat the concept of time quite differently than even our recent ancestors with their sundials and linear constructs. I am not a physicist, however, or well versed in the spacetime continuum. What little I know is theorists suggest time cannot be detached from three dimensions, and our Universe may have more dimensions than the three of which laypersons are aware. Our understanding of time and the passage of time is severely limited by our mental capacities and expertise.

I am appreciative yet apprehensive of the knowledge that time and the curvature of spacetime is illusory. Time as integral to a single conceptual scheme is dependent on the position from which we observe. What this difficult, factual, but theoretical construct of time means to the layperson is that things are not necessarily what they seem.

Ironically in this context, a particular prized possession of Blaise's was a beautiful gold watch he bought himself. He never seemed to care as much about recorded time as the style statement the watch made, a handsome piece lost and later lost only rediscovered by his father a year after his son's death. Time, too, was valued and stolen from my son. He was stolen from all of us.

After Blaise's death, I wanted both to extinguish time, reverse events, somehow bring him back. I wanted the impossible. For an indefinable period, I perceived my life outside of time, floating in an imagined transport between plains. Between waves of despair and less despairing experiences.

Here at a singular juncture, I return to the end of earthly life of my much-loved, 32-year-old son over and over in a time loop in which existence is no longer a formalized, linear construct. Loss of my son is sufficient cause to draw up, like the moon, tidal waves of negative emotions. But I slip back along a looping string, rummaging for another photo, another flash of recognition when he was perfectly alive. Life comes "gushing back."

"In all these other moments, he's perfectly fine." One picture of him at six years old, one at twenty-two. In one particular photo, Blaise is emerging from the Atlantic Ocean, broad shoulders, tanned, muscular, and he holds a wide smile: more than fine. He looks like a young Atlas before being tasked with holding up the world.

For all the brilliance of physicists and authors quoted in my text, and for all their resonance, I am grateful. I borrowed or bought many books on dealing with grief. Natasha Trethewey reminded me of the paradoxical intimacy and distance needed to write about such grief in her new memoir about her mother's tragic death in *Memorial Drive*. We learn by living and by reading.

Trethewey is a master writer and poet. Yet, nothing fully prepared me to write this book. I wrote because I had to write it down. There is no book, holy or otherwise, that fully manifests the enormity of the loss of a child. Still, I am a writer and continue to seek, heal, understand through written words. Blaise would have approved of my pursuit even if he shook his head slightly at my persistent folly of trying to capture life through words. He also believed in me as I always did in him.

Finally, the unusual ordering of my book requires a summation: anarchic ordering closely resembles our lived experience of continual interruptions of slivers from our "past," of repetitions or refrains of significant moments. It is reflective of the chaos that human beings continue to try to harness and subdue. Yet, neither life nor death will be subdued. I am focusing on the life of my son, all of those moments in which he was and always will be, for me, in my present as well as my past.

One

In All These Other Moments,
Blaise is Fine

I had three children, and then, there are two. Searching desperately, I find a photo. There is a crease near the edge where it was accidentally bent. Here is a picture of my son Blaise Martin at age four. I am kneeling beside him on the wide dock attached to our sloping lawn with the other end of the dock hanging precariously over shallow water. One of the supporting legs is tilted. Blaise, as a little boy in this photograph, looks skeptical, likely about the possibility of catching a fish, but I was certain he would, my younger self all smiles with anticipation for the day, his future, because I cannot imagine an unfolding of life in which my son does not exist looking for adventure, for the next fish.

Deep breath. Looking everywhere for photographs of Blaise, digging through old albums and a drawer filled with loose pictures, I sense rising alarm. "We don't have enough photos of him," I yell, feeling helpless.

"What are you talking about, Mom? There are pictures of Blaise in every room," my daughter Nicole said, trying to calm me in the days following my son's death.

My lovely second child was right, of course, but what she did not acknowledge in the moment was why I was so frantic: there would never be enough photos of Blaise again. I needed to see him everywhere because I could not see him anywhere.

Having to rely on my memory alone for my son caused such pain that I had to stop and sit to catch my breath every few minutes. I am acutely aware of the imperfection of our recollections, no substitute for the physical being, the present tense. As Proust wrote in *Swan's Way*, "these shifting and confused gusts of memory." My own gusts of memory come in rogue waves that drown me and disappear, leaving me drenched in grief.

"The real person is so very different from our imaginings, from our flawed memories that pick and choose the frame," wrote great British writer C.S. Lewis in his memoir *A Grief Observed* about the loss of his wife Helen Joy Gresham. Lewis, too, was unsatisfied with memories as his only link to his beloved.

What would happen when my humanly flawed memory could not readily bring forth images of Blaise's face exactly, his voice, his gestures, his words? Even considering this eventuality causes the kind of fear in which my stomach churns, my head throbs, my heart appears to be trying to crawl out of my chest. This physical manifestation of emotional havoc is the reality I experienced again and again after the death of my son.

Watching *JoJo Rabbit* to calm my nervous anticipation on an airplane, I startled at the ending quotation appearing on that small screen on the back of an airplane seat: a quotation from Rainer Maria Rilke's poem, "Let Everything Happen." Yes, I thought. I have let everything happen. I have remained open to love and loss. Only later, when I read Rilke's exhortation to let everything happen to you in his poem, I discovered a different meaning than the interpretation I took in as I attempted not to cry in that private-public container flying above the Earth.

Of course, I had accepted "beauty and terror," locking out no emotion, as difficult as that can be. If I am to be repeatedly menaced, often unexpectedly, by repetitions of the scene of my son's death, I have also remained cognizant of the beauty of his life, beauty he brought to me in daily acts, athletically graceful movements, kindness to people he knew whom I did not know at the time but am now welcoming. Rilke's words address a lack of finality which I pushed back against initially. Of course, death is final, and yet, death cannot steal every memory, the will to recall. Blaise is just "unstuck in time," as Kurt Vonnegut wrote about Billy Pilgrim in his novel *Slaughter House-Five*. Blaise's friend Alena Turturro reminded me of this alternative manner of perceiving life and death.

I, too, came unstuck in time but in less positive connotations, as in unglued, come apart, rattled, floored. Forward motion seemed impossible for a considerable period, not simply difficult after my son died. Even when I was physically moving, I had no recollection of having gotten from one place to another. Lost. I made myself consider other parallels to the strings of time that could loop back upon themselves. I followed my senses to the stories of my son's life.

We wake daily to an assault of information, pictures of violence from tragedies of the world constantly coming at us through our media sources. If we are decent human beings, we are aware of and empathic with others' sorrows and great misfortunes. On some level, however, we delude ourselves into believing this or that calamity will not happen to us or those we love. Then, tragedy strikes directly into our busy lives. In the face of great loss, what we previously thought of as catastrophe is suddenly less than. We cannot insulate ourselves, after all. Moment to moment, we are caught in tornados of emotion and memory. We no longer have the comforting distance of third person. I am. He was.

Deep breath. Opening an album, I am struck by an 8x10 black and white photograph someone took of me and Blaise as a baby. Remembering the scene, I reflect on getting that call from the Cortland City School District to cover a story for their newsletter. I do not have a babysitter, and I have limited time to get to my client's. I head out with Blaise in his infant car seat.

When I arrive at the high school parking lot, I settle my 8-month-old son into a backpack and walk up the hill with camera around my neck and notebook in my left hand. Blaise is quiet, surveying landscape behind us. Inside the gymnasium where I am taking photographs and interviewing people, curious students surround my son. Another photographer for the community newspaper takes my photo while I'm taking photographs of students, like a painting of a painting by Magritte. Blaise's head is turned in the opposite direction, his arms hang loosely, relaxed, as he looks out curiously at the students from his child carrier affixed to my back. The teenagers talk to him as they decide my toddler is more fascinating than whatever occasion they had been told to gather in the gymnasium.

We were gone for an hour, and Blaise never said a word, remained open and interested. He must have decided he liked riding in the backpack because he always wanted to go with me and not to be dropped off at his babysitter's house after that morning. Whenever I could bring him with me to cover a story, I did. He was always a draw but never demanded attention: what people term, "a good baby."

Here in a scrapbook is a card from Dr. Wang wishing his patients a Merry Christmas. In this photo from years ago, Dr. Wang is a young man. My children's pediatrician, Dr. Wang measured my toddler and remarked that he thought Blaise would be 6'5" when he was grown. How the good, perceptive Dr. Wang so accurately predicted my son's adult height is uncanny. How he later missed multiple early signs of Marfan syndrome is completely understandable but, on another level, unforgivable.

Blaise was a quiet and calm baby. Big for his age and verbal, Blaise convinced strangers he was older than his chronology. At his nursery school graduation, he literally stood out, taller than the others, as if an older brother had hopped up on the stage to join in the celebration.

Deep breath. Closing one photo album, I open another. Another black and white photograph I took and developed in my make-shift dark room. This picture is of my friend, poet Gwynn O'Gara. She happens to call me at this particularly serendipitous moment. Gwynn begins telling me about an intricate hand gesture in Tantric Yoga, approximately called *Anahata Chakra Mudra* or, in English, the "wheel of un-struck sound." As soon as she heard me say Blaise was "unstuck in time," I could hear her intake of breath in amazement. She very much wanted to describe and share this other concept that seemed akin but also paradoxical. What is the sound of unstruck sound if not paradox? Gwynn asked me to consider aspects of this notion: the wheel of unstruck sound is believed to open the center of being, presenting potentiality. What is possible is that which is not yet limited by choice or action. Any potential sound or all sound unfiltered by our constraints and desires. All of us exist in that wheel of limitless possibilities before we take action, before we resolve to consider, before we proceed.

Like unstruck sound, could unstuck time be at once devastating but freeing? Thinking of my son as freed from the burdens of life, from his cancer, from his particular genetic mutation, from his period of struggles with alcohol and drugs, was assuaging, but that small comfort was also too limited. Being freed from burdens was also from my perspective, not his. He had lost everything. I imagine, if he could follow this line of reasoning, he would find it entirely unreasonable.

Deep breath. A photo of my son at five. His smile is faint as if he is only trying to produce the desired effect because his mom asked for the camera, but the day is not quite what he had hoped. His little brows are knitted, and his eyes glance to the right as if there is something out of camera range that is causing concern. But he appears to be the picture of a healthy child. I do not remember the moment I took this photograph, but here we are again: my little son holding his worrying secret matter, and someone capturing that close-up moment. Maybe he just did not want his picture taken again. Perhaps the shadow across his face is not worry but something else entirely, a mistake of interpretation.

Knowledge of his sudden death at thirty-two impinges on every photograph of him, at every age, now. This is not foreshadowing or omen, I tell myself, just a child not wanting to hold still any longer. I can almost hear my entreaty: "Just one more picture; just a little smile."

Joan Didion famously wrote in her memoir *The Year of Magical Thinking* about her husband John Gregory Dunne's death, "Survivors look back and see omens, messages they missed...They live by symbols." I did not want to read Blaise's death into every expression my son made as a child, teen, or young adult. I needed to let go of perceived omens.

Run, Blaise, run. Run fast. I arrive at this entreaty: "outrun death."

Deep breath. Sorting and storing photos, I come across one of Blaise proximate to the time his nose was broken when he was a junior in high school. Our sixteen-year-old son would not tell his father or me how it happened, but a third-party witness confessed to us. Teenage years are hard for everyone. Blaise was, in the words of a witness/bystander, "sucker punched when he turned his head away, saying he wouldn't fight." The other boy, a senior in high school and teammate of Blaise's, did not want Blaise to date his sister. Perhaps, the anger went deeper and was for another reason entirely, but such was the story we got from those witnessing the scene.

Funny, that same boy who sucker punched my son won the character award later that year, nobody but four people knowing about this incident. Ultimately, the girl's brother was right. If Blaise and that boy's sister had dated and fallen in love, she would be crushed now, left horribly bereft without Blaise. She is a lucky girl, a fortunate woman in that her brother could see so clearly into the future.

In spite of a broken nose, Blaise is still fine in this photo, a fine young man with a broken nose that will eventually heal but never again be perfectly straight. In all these other moments, I try to finish the phrase. I cannot.

Deep breath. Run, Blaise. I always wanted to protect him, only occasionally acknowledging our inability to safeguard our children. Pulling out a photograph of my son running up and down basketball courts, another picture of him on ball fields, one photo of him climbing a hill across the countryside straight past those esoteric and worldly, man-constructed boundaries until he could not run anymore. How he loved playing sports. All while his heart was growing larger, tissues spreading dangerously apart without anyone's knowledge of it happening.

I do not know where that freedom from boundaries took my son, but considering death as a type of freedom returns to the forefront. No one can ever hurt him again, I remind myself. Yet, this fact is not comforting. Blaise will not fall in love again. He will not. I stop midsentence, not wanting to go there.

"Photographers deal in things which are continually vanishing," wrote the great humanist, French photographer Henri Cartier-Bresson. But we work so hard to keep the vanishing from unfolding before us. Leafing through photo albums, I come to an image I took of Blaise staring at the Korean War Memorial's mural wall in Washington, D.C. What is seen in the photograph are reflections of other lives, with the black marble depicting sandblasted images of soldiers appearing and disappearing on shiny surface, my son moving in line with them. From the album, the photograph looks as if these ghost soldiers are on the move, and my son stands too tall above them, only his head turned the opposite direction. If you did not know the nature of reflective surfaces, the image is disorienting.

I think about how wordsmiths, like photographers, deal in the vanishing.

Deep breath. I place a photo back in an album and remember that precise moment: "How was work?" I ask as my son leaps up the steps two at a time to change clothes.

He does not answer immediately, then descends the stairs in swim shorts. "All good," he says before tossing a towel over his shoulder, pontoon boat key slipped into his pocket. We are continuing the conversation through gestures rather than words. Bogie, his little rescue dog, leaps off the couch and races Blaise to the door then down to the water, beating him onto the boat. Quick flick of Blaise's wrist and ropes come undone. I'm standing on the porch and watching my strong son. One push away from our weathered wood dock, and the two of them are floating, warm sun on their backs, cool lake beneath, dog's ears flapping in summer wind.

They are out on the water again, perfectly fine. I snap a mental picture. I close albums.

Two

How to Tell the Story

Where are the faces of mourning? "He died, and the world showed no outward sign," wrote the author Mary Shelley in the preface to the book she created from her husband Percy Bysshe Shelley's complete works. Mary Shelley's words about grief resonate. How could everyone seem to continue with "no outward sign" after the death of my beautiful son? Yet, friends, acquaintances, strangers did go on without sorrowing and will, even must, continue in that manner. Life does not wait.

Hospital ICU room at the end of a long hallway. Surreal tubes, IVs, monitors, chemical cleaning smells, plastic bag hanging below the bed with dark matter collecting, beeping noises from other nearby rooms, nurses everywhere, and in some recess in my brain, I started to foolishly think, "hope." If I had read the statistics on comatose patients and length of time of depressed brain stem reflexes, I would not have indulged in that most cruel instance of feeding into the prospect of anything that held promise. Yet, my son looked perfect, strong and healthy in nearly every outward aspect as he lay in a coma on the bed not long enough for him, his feet sticking out. He appeared to be sleeping.

I knew better. I should have known better. The flurry of activity dissuaded me from reality.

Distance desperately needed. Start again in second person narrative: You recognize you are "unstuck in time," no longer moving along some arbitrarily constructed line but caught in impossible whorls in which life is replayed, and death is repeated scenes along this continuous, temporal loop. Your son's death again.

Too personal, demanding first person even while hiding behind a narrative point of view. Within months following Blaise's death, I found myself compelled to scratch out notes, lines of poems, anything to recall him, move out of a state of dread and hopelessness.

Writers keep searching to create order out of chaos. Death reintroduces chaos and the natural disorder of the world.

"You sit down to dinner and life as you know it ends," Joan Didion wrote in *The Year of Magical Thinking* in which she emotionally explores and intellectually responds to the sudden death of her husband, the writer John Gregory Dunne.

Yes, Joan, I think, joining her in the more removed second person narrative: you go to bed, snuggled under clean, soft covers after a good, productive day of giving writing workshops and interacting with some lovely people when someone below cries out, "He's not breathing."

You do not remember running down your stairs, but you experience again seeing his face, his long body lying there in the living room at an awkward angle. You comprehend you are useless, abstract in a surreal world that has grabbed hold of life as you have known it. Your son does not move. You are pushed to the side. Yes, Joan, "Life as you know it ends in that instant."

Shifting again, I hear a voice but not a word, a piercing yell, before words are discernible. The obstacle in creating memoir is that the events happened. I am struggling with the enormity of the loss of my son, trying to formulate statements.

Gone at thirty-two, Blaise had lived with his dad and me. Unusual circumstance for a lot of families, but our son was recovering from addiction and had moved home to survive, to try and get through this trial. We wanted to help.

Following his recovery, the last nearly three years of his life, Blaise was the easiest person in the world with whom to live. Quiet, respectful, responsible, funny, and helpful, he floated in and out of rooms without disruption. It had not always been so.

Struggling with how to tell this story that is not story but life, "I" locator back into hiding: Your son won't wake. Everything you have ever known or believed has seismically shifted. You clench and unclench your hands. Time itself has disappeared into whirlpool of darkness. Screaming. Not you, but that voice has become unidentifiable. His friend Rachel is hyperventilating. You are following an ambulance, racing into the darkest of dark nights.

Only much later, I write.

***

Late Afternoon in November
Kittiwake Gulls silhouetted against solemn sky,
white wings steady in slow descent,
streaming on winter winds. Too far from shore,
they looked not lost nor displaced but temporary.
Not symbols of hope nor peace
but comforting, nevertheless, in aerial display.
Snow covering arrives early.
Death should only take place in winter,
short days and long nights
in which hush descends.

There is a pattern to the gliding gulls. I am seeking pattern, order. A chapter about the act of writing, about creating in the midst of sadness, disorder; no neat separations of chapters, even vignettes are mingled, chaotic ordering of the world, of lines conveying our emotions and sense of living fall into tangles, doubling back upon lives lived and living. A story of disorder, turmoil, and tumult, grief never settles into a routine or neat narrative.

Crow caws unexpectedly in Max Porter's book *Grief is a Thing with Feathers*; crow cries, sings, balks, flees and returns, always portraying the paradoxical, familiar stranger, beyond rival for every thought and emotion, refusing to agree to any premise. No choice but to accept grief's arrival.

Porter's fiction feels more real, more immediate than a clinical study of grief. There is a time and place for reading the well-researched book, such as George Bonanno's *The Other Side of Sadness*, but it is not yet, not yet. Porter's little novel is more attuned to what you experience. Discussing chemical reactions is helpful to a doctor but not to your suffering.

Order narrative about his death around Christmas and vignettes about Christmas, I jot down old lists of Christmas gifts appearing in journals. I am looking for something, but I am not sure what I am seeking. Blaise's name is marked next to gold chain, that year I spent too much on presents and finally got him just what he wanted. My son was so easy to buy gifts for because he let me know exactly what he expected. No equivocating, he would leave an Eastbay catalog on my desk with the items he chose circled in red marker, folding the pages over, so as not to be missed. He was extremely thoughtful in his giving, as well.

On Christmas morning, Blaise handed me a package from him. Inside the careless wrapping was *The Nix*, a novel by Nathan Hill. I had never heard of the book, but Blaise proceeded to tell me an anecdote about how he had been all over the mall a few weeks earlier, asking store owners and people in the book store their favorite books for a mother who is a writer. "About five people recommended this book, so I knew it had to be pretty good," he said. "I bought it and read it. I think you'll like it, too." He smiles that little half smile that is almost smirk.

There were two remarkable qualities to this gift from my son. The first was its appropriateness. I love reading novels and to have one about mother and son protagonists was particularly affecting. The second quality I will never forget is the fact that Blaise read a 620-page novel to make sure it was right for me. He at least skimmed it. By way of context, Blaise did not like to read novels. In fact, he seldom, if ever, read fiction. Although, toward the end of his life, my son became a good reader of nonfiction articles, he never picked up novels and short stories that I am aware of.

The Nix is a convoluted, sprawling story of a mother, Faye, and son, Samuel, in which "disappointment is the price of hope," according to author John Irving, who reviewed Nathan Hill's book. It took me forever to start reading the over 600-page book, but when I did, I did not want to put it down. I appreciated the fact Hill's characterization of the mother is not carved from some tired trope of motherhood. Faye is a political activist, abandoned her son, is misjudged by her son, but also inspires him once he uncovers her past. This mother is much more than Samuel mistakenly assumed she was. She is flawed, brilliant, and alive. I thought this last idea of a brilliant flawed mother was rather surprising and one that resonated.

Hill's novel reveals themes of change and trans-formation. In the end of his story, Hill wrote, "Any real change should make you feel, at first, afraid...and we're in for years of pain...Okay, Faye thinks, that's probably the way it ought to be...That's how we find our way back...Eventually, all debts must be paid." Even at the time I read Hill's work, I thought it was prescient and apt. A couple of years after first reading, the novel seemed attuned to what my son was thinking. Son forgives his mother. Son forgives himself. Mother forgives herself. To this day, that book holds a prominent position in my readings.

Blaise indulged his mother as a teen and in his twenties by waiting on the stairs Christmas morning, so I could take a photo before the stockings were opened. It was not always easy to tell what Blaise was thinking, but nobody doubted he loved everything about Christmas: giving gifts as much as receiving them. He picked out his own gifts for others with meticulous care and was overly generous, especially with his little nephews. Only one lone gift could not be given. His one miscue was a Red Ryder BB gun Blaise bought for his nephew Truman.

"You can't give him that!" I said as Blaise was wrapping his presents, tape everywhere.

"No?" He genuinely looked surprised.

"Truman's too little. He'll shoot his eye out," I said, quoting the mother Melinda Dillon's line from *A Christmas Story* movie. I knew Blaise loved the movie which inspired his gift.

Although Blaise was certain Truman could handle the Red Ryder, he did not protest but tucked the BB gun away in his closet. "Next year," he said with a mischievous smile.

Blaise did not live to see the following Christmas, and the Red Ryder remains on the top shelf in his untouched closet.

One Christmas ago, he was alive, I say to myself. One Christmas ago, he gave me a knowing glance and smile when his sister Colette asked me, "How did you know just what he wanted?" One Christmas ago, he was perfectly fine. One Christmas ago, I will say again and again, only changing the expanding distance. It will become, two Christmases ago. Three Christmases ago. The distance will change but not the absence.

This chapter in my memoir about my son is thematically tied to the act of writing and Christmas' past with Blaise; I falter again. I'm not writing some postmodernist novel, but a memoir, I remind myself. Still, I find my annoying traits spilling out on the page: self-referencing, authorial intrusion, unreliable narrator. I want to scream, yell for my son. "Stop. This is impossible." Then, "Come, sit with me, Blaise, help me find a way to tell your story and mine." I have all the words, may choose at my discretion. Nevertheless, not one of my words seems right, disorder expanding as I watch every reasonable line scramble, imploding like the present before they reach the page.

"Don't be afraid," Blaise says out of nowhere.

I hear him.

Something about gulls floating over a frozen lake. I return to the image and just when I start to wax poetic about my grief, a detective walks into the room. He is acutely aware I have written murder mysteries and am comfortable with that genre. Taking off his hat to run a hand through his thick, disorderly hair, he says, "You have forgotten a few things. Clues left behind. I think you know."

I know, but I'm too stunned to respond for a moment. He is tall like my son.

"This isn't just about you," he cautions, adjusting his Fedora, accentuating its crease, his dark eyes staring below the brim. He is straight out of a 40s, hard-boiled film noir, but this isn't a murder, not even an accidental death. It is monumentally death, paradoxically unnatural yet natural death.

I know. Then out loud, "I know. I don't want this story to be just about me."

"Why 'I…I…I' everywhere?"

"Not sure how to get at my son's voice. I miss that sound. I miss him. What I want," I respond, faltering.

"You'll get there. Keep looking," he says nodding before walking out as unceremoniously as he entered.

"In order to keep moving, to keep doing the things you're supposed to be doing, you're going to have to give yourself orders, imperatives," wrote poet/ educator/ novelist Mark Yakich in his novel *A Meaning for Wife* about a widower and his two sons. I am surprised again by how fiction resonates. My only task is the imperative to "keep moving." I move but don't remember where I'm going, only where I have been.

Recognizing I am scarcely stemming the tide of chaos, I still attempt to shape experience, create a form for this horrible grief and long to pull up memories of my son. This is what writers do even when we do not want to revisit those scenes.

"It's okay, Mom. Just write," Blaise says. I hear him as clearly as if he is in the same room. I sit back and listen for more. Silence.

But the door opens as I type, and for that half second, I hear Blaise walking in, his Nike shoes clunk as he pulls them off in the entrance, before he stuffs them under or near the bench. He's home.

No, it is only my imaginings.

Three

Hope, Not Optimism

Stopping and kneeling at the bier holding Blaise's coffin, my son-in-law David reached for and removed his own gold chain. David took the cross from his neck, a cross he had worn for much of his life, one given to him by David's grandmother when he was thirteen. My son-in-law gently placed his cross on Blaise's chest. This small-scale gesture was an extraordinary act of generosity and struck me powerfully as I stood back. Considering the gifts I might have placed with my son before his burial, I felt as if nothing was adequate. I suddenly realized I was unprepared for this custom, reaching another level of panic, even as I had attended to so many others in the worst moments of my grief.

I wanted to break down again, but then I thought about what my son might say to me at that moment. Blaise would have been extremely grateful and touched by his brother-in-law's offering, but he would also have said something along the lines of, "You don't have to leave anything with me, Mom. You gave it all to me in my lifetime." I comforted myself, hoping those words floating in my head, those words coming from some place of knowing my son were honest.

Following Blaise's death, I lost optimism. I no longer expected things to work out, anticipating a brighter future. Strangely, however, I had not entirely lost hope. What made the distinctions, and why were those delineations so important? Trying to reason anything for a while was absurd. My thinking felt so muddled even as my emotions were keenly honed. I wanted to hold onto hope, regardless of how foolish that concept seemed. Eventually, I started to think about distinguishing between hope and optimism because I needed to find that boundary. Perhaps not for myself but for my four little grandsons and my daughters, for the larger world.

I begin to think deeper about what separates the two concepts while I was talking with Marilyn, my sister-in-law. She, too, had suffered an unbearable, devastating loss when my brother, her husband, Emerson, Jr. died young. "I no longer think of myself as an optimistic person," I said. She agreed, noting she felt the same. Then I added, "but I'm still hopeful."

"Well, what's the difference?" She asked. Knowing there is a distinction, we struggled briefly to try to define that line.

Attempting to articulate how hope diverged from optimism, I fumbled but arrived at the place in which I could suggest hope is tied up with beliefs and the last shelter from complete destruction of everything. "Even people in a war zone, with their loved ones lost or maimed, don't seem to give up hope, but they are not optimistic about outcomes."

Marilyn agreed. "Yes, we see people who are not optimistic for their futures, but they retain hope.

After leaving my sister-in-law, I continued thinking about those notions because I wanted to hang onto hope. Psychologists discuss the elements of the "cognitive processes" involved in hoping. But I am not a psychologist nor am I a scientist, but I have a lay person's understanding of the distinctions between hope and optimism.

If I was writing a treatise on hope, however, I would have to go back further. Ancient philosopher Aristotle used a Greek word for hope that carries the weight of "expectation" in the way that optimism does for us today. Perhaps these two concepts— hope and optimism—were once thought of as one. Finding the separations involves a study in etymology and languages that is not intended here. I am not writing a treatise, just trying to figure out why I had lost one aspect of future after Blaise's death but not another.

"Western religion, in particular, elevates the sort of hope that thrives in the face of adversity, turning it into a virtue," writes author Nikki Stern in her nonfiction text *Hope in Small Doses*, published by Ruthenia Press in Princeton (2018). Stern's comments felt like a criticism of human beings who take a basic emotion and elevate it to protect themselves. Perhaps Stern's statements refer, instead, to how institutionalized religions use basic human emotions to promote an aspect of dogma.

After my conversation with Marilyn, I did a little research as to where these words diverge in connotation as well as denotation and, surprisingly, found there is considerable research on this topic. I had not expected to find anything. Instead, there is a treasure trove.

Life makes us all hypocrites or, in the very least, contrary. Even William Shakespeare, when it came to "hope," vacillated between extremes on the interpretation of hope. One may quote Shakespeare to prove a point about the utter absurdity of hope: "And so, by hoping more, they have but less," (l. 138) Shakespeare wrote in his 1,855-line narrative poem "The Rape of Lucrece," in which the characters are "full of foul hope." Hope as a foul emotion is ugly. Point demonstrated by Shakespeare: hope is useless and humans foolish for succumbing to it.

We could also quote Shakespeare, however, to reinforce mankind's propensity and need for hope: "True hope is swift and flies with swallow's wings" (Act. V, scene ii). Yet, an interpretation of this quotation may also mean that hope flies away as swiftly as it arrives. A Shakespeare quotation from *The Two Gentlemen of Verona* appearing more positive in consideration of our prospects is Proteus exhortation, "Hope is a lover's staff; walk hence with that and manage it against despairing thoughts" (Act III, scene i). Hope is to be found everywhere: on the battlefield, in the midst of famine and even in the agonies of torture. Without hope, man and woman cease to exist. But, was even "seeming necessity" just delusional?

"Hope is the most evil of evils because it prolongs man's torments," wrote German philosopher Fredrich Nietzsche in his book *Human, All Too Human: A Book for Free Spirits* (1878). Nietzsche was more than a little extreme and pessimistic even though brilliant, but hope does seem to place human beings in a quandary.

Arbitrators fall somewhere in the middle, naturally. One such statement found in seventeenth century French writer and philosopher Francois Duc de la Rochefoucauld's *Reflections; Sentences and Moral Maxims*: "Hope, deceitful as it is, serves at least to lead us to the end of our lives by an agreeable route." Practical. We need hope even if we know we are deluding ourselves through our beliefs and desires. That "agreeable route" may keep us from suicide or murder.

Optimism, however, speaks of agency and expectation. Optimism is outlook that positively colors even the bleakest situations. Optimism suggests in arrogance that we are able to control outcomes or at least alter the course. Certainly, during periods of my life, when I was younger, I would have described myself as an optimist. I expected good results based upon a set of conditions that were reasonably likely to continue until one day they no longer were. Optimists do not deny the reality of death, but they expect a good death, a just death.

I have not reached the same conclusions as Utpal M Dholakia, Ph.D., Professor of Marketing at Rice University, who wrote, "the concept of hope seemed to me to be a decidedly inferior concept, like a cocktail of optimism mixed with a bit of desperation and a dash of wishful thinking." Dholakia used impugning language to express the "decidedly inferior concept" of hope.

Dholakia's paper "What's the Difference Between Optimism and Hope," printed in the February 26, 2017 issue of *Psychology Today* journal, is, on the whole, erudite and well-reasoned: "Social psychologists see optimism as the individual's core belief that their future will have good, positive experiences, and won't have bad, negative ones." Dholakia went on to state, "hope is invoked by people when they expect positive outcomes as less likely to happen."

With Dholakia's last statement, I could agree. I no longer expected positive outcomes but clung to hope. I suspect hope is more basic to humanity, rather than inferior in its genesis. Hope is the last refuge of our human experience before death. Undoubtedly, religions are born from it, arising out of fears of death. Hope helps to sustain us in the middle of a crisis, in pain, trepidation, and most terrible grief. Intellect for all of its superior qualities is nowhere to be found in the midst of personal losses to death.

I wondered if Anne Frank could have written her diary in that attic, knowing full well the approach of Nazis meant her death, without hope? Speculating about Shakespeare's master works, I was aware the Bard created *King Lear* while quarantined in London during another outbreak of the plague. Was Shakespeare optimistic in expecting a positive outcome or "merely" and powerfully hopeful his words would again be spoken on stage? Foreshadowing death and our foolish hope, Shakespeare wrote in *Lear* these insightful, punning lines: "When we are born, we cry that we are come to this great stage of fools." Yet, Shakespeare hoped these lines, this cynical wisdom would be heard by audiences in some vague future. Our great stage of fools is an apt metaphor for our human experience.

Of course, intellectually accounted for, we are all rather foolish to hope since the outcome of all of our lives is always death, but, like the great and self-effacing American poet Emily Dickinson wrote, hope allows us to "dwell in possibility." Hope is a "thing with feathers" that might allow us to fly away in the direst situations. Hope seems to me to be a gift from the imagination; whereas, optimism is handed down from reasoning's cause and effect.

I reach into my imagination for words about my son's loss that express death while retaining a glimmer of hope.

***

Gravity

He was.
Tensing from this past tense,
I move slowly
like some ancient,
weighed down,
collapsed by grief.
English commands: I am,
I think, I sorrow for my son.

He was; I am.
Abstractions distract,
making it possible to continue
moving out from paralysis,
stone cold inertia.

In Gaelic ethos, sadness
is upon me, laying its heavy cloak
over landscape and imaginings.

That poetic language
passive in aspect;
seismic shift is now upon me,
roiling inside;
what that means,
what departs, bereft
when world tilts on its axis
until something, no, someone
tall and beautiful disturbs it,
stops all motion before being swept away.
I so want to see him again,
searching night sky
until my eyes catch the moon
holding oceans; gravity pinning this body,
pulling fiercely downward.

Spinning, earthbound, tethered, I look
for my son further out, out past
a whirling earth, out beyond.

***

For an extended period after Blaise's death, I knew my
sense of optimism had forever disappeared. Perhaps that outlook
was lost to me even before the fateful night of my son's death,
but, strangely, I held onto hope. During those most terrible days
immediately following our great loss and the days after, I
considered what leads people to be suicidal: that utter loss of
hope.

During calling hours for my son, a slide show played on
continuous loop on a television in the back of the room at the

funeral home. I could not see the slide show due to a throng of people who came to offer their condolences standing in front of me. At the end of the evening, I stopped to watch the program my daughters had put together. Beautiful images of my son full of vibrancy come up. I am reminded he had his grandmother Dafoe's Irish nose, that he looked a lot like his sister Colette and father Daniel. Then, the show ended with a photo of Blaise wearing the hood of his sweatshirt pulled over his hair as he turns to look back before walking away. That photo I had not seen before, a picture of his head pivoting as he leaves us is stunningly beautiful and agonizingly final. Blaise departing; now he is gone.

Four

Ice-Covered Land

Bleak, cold winter is typically something to avoid, to escape from, to fly to Florida or other warmer climes, or at least steer away from biting winds. During mourning, however, winter feels like the only reasonable season.

Writer and artist Rachel Dickinson photographed and created watercolor scenes in Iceland, as well as near her home in Central New York. Online, she shared a few of her works: a photograph of Gullfoss Waterfalls in Iceland in which rushing water transforms into ice in the midst of dropping into deep ravine. Bitter cold penetrates.

Rachel and I went to the same college but have only recently come to know each other. We share more than a college and mutual interest in writing and art. We have both lost our sons, creating an unlooked-for intimacy. Rachel's winter scenes are especially riveting, stark, and transcendent. In her Iceland photograph, a road becomes ice river, glistening with partial light from a distant sun struggling through high, gray cirrus clouds, snow tinged with blue in its wavelength of scattered light. Staring at Dickinson's images, I slip inside them, lost to the comfort of my physical surroundings of my home near the fire and inhabit surreal Iceland of frozen speculation.

Waking again to loss, I study Dickinson's images intently and compare them to those I see outside my window: our frozen lake. I am aware that beneath layers of snow, there is still subnivean life, burrowed, hidden. Winter scenes are suggestive of substratum, of mystery waiting for our eyes through long hibernation.

Sheets of snow, like metaphors, like poetry, cause conjecture, contemplation, leading me below surfaces. In winter, I have thought an entire universe about my son, what we have all lost, the immensity of grief, and the boundlessness of love. I want to remain in this snow-covered landscape, cloaked, and in some metaphorical manner, buried with my son. I have no desire to shake off the cloak of grief, even as self-protection.

Another friend, Rose, sent me a photograph she had taken while she was in Iceland, "one of the most beautiful places on earth," she said. I suddenly wonder why all these people I know are heading to Iceland when we live in one of the coldest climates in the lower states of the United States? In Rose's picture, large, uneven blocks of blue-white ice chunks are abutted, jammed into a bay by black water presenting only in spaces between these floes. Further out at sea, color appears deep bluish green, light blue sky above in sharp, crisp contrast. Shadowy white clouds mirror ice beneath as if in imitation.

Percy Bysshe Shelley's phrase from *Prometheus Unbound* comes to mind after I contemplate Rose's photo: these broken away parts of a glacier, "with the spears of their moon-freezing crystals." It is a gorgeous scene but terribly forbidding. I recognize the familiar in those scenes of frozen, concealed seas and landscape.

Living in a part of the country where snow covers ground and the sun is seldom seen for nearly half of the year, I have repeatedly reflected on how winter is the season for grieving. Rachel's watercolor paintings, in shades of gray and white imbued with faint blues, resonate. Missing my son so terribly, I am oddly consoled by these severe, wintery scenes: pale shapes, pale winter, punctuated only by black lines of bare-limbed trees reaching upward in entreaty.

Not in Iceland but in the Central New York region, winter arrived not long after my son's death. Although winter came two months later by calendar, I had already fallen deeply into this chilling season. When snows fell in November, it snowed for days. Ice quickly formed on Little York Lake thick enough to walk out and across.

Death is paramount in winter, short days and long nights in which we seek shelter, hidden in this whiteness, without causing neighborly concern. As far as the eye can see, miles away, hoary cover. Deep snow silences, and that silence gives way to mourning, to contemplation, to unstruck-sound, unstuck time. The snow covering leads me to consider the title of Milan Kundera's novel, *Life is Elsewhere*. Yes, I think, life exists in other places. It is not here. No need to search.

My daughter Colette bought a weighted blanket claimed to be therapeutic. The heft of it appeared to work; she bought a blanket for her sister and another one for me. Late afternoon, I folded myself under the weight of sorrow and beneath that soft, gray blanket. Underneath the heavy comfort, I was reminded of snow outside and repeatedly told myself that life still exists below surface.

Blaise's body lies beneath a winter covering now, but I do not believe he is there. My son is not living underground. He is gone. Still, I will visit his gravesite and talk with him.

In the ensuing months, I had made no discernable "progress," could not accept my son's passing, this gigantic lack in my center. Everything seemed impossible. Of course, the "center will not hold," I told myself even if it appeared to do so for many others around me. W. B. Yeats and Chinua Achebe come to mind from my use of their phrasing, but I'm not ready, not ready to move or talk, read literature, nor once again be inquisitive and analytical.

A few years ago, my parents died, my father first in a tragic fall and my mother succumbed after lingering illness, Alzheimer's disease. I was, at an older age, an orphan, feeling the way many feel when they have lost both their parents: adrift for an indistinct period of time. There was, however, the realization that both my parents had lived long, joy-filled, successful lives in which their love for each other was an evident and defining factor. Not minimizing the deaths of my mother and father, the death of my son was entirely different, a substratum catastrophically lower than even sorrow.

Going out for a drive with my husband Dan on Sunday mornings, I look for hawks, a bald eagle if we are really lucky. I thought about Rachel Dickinson's book *Falconer on the Edge*. We could try to spot hawks in our region any time of year, but in the winter, Red Tails are more likely to wait out the snow storms, hawks perched high in pine trees. I could almost always find a hawk with bird's broad wings folded, head tucked, and eyes scanning snow-covered fields for movements beneath white powder.

Hawks are said to have 20/2 vision with the ability to see four to five times further and sharper than humans. No matter how I try to sneak up on resting birds, they always spot me the moment I step toward them.

Sometimes, I would jump out of the car that Dan had pulled to the side of the road and try to take a photograph. The hawk would then fly off at my approach, but I often got a few pictures that are stunning, not the National Geographic quality, but the type I would term decent amateur photos. I called this activity "winter hawk hunting" although I never hunted, just looked for these magnificent predators in wintry storms. I never clinically tried to assess why this endeavor so soothed me and made me feel very much alive.

Dan and I drove back from breakfast in December only a couple of months after Blaise's death, and my husband asked if I wanted to look for hawks again. Our son had been gone for a while, but the idea of pursuing beauty was still impossible for me. I said, "no." I turned down something that I loved to do, that was beautiful and not harmful in any way. I knew I was in trouble; landscape scarcely noticed.

Having difficulty reading, reading anything let alone poetry or a novel, I let books pile up, trying to get my attention. Their efforts are, at first, in vain. My agitated brain did not seem capable of holding more than a few isolated sentences at a time, overwhelmed as it was with emotional turmoil and pain. I also felt guilt. I am not sure why or what that guilt was attached to, other than to me. Guilt and death. How could my son die before me? Where was the natural order? Things fall apart. That phrase should have read, "things fly apart," "things are ripped apart."

Mary Kennedy, friend and former professor of mine, sends me Gregory Orr's *How Beautiful the Beloved*, a book of poetry in which the "beloved" changes shape. I start with one short part of this book-length poem of permutations. Then another. By the end of the day, I have read the long poem in its episodic entirety. I do not know if it helped with grieving, but I remember thinking that my brain was somewhat functioning again. I do know. It helped.

My sister-in-law Philomena Mantella mailed me Martha W. Hickman's *Healing After Loss*. At first, I was too weary to read another book about loss, but then I picked it up and was awakened to all of the amazing words of famous writers, poets, philosophers who had written lines about grieving, and those lines largely felt true.

I began reading all of it, every book I could find about grieving. Some have stayed with me. An anthology of poems, *The Art of Losing,* edited by Kevin Young have made this long passage in grief easier to bare because I have companions. Owen Dodson wrote a long poem "For My Brother Kenneth" that is ghostly and resonant, phrases echoing across empty rooms.

Reading often gives way to contemplative walks. I watch for osprey over the lake. This morning, I saw a Loon, thought it was a male Merganser before I heard its deeply forlorn call. I realized without joy that I was looking for life again.

April 7th and the largest supermoon of the year appears, this bright full moon at lunar perigee. I go outside in the cold to witness this event. It snows again. Landscape of the moon shows its face, and my son feels as far and as close as that Pink Moon. He is there with me as I stand in our old asparagus garden gone to weed.

It is snowing in April, on April 10th to be more precise, and it is not just snowing, but the ground is covered, and the wind is blowing from multiple directions, so no matter where I turn, my face is exposed to bite and snowflakes. I walked this past morning and this afternoon despite the weather. I actually told myself, I faced the death of my son, I can face a gale.

By the time I got back to my house, the tips of my fingers in fingerless gloves were frozen and red, my face also red and wet, my hair soaked even with a hood on, and I sat by the fire for an interval to take away the chill that would not leave.

April 16th and another snowfall, winter disregarding calendar days. I walk along an empty road, a scarf pulled over my mouth, wool hot and moist. My thoughts fall below my bootsteps.

Colder still, I finally look up to see an osprey hunting over the lake, its huge wings fluttering above its head, maintaining body position, as it prepares to dive. I see the bird plunge but not its catch, bird and prey hidden by trees and brush.

Osprey wakes me from a stupor. I recall Blaise's words repeated to me near his end, "You don't have to worry about me anymore." I no longer have to worry about him I tell myself. The thought is filled with unanswerable sorrow.

April 21, and the snow is coming down as if it was February. How is it that Winter returns after Spring? How has the world abandoned reason and order? Then I thought about the many moments in which I felt like I was doing okay when everything suddenly turns, my breath catches, my stomach churns, my eyes burn because I know with very fiber of my being, I have lost my son. The body ends, but love does not end.

April 22nd and no snow plows have come through, our road nearly impassable from cover. It is snowing as hard on this Spring morning as the middle of January. Buds on trees look like round white balls, entirely encased in snow. I woke to snow and went to sleep in snow. It feels as if there is no forward motion, only stasis.

Too many nights occur in which I try neither sleep nor arrive at wakefulness. I push myself to read even though I don't want to go there. I need something to nudge me in another direction, give me something to talk about other than the sudden death of my son. A white cover stands out on my bookshelf. I have read *Erebus* before, this hybrid memoir/poetry book, but something compels me to open it again: whiteness of its cover.

I know a little of the true story of this narrative written by my friend from college, Jane Summer. Historically, Air New Zealand flight TE901 took off in the morning to fly 257 tourists, adventurers, and flight crew members between two mountains in Antarctica. Radio contact was lost. Exact cause of the crash into

Mount Erebus is still under debate, but, in 1979, the plane crash
and loss of life was one of the worst in history. Summer wrote her
hybrid poetry/memoir of these historic events from the personal
perspective of knowing one of the victims. Her book is entrance
to grief, to loss. Summer's book haunted the first time I read it but
resonated in an entirely different way on the third reading.

     After *Erebus*, I wrote a poem for Jane, for Kay, for Blaise,
for all of us.

***

Mount Terror

Stark white cover confronting me.
Unidentifiable figure with her back
to me struggles and searches in deep snow,
narrative and poetry on matte stock:
overlay of Antarctica's Ross Island,
topographic map. On either side of figure,
Mount Erebus and Mount Terror appear
as symbolic threats of death surrounded
by wavy lines indicating sudden changes
in elevation, "ominous calm, a little death
in every object," as poet Jane Summer
wrote in elegy to Kay Barnick, her friend
among the doomed, on flight TE901.

For months after reading Summer's
remarkable memoir/poem, I could not shake
the rawness of tragically lost men and women,
of one adventurous young woman in particular.

Final photograph of impact was a mistake,
an automatically clicking shutter capturing
beaded window image of streaking moisture,
annihilation in which the "three-dimensional

are made two," Summer tells us as I read,
author presenting blank pages of found journal
unstuck in time, even with date affixed
to the top of the page: 1979.

Impact of those extinguished lives move
the Earth like aftershocks from earthquakes,
displacing multitudes as magnitude of loss
arrives as unintended tsunami.

***

Finished rereading Summer's *Erebus* epic, I fear for my son again. As if he is on that plane, and there is nothing I can do to alter symbolic airplane's trajectory. I want to scream to the pilot, this trope of higher power, directing everything, "Who is in charge? Why are you going off course? Manually adjust! There is time. Why? Why? Why are you flying straight into a mountain?" Pilot is incapable of listening or indifferent to hearing anyone, symbol as he is, directing flight over and over, each time I read, into unmovable Mount Erebus in that ice-covered land. Explosion immense: there is no one to hear it. If a plane crashes, and there is no one to hear it, the concussive explosion is still immense. None survive.

***

Pulling a book of Neruda's poetry from my shelf, I started reading "If You Forget Me" before stopping. The poem is one between lovers, not parent and child, but the title leaves me in another, familiar domain. I am lost in that poetic country. Am I writing so as not to forget?

"Reading a good poem doesn't give you something to talk about. It silences you," Mark Yakich wrote in *Reading a Poem: Twenty Strategies*. "Reading a great poem pushes further. It prepares you for the silence that perplexes us all: death," Yakich continued.

Perhaps that is why so many people refuse to read, I thought. They really do not want to consider death or be prepared for the inevitable. I met Yakich, a remarkable poet and teacher, a few years ago in New Orleans, and open one of his books to read again because my writing efforts and thoughts have coalesced into swirling, muddy streams of doubt and confusion. When there is nothing solid, there is no place even to stand, to sit, to be in place.

I close Yakich's book and continue to think about his truthful, annihilating statements. Tackling the reading of verse was not what I wanted to do but what I needed. Everything hushes, and I slide deeper into silence. Winter inside even as ice on the lake withdraws.

None of us survive ultimately. A sole death is all of our deaths foretold. Yet someone tells our stories. Because Blaise's life was stopped before he had reached where he was going, I am telling part of his story, but only the part from the immensity of my loss and love for him.

Five

Grace

Spare, honed to the bone poetry of Jane Kenyon sits on my desk.
I think about her bravery: writing detailed observations,
unadorned, as her disease, growing cancer, settled on a bough
above her like the prescient, flying owl in her poem "Prognosis."

Writing a memoir takes some amount of bravery, too, I
remind myself, tormented with unanswerable questions. Would
Blaise want me to tell these stories, even those in which he is
nothing short of heroic? Hesitating again, I write about my son
but get up suddenly, unable to modify the image I see of him
looking troubled. I can picture Blaise slowly shaking his head in
disbelief, or is it disapproval? He was not ready to write with this
kind of intimacy, I know. At the moment, I am not sure he was
ready for me to write about him either.

"I want others to know what a good man you are," I tell
his ghost. I consider the meaning of the word grace as tied to
goodwill. My son was filled with that kind of grace.

"Was." He reminds me. "They know what I was like if they
knew me. If not, why do you care what others think? What matters

is what I came to understand about myself. What matters is what the people I care about think."

But I care. "I want everyone to know." The room is silent again, without accusation or query. I cannot see or hear him.

After Blaise's funeral, my sister-in-law Marilyn told me that people in our community were talking about what they believed was Blaise's overdose. Marilyn is upset because they are gossiping about her nephew, and they are wrong in their assumptions.

"He didn't die of an overdose." I snorted because I could not laugh about such an obscenity. My son could have overdosed at one period in his life, but he had three years earlier made the hard climb out of that darkness. For those last few years of his life, he had been fully himself. He had been, in fact, his best self: generous and thoughtful.

"I know," said Marilyn. "I just wanted you to know what some people are saying."

"Don't write about me to excuse or dismiss my addiction," Blaise would have said. He wanted it laid bare, and he was proud of moving through his trials of addiction. I still struggle remembering those hard moments. There were some instances of his behaviors during addiction that were monumentally negative. He missed his sister Colette's birth of her first son Enzo because he was out drinking. What was worse, he would remind me only once, was that Dan and I had to leave shortly after our grandson's birth to try to get our son out of trouble. He had been stopped and charged with a DUI. "I was an a-hole," he said. His honesty and contempt for himself was abrupt. He was done with excuses.

Blaise never tried to diminish his actions or the consequences he paid. He knew full well the hurt he had caused others and the damage to himself. Yet his truthfulness about it later was almost startling. His honesty also made it easier to forgive. "Don't make me out to be more than I was," I could hear him. But he was also so much more, so much braver than I could ever write. He was, in fact, better than even he knew.

agree to my daughter's request that I see a grief counselor she has found for me.

Talking with my counselor Ann, I was struck by just how seldom she spoke during my visit. Her office's private, quiet space and her patience allowed me to go in any direction I wanted or needed without hindrance. I could utter a statement, cry, blow my nose, start up again without having to censor myself. Her expansive listening was a gift. I recognize few people receive in this manner. Largely unintentionally, people cannot wait to jump into any opening in order to tell their own stories, relate their anecdotes. How often we interrupt each other, breathless with excitement over our words. Ann was not waiting to speak, thankfully. She listened.

A second remarkable aspect of my session with my grief counselor: her few words seemed just right. At one point, I had been describing my son's horrific death scene, and I was emotionally drained, struggling at the bottom of a deep, empty well. I looked up and asked, "How do you do this? Listen to these terribly sad incidences in people's lives day after day?" I really wanted to know.

"It is a privilege," she said without gesture, no movement of her hands, nor her feet; her face tranquil. "I am allowed to experience grace in your presence." Her words appeared genuine. I had not thought about what a state of grace sounds and looks like until that moment. Knowing, however, everything else is stripped away in the intimacy of great sorrow: life's trivialities dissipated, I exhaled and breathed in long and slow.

"Privilege of grace," I said, almost a question.

"Anchored in love," she answered, as if in Catholic Mass service and response.

On the way home, I recalled Annie Dillard lines from her book *Pilgrim at Tinker Creek,* a book I had read multiple times: "The answer must be, I think, that beauty and grace are performed whether or not we will recognize or sense them. The least we can do is try to be there." My grief counselor was there to witness. Another meaning of grace: that unmerited favor of spiritual blessing. I have felt it more often since my son has passed away. I felt it in my son in the last years of his life almost as if he knew what was ahead. I have felt it throughout my family and with friends.

Not long after Blaise's death, Dan and I were in Washington, D.C. having lunch with my daughter Colette and son-in-law David. The playoffs before the World Series were still going on, and the Yankees were playing their last game later that day. A young waiter approached our table wearing a Washington Nationals baseball cap. He looked to be about Blaise's age, and something about him seemed familiar, or perhaps, I was subconsciously looking for my son in every young man's face.

When the waiter asked for my order, he tapped his cap in enthusiasm, and I responded to his gesture, "I'd rather have the Yankees win."

"Aw, noooooo," he laughed. "Not the Yankees. You're in D.C. It's the Nationals going all the way this year. Why the Yanks?"

"They were my son's team," I said before my husband or daughter could stop me. "He died recently, and so I want the Yankees to win for him."

Everyone at the table, as well as the waiter, became momentarily stunned. The waiter opened his eyes wider then left hurriedly to get our drinks.

Dan was visibly mortified at my sharing such personal, painful information with a stranger. "I am going to talk about Blaise," I said defensively. "I'm sorry if it makes you uncomfortable." Colette's eyes watered, but I knew she understood, or, rather, I hoped she did. I did not look at David, but I knew his suffering, too.

"Talk about him to me, not to a waiter," Dan said, a little exasperated with my unwanted sharing.

Despite my poor social form, we had a lovely time with our daughter and son-in-law during lunch. When the waiter later brought us desserts, he said nothing, setting them down as if he had filled our order.

My daughter looked up at me and laughed. "Did you slip in a dessert order for us?"

"No," I said, honestly not remembering if I had hinted that I wanted dessert or not.

When we finished, our waiter returned with the check. "Desserts on the House," he confessed with a wry smile, his Nationals baseball cap missing and his curly dark hair flopping over his ears.

I looked down at the check and written across it in large letters were the words, "Go, Yankees!"

All of us at our intimate little table had tears welling in our eyes. It scarcely mattered that the Yankees lost later that day. The young waiter's generosity silenced us but filled us with more love. That young man and our interactions are what grace looks like. I will remember him and his kindness.

Concepts about grace, for me, are inextricably linked to thinking about Blaise Martin. "Grace" in all these permutations of the word. Being very tall is frequently associated with being a little clumsy. Blaise never was ungainly, not even in adolescence. I could see him moving from one end of a basketball court to the other almost without comprehension of how he got into position to block a shot, so elegant his form and swift his deceptive movements. How many games had I watched over the years, sports in which he gradually came into his own, always with fluidity of economical movement? Grace, here, as refinement of movement.

Beautiful, polished movements are not always culturally accepted in men, however. Males with the dexterity of ballet dancers, whether or not they take ballet, face an uphill battle in our culture. Blaise had that type of grace combined with power. Yet, he was never a coach's favorite. He did not have the kind of "hustle" with which they were all so enamored. He often appeared not to be "trying" hard enough.

As a four-year old, Blaise wanted to hit a few baseballs. I took him out in the field, not wearing a baseball glove, and tossed a ball to him. I did not expect him to be able to connect, let alone hit a baseball squarely. The line drive did not hit me directly, fortunately; ball barely glancing off my cheekbone, but even the glancing blow stunned and unbalanced me. I stopped, held my cheek, wondering if anything was broken. It was not, but that was one of the last times I underestimated my son's athletic ability.

Blaise was wearing number 81, grinning, in his bright green Jets, Homer Small Fry Jersey. The team ended up Pee-Wee football champions for two years in a row. My son was eight years old at the time. His heart was strong. His future looked bright. His coach thanked him at the end of the season for playing, "one of the non-glory positions and helping our team win."

An influential parent told one of our school coaches that Blaise was "lazy and slow. He doesn't hustle." That baseball coach decided to cut my son from the junior high team, based upon this other parent's intrusion in the decision process.

I know this fact because the coach later confessed. "I think I made a mistake," he said with some humility, long after the damage. So many mistakes made. "I thought he didn't hustle," his voice trailed off as I restrained my anger and hurt. Let it go, I tried to tell myself.

When 12-year-old Blaise found out his name was not on the baseball team's list of players, he sat staring at a blank computer screen. Coming into the library, I found him silently crying, tears streaking his face. Mother's protective instincts took over, and I wanted to fix it all for him. It was good that the bad-mouthing parent and coach were not present. I seriously wanted to lash out at them.

The boy cut from the junior high baseball team was the same one who had a huge impact on his team winning the Little League home town tournament with his pitching and hitting. This was the twelve-year-old who could stretch out and catch almost anything thrown to first base, the same kid who could hit a baseball effortlessly and watch it fly for a homerun or triple. Quite simply, he did not have to be the fastest kid or the one with the showy hustle when he hit for extra bases consistently. He did not have to appear to work incredibly hard when it all came too easily.

When you are very good at something, you do not expect to be cut. Nothing new in this indifferent universe, but it hurt Blaise, and because he was hurt, I ached for him. His dad and I took a different tact, however, and pointed our son in another direction. We convinced him to try out for lacrosse. Blaise did go out for the team and played lacrosse until he graduated from high school.

In retrospect, I am still not sure if ours was the right decision in convincing him to play a different sport. Playing lacrosse, however, kept Blaise busy and prevented him from dwelling on the first time he was unfairly cut from something he truly loved. Looking back, I thought he took the blow with considerable grace for a kid, handling the wound much better than his mother and father. He never said a mean word about the coach who cut him.

Blaise was good at lacrosse without a lot of effort or previous experience. I knew he was not crazy about the game, but he always wanted his team to win. He did like the helmet and being able to hit with his stick. And he was not just good, he was very good.

During his senior year, more than one college coach approached and asked if he was interested in playing lacrosse for them in college. He was not. Although we knew he was talented, we understood Blaise never loved lacrosse the way he had loved baseball, but he adjusted and left the hurt behind.

Yet, for one more summer after being cut from the junior high school team, Blaise played baseball. A local summer league team ran short of players, and he was asked to join to fill out the roster. All of the other players on the summer team had been playing on the school team that had just finished their scholastic season. From the pitchers' mound, Blaise dominated, striking out batters with seeming ease. He had not lost his long stride from the mound and natural stroke at the plate.

Blaise and his great childhood friend Nick Triolo combined for a one-hit shutout in the summer Babe Ruth League. The triple Blaise hit in the game made a difference to the team and to the boy who had been cut from the school team earlier that spring. I remember sitting in a chair to the side of the bleachers, not feeling part of the parent group that cheered the team on, but I was so proud. I believed he had his whole life ahead of him.

The kids on the team told him to try out for baseball again, but, at the end of the summer, Blaise signed up to play lacrosse on the school team. Once he made a decision, he moved on.

By the time he graduated from high school, Blaise had been named to many all-tournament teams, both in school competitions and outside school competition in AAU play in multiple sports, but particularly basketball. An opposing basketball coach from our league told his ex-wife, who happened to be my teaching colleague, "Where did that kid come from? Dafoe was the best player on the court." This comment was particularly high praise since one of the players on that coach's team went on to play in the NBA. The opposing coach's ex-wife shared his compliment with me. I thought it strange that praise for Blaise always seemed to come from rival coaches.

Playing basketball in college for a few years, Blaise never let go of his love of that sport but had grown weary of playing under whims of volatile coaches, men who too often acted younger than their players, throwing temper tantrums, flinging water bottles, shoving players, spitting while berating. When Blaise did not go out for the college basketball team in his junior year, his interest in college dissipated with the loss of basketball. Sadly, he walked away from formal education during his senior year of college, a choice that hurt both his father and me.

Just once, I recall thinking, if just one coach or professor had shown that he or she really cared about my son enough to talk with him and listen. In fairness, Blaise probably made it hard for them. He never tried to flatter or worm his way into a lineup or "suck up" to a teacher.

Only much later, after he had beaten his addictions, Blaise quietly began a journey to self-education, hungrily reading every issue of *The New Yorker* and *Atlantic* magazines that arrived at our door, watching documentaries and podcasts of topical importance to history, reading online journals and articles. Then he would ask questions of his father or me, test his theories out in the way he might have while in college.

There was, at the time, so much neither Blaise nor his parents knew about his body. Blaise generally had a calm demeanor. Although he loved sports and was physically gifted, I discovered after his death, he should never have played competitive athletics. His heart and undetected Marfan syndrome should have precluded action games. Yet, I cannot imagine my son would have chosen to remain on the sidelines no matter the consequence.

As a result of our inability to know about the danger he faced and inability to protect him, Blaise dominated in athletics but continued to strain his heart. Only after Blaise died did I come to know that Marfan syndrome causes fatigue, the heart working too hard.

All of that cheering from the sidelines, cheers for his magnificent movements, those sometimes-astonishing acts of athleticism were accomplished under duress. His heart was in a fight with the rest of his body, and only in looking back do I speculate as to whether or not he instinctively knew.

Did my son's coaches' critical appraisal of his supposed lack of "hustle" have something to do with Blaise's instinct to protect himself without fully knowing why. Fatigue is always a factor with an ailing heart. Without demonstrating the coaches' love of "hustle," Blaise caught four passes in one football game for sixty-six yards, against a tough Jamesville-DeWitt football team, for the win. He covered the length of a gymnasium basketball court as if it was measured with inches, not feet. Was he making calculated decisions or subconscious ones about when he exerted himself? A long stride, long arms, long fingers, and perfect timing allowed him to make it all look too easy. Achievement is never supposed to appear easy.

He, too often, made life appear easy. I think his teachers thought he believed everything was a joke, but it was a philosophical one in which the jester is the most aware of the end.

Grace in athletics transferred to everything about his being. Blaise was smooth and dexterous even in the manner in which he took in the day, entered a room, left quietly, often without speaking, a wry smile caught only in the last moment glance. I was always aware, however, of my son's large presence, his too big of a heart, and, since his death, the vast hole left by his absence.

Six

Grief's Appearance and Disguises

Stomach churning, dizzying dread. Grief and fear are wed. "No one ever told me that grief felt so like fear," wrote C.S. Lewis in *A Grief Observed*, about the loss of his wife Helen. "I find it hard to take what anyone says," Lewis admitted, giving into honesty even as his words conflicted with his faith. For Lewis, for me, all this "helpful" advice and religious platitudes from others too often, "vanish like an ant in the mouth of a furnace."

Kind words from friends and acquaintances have been extended, but lessons and warnings of caution to accept someone else's notion of heaven and hell do not go down well. I am not so much resistant to their exhortations as dismayed that such superstitions still dominate our culture. I recognize that people need something to hold onto during the onslaught following loss of a loved one, but assumptions should not be made that everyone has or should have the same belief system.

Considering Lewis's choice of words, "fear" is closely aligned with grief. What I most feared had already happened. I did not fear hell but the loss of my child. Grief is the aftermath of fear; it is an obliteration.

Matthew Dickman has grief arriving as a "purple gorilla" of all things in his poem "Grief." The purple gorilla should be funny, but it is not, and Dickman knows it, plays with our abhorrence until we are stricken from just one poem. I read on, searching for an answer that does not exist although I like Dylan Thomas' promise, "And Death Shall Have No Dominion." Yet, death always has the final say.

Max Porter suggests Grief with a capital "g" comes in the guise of Corvus corax, an absurd member of the species, hopping out of that "murder of crows," cawing and flapping its way straight out of some Ted Hughes' poem. Porter's grief is a crow metaphor relentlessly agitating and aggravating a widower and his two young sons in Porter's novella *Grief is the Thing with Feathers*. The author's title is a play on the words of Emily Dickinson's poem "Hope is the thing with feathers, poem 254." Porter's Grief is personal and intimate even when it is maddening and absurdly incoherent.

I am working to identify my grief, lowercase but ever present. How would I characterize it? After reading Porter's book, I wonder if every instance in which I see a black feather, I will think "Grief." Fortunately, I do not. Grief is unlike a crow to me, but when grief walks in, I find myself anthropomorphizing, cursing it, begging it, trying to, alternately, make unholy then holy bargains with this creature with multitudinous arms and legs, a wide mouth that will not coalesce into frown nor grin.

No, I reassess, having lived with grief. Grief does not have multiple arms and legs. Grief is shadow, usually amorphous, by odd turns taking the shape of a being. What little I have learned about this shapeshifter is that grief is always lurking about, behind some closed door, under a bed, putting holes in a boat over water, squeezing between you and the other passenger on an airplane, unexpectedly turning up. Grief is terrifying one moment, a companion I do not want to leave in the next. Grief appears suddenly, refusing to exit, then, just as unexpectedly, slides out through some crevice, only to return when I open my eyes in the morning or when I close them for another sleepless night.

There is no accounting for this unsubstantial shade that, at intervals, wears distorted human face then appears across a field of snow on which ice has formed, causing glassy, unreadable surface and then a treatise on loss.

Religions institutionalize reactions to grief as if such a complex emotional reaction could ever be harnessed for propaganda or utilitarian reasons, made to work for man's purposes. Yet, indoctrination has worked because grief is universal, and we are all variously afraid of the reason grief is with us: death. Cause people to fear death, offer an alternative, and they will follow, however illogical the dictate. Ultimately, death triumphs over every human endeavor.

I remind myself that birth does, as well.

Tom Petty's "Buried Treasure" Sirius radio show is playing in the background. His wonderful voice feels so alive, yet I know Petty is no longer in this world, these recordings taped and replayed. I'm at the computer, and Dan comes into the library to read after getting the mail. I open a card from a neighbor. It is a sympathy note for us and a tribute to the affection earned by our dog Bogie. I stand the card on the desk. Dan cries, trying unsuccessfully to hold back tears. "I can't think of losing Bogie without thinking of losing Blaise," he finally says. Bereavement looms larger than anything in our house, larger than the snow-covered landscape and frozen lake beyond our windows. Grief sits on the couch behind me, so I do not turn around. I am aware that at any moment, grief will leap out at me or at Dan. We cannot prepare for its tumultuous comings and goings. One of us is wrapped up in it at various points during the days and weeks and months since our loss.

"That Discomfort You're Feeling is Grief" is the title of an article by Scott Berinato in the March 23, 2020 issue of the *Harvard Business Review*. Berinato's article refers to a national, collective grief being experienced by the country during the unsettling conditions brought on by the novel coronavirus, COVID-19. Hard to look anywhere since March 2020 without confronting our national pandemic horror in the news, in editorials, and nonfiction work through the lens of loss. Within that wider view of sorrow mixed with anger and fear about loss of jobs and uncertainty, there is the deep grieving about loss of loved ones.

Almost as if these writings about grief seek me out rather than the other way around, I look up to my computer screen to see a review of Jason Rosenthal's memoir about the death of his wife in *The Washington Post, Style* section, April 21, 2020 issue. *Style* writer Karen Heller gave her review of the book a lengthy title: "He became one of America's most famous widowers—thanks to his wife. Now he's trying to teach us about grief."

After reading Heller's review, I reflected on her title. Was Rosenthal really, "trying to teach us about grief?" Or was he, rather, sharing his love and loss? Heller's words also caused me to consider again why I was writing my memoir about the loss of my son. But I had never once thought that the purpose of writing my book was to "teach about grief." I am not a grief instructor, nor an expert, neither a psychologist nor a counselor nor clinician. I have no medical expertise. I also do not believe you can teach grief. You experience suffering or you empathize with others who are in pain. I had only my own powerful lived moments to reveal and the compulsion to document.

Heller noted that Rosenthal, the "world's most famous widower" had his book published "during the coronavirus pandemic, when the world is going through its own protracted grief." Yet Rosenthal was engaged in writing his book long before anyone in this country knew about or even imagined this pandemic. It is more than doubtful Rosenthal set out to teach the world about grief experienced during a pandemic. Because of the fame of Rosenthal's wife, Amy Krause Rosenthal, a children's book author and blogger, Jason Rosenthal was aware the world was watching and waiting for his words. His dying wife had written perhaps the most famous, published valentine in contemporary culture: "You May Want to Marry My Husband." In his book *My Wife Said You May Want to Marry Me*, Rosenthal first referenced his wife's title in his own, then stated, "I realized the world was grieving with me." How powerful that must feel. I was trying to imagine but could not find such a profusion of evidence in my own life.

Why did I set out to write this book? Only after long contemplation and multiple false starts, I am able to define a bit more precisely what led to this writing: love for my son and a need to search for answers. I had to write it down. I also wanted to give Blaise something I was unable to give him during his life. An unnatural, spontaneous gene mutation shortened my son's life. No one knew about the imminent danger he faced during his lifetime. Looking back, I recognize we were fortunate we did not lose him while watching one of his lacrosse or basketball games in high school. His heart kept beating even when he was tackled in football, or he sprinted down the field, or he leaped to block a shot in basketball. It kept beating.

I could not eliminate the horror of his death, but I could show the fullness of his quiet, yet remarkable thirty-two years, a story few people knew. The process of writing is, of course, therapeutic, but writing also opens wounds that long for salve. I had to be willing to go there, in that dark place again and again, to write a memoir of this nature. Then, I knew I would do it out of love.

Initially wrapping myself in silence and inaction, I woke to a demand, a need. I feel as if my son has been encouraging me, looking over my shoulder throughout this writing. He has made gentle suggestions and let me know more than once when I went too far. He suggested I delete a whole section. I did.

Although I was a teacher in high school and, for a brief time, in a community college, I would never presume to "teach about grief," but I tried to share as honestly as possible my own journey. I humbly offer my experience and love because that is what is most real. In sharing stories about my son, I did find other people who felt comforted or entered into the story through connections to their own experiences with great loss.

"Grief for a while is blind," wrote Percy Bysshe Shelley in *Prometheus Unbound,* his lyrical drama. Grief's blindness is evident, but what struck me reading Shelley again was the phrase "for a while." Embodied in that phrase is the expectation and hope that grief, too, is mutable. For now, it is with me as a constant. There is the expectation it will at some point leave me, but what then? When grief exits my metaphorical and literal house, will I still sorrow for my son? Will I laugh over his antics and wry sense of humor? Will I remember with fondness his spontaneous huge hugs? Will I struggle to recall his voice, his expressions? I prefer Grief or grief to blurred images, to no longer recognizing Blaise.

How many moments of my son's life have already disappeared? This hideous contract we have with our memories. If the tradeoff for leaving grief behind is forgetting, I determine to keep grief, however painful, as close as possible.

At moments, grief seems other than hostile, more like an ancient being who is weary of listening to the world's sorrows but will reluctantly settle in for just one more session. Naturally, grief is very old. Grief is patient in the sense that it seems to know it will be around a long time and does not have to draw out your responses immediately. As soon as humans could form attachments, grief made a permanent arrangement with us.

***

Your presence in silent rooms

Your presence in silent rooms,
the surprise of you again and again
is unsettling, yet comforting, even as we weep.

How did I not remark with growing dread?
"His long, slender fingers; his long, slender toes?"
How did I not know what remarkable beauty portends?

My son, I knew so well and did not know
those gestures you made, those unexpected gifts
of stories told by strangers who knew you.

Mourners filing in, "patron saint of the struggling,"
someone remarked because you were tender, generous
to others who were swimming in deep waters.

An addict in the mourning room, shuffling his feet
in the back, unable to approach. "You did nothing wrong,"
my daughters told him. "He did not die from an overdose."

"He was king of the sauna," another remarked,
uncomfortable, stifling laughter. "Made us all laugh,
made our jobs more bearable," a dark-haired man said.

Delivered pizza after work to a boy with cancer
and never said a word about this kindness;
the boy with cancer living still, but my boy gone.

"He was my best friend," they said again and again,

59

as if my son had been a dozen men, not one
who could seem so alone and inconsolable.

How could I not have known about his many expressions of
benevolence, his politically savvy Tweets, his practiced humor?
How could I not have apprehended he would leave us in the night?

Am I honest here? How could I know this child I loved so would
conquer addiction to fall to some rare syndrome, yet find scarcely
attainable balance and grace?

Bird, shadow, amorphous creature, draped urn, open gate,
endless voyager: however it arrived and in whatever form, grief
overstays its stay. I fall asleep to it hovering, open my eyes to its
face, ride with grief as my shapeshifting companion in this liminal
space.

Seven

Safe at Home

Christmas, a thousand years ago, at least that is my skewed sense of its placement in my unstuck ordering, my father got a call during dinner. My childhood family members were sitting around the dining room table with our turkey and mom's perfect mashed potatoes before us. Everyone talking at once when my dad got up. My mother was annoyed he left the table to answer the phone. When he returned a considerable time later, she asked what was so important that he had to be interrupted during our family's holiday meal?

He said with a tremor in his voice, "Mr. _____ died. His wife called. They had been sitting together when he said he was tired, got up, went to his bedroom, and died. Just like that." I still remember the welling of tears in my father's eyes.

My mom was not satisfied with that answer, pressing, "Why did she call you? Why would anyone call a lawyer on Christmas when her husband dies?"

My father said simply, "She didn't know what else to do."

Our noisy, large family became suddenly silent, everyone thinking about this other family, not so very different from ours, this family that had suddenly fallen into another dimension, one without joy or presents or laughter. There would be no further holiday celebration for them, no "goodnight, John Boy," echoing throughout their big, many-roomed house that evening or the many evenings to follow.

Home is the safe space, a sanctuary from a troubled world. We tell ourselves this comforting lie repeatedly. Just get home safely, we whisper. Yet, the terror is always there, tucked into our own beds.

***

Years, not months, went by while my son battled with addiction. Dan and I were in the struggle, too, not simply as bystanders, but unable to make moves of any lasting consequence. We tried everything we could think of except to turn our son out of his home. On more than one occasion, we verbally battled each other because there were no easy answers, and we had different ideas about the direction to turn in order to help our son.

Angry words once broke out between Dan and Blaise after he stumbled into the house. Accusations went flying around the dining room. I stood beside them physically but between them in emotional space. Suddenly, Blaise turned and said, "That's it. I'm leaving." He walked unsteadily but managed to shut the door and set out down the road.

I looked at Dan pleadingly but could see only angry resolve in his face, not the fear. Then I followed my son out the door. I had no plan or thought of what actions I should take beyond going after him. I just knew Blaise was in trouble, and I could not let him go alone. I knew even if he was walking straight into Hell, I would go there, too.

Walking over a mile down the road, I could see the figure of my son growing fainter as his strides, even in an inebriated state, were so much longer than mine. I would never be able to catch up to him but neither could I stop and go home without him.

Just then, our car pulled up beside me. Dan rolled down the window and commanded without anger, "Get in."

I said something to the effect of, "I can't without him."

"We're going to get him," Dan said. Within a few minutes, we caught up to our son, and Dan helped Blaise into the car where our grown young man flopped over on the seat. We drove back to the house where Dan took off his shoes and lifted his son into bed. I thought my husband was going to yell, but instead he said while looking straight ahead, "We're never doing this again."

Starting to protest, I thought he meant we were never going to bring our son home again, but then he finished his thought. "We're never going to let him come between us again. We will always bring him home." And we did.

I could never understand what started Blaise down this treacherous path of addiction. How was it that his sisters moved so effortlessly to successful careers and lives without this problem? I questioned myself and my parenting. Had I unintentionally acted in a way that made Blaise more anxious than his sisters? Did his birth position as the last of my children alter the way I treated him? Yet, that made little sense. Unlike my first child during which time Dan was on the road working for his family much of the time, Blaise not only had his mother's and father's attentions, but his two older sisters were like little mothers watching over him. They put sunglasses on him, dressed him up for plays, and had tea parties. It is not so strange that Blaise grew up gentle. But each of us is more complex than a single set of factors.

As for his relationship with his father, I once asked my son about whether Nick or Jesse was his best friend. He just smiled that impish smile of his and said, "Love them both," then definitively said, "Dad is my best friend."

We lived on a lake, but Blaise was not really a fisherman. He never hunted, as did his grandfathers, father, and uncles on both sides of our family. Killing anything held no interest for him. He preferred the fish swimming about rather than on a hook. Even as an adult, Blaise kept that gentle aspect of his nature.

Then, how did he become so terribly anxious that he sought relief in drugs? Looking at his anxiety from every point of view without knowledge of his condition, I kept coming back to my fears that I had not been a good parent in some way to my son. I did not know what was affecting his health, the secret of his ailing heart not discovered during his lifetime.

When the medical examiner told me, "Undiagnosed people with Marfan's are frequently addicts. They are looking for something to relieve the pain and issues related to the syndrome." Although I cried like a forsaken child when she said those words, part of me also experienced a great weight lifted from me. All those years I had partially blamed myself for my son's pain and addiction. How had I made him so anxious that he sought out Xanax? My daughters were so grounded, I could not understand what had happened with my son.

Blaise could not understand either, but he once told me, "It's nothing you did, Mom. I did this to myself." Then, when it was too late for him to know, we finally had some explanation. It was not anxiety. That pain in his chest was his ailing heart, tissue splitting apart.

If Blaise could only return for a minute, I wanted to give him that knowledge, let him hear the medical examiner's words, as well. "He must have been in terrible pain," the medical examiner repeated. "I don't know how he was walking around. What courage." Yet, Blaise had more than walked around. He cut down trees, lifted logs, carried immense, physical weight in addition to the weight of anxiety and an enlarged heart, without complaint, on that last day of his life.

Only after his death did I fully comprehend the extent of my son's strength and bravery in life. If I set out to write a memoir about my son, the previous statement is the one I most want any reader to take with him or her. I could not give my son his life back. I could not take away his pain in life, but I could let others know how magnificent he was, how selfless near the end, how strong in his suffering silently.

At my nephew Michael's wedding, Blaise brought his friend Alena. They both looked so beautiful, radiating joy and good health. They stood out because both of them were tall. One of my late brother Emerson's friends remarked to me, "Blaise looks really good. Is he working out? What's he up to now?"

I nodded my head, unsure about what to say or how to answer. Blaise was not working out during that juncture, but I knew he was too thin. Thin but handsome. What I did not know was he had moved on from taking Xanax to calm his anxiety to heroin, due to the expense of Xanax. He had already entered a nightmare, and I was only suspicious, still largely ignorant of his imminent peril from multiple directions.

Finally, I smiled at the friend and said, "thanks" as if the man had been complimenting me and not asking a pressing question. I avoided an extended conversation about my son because I wanted to avoid inevitable and unanswerable questions. What was he doing now? It was not out of embarrassment, however, but fear. If I said something out loud, would it be true?

My son knew I wrote poetry. He listened to many of my poems but never the poems I wrote about his struggle with drugs and alcohol. "I'm not addicted to alcohol," he would firmly remind me much later, as if the addiction to Xanax was more than sufficient, admitting his dependence on the drug.

Dan and I were not unaware that our son was drinking too much earlier on, but we thought that if we could just help him get through the self-destructive impulses that race through too many adolescents and young people, he would be fine.

It is also relevant to note that during the time Blaise began his descent into addiction, tentative at first and then finally, with abandon, my mother's Alzheimer's was diagnosed, my father fell down the stairs and died, my husband's father died, and I was responsible for determining my mother's care while I was working full time. My younger brother was dying. It is not that I did not think about my son and worry about his secrecy but not enough. Chaos whirled around me. Looking back with perspective now, I am able to see how overwhelmed I was and unable to pay significant attention to what my youngest child was doing or feeling. I was distracted. I can also imagine that Blaise was looking for something to relieve pain during that period of time, emotional pain of what our family was going through, as well as his undiagnosed physical pains.

Blaise's struggle with addiction chewed chunks of his life and left his father and me frequently upset as to how to deal with fraught situations. We were frustrated, scared, angry, and confused. I could not help thinking that our beautiful boy had turned in this destructive direction because of something I had done. More guilt mingled with fear. Why was he so anxious? If only we had known that Blaise's anxiety was not anxiety at all but a heart in terrible trouble.

Although he was not entirely himself as an addict, Blaise was not cruel or disrespectful to us. I still find it remarkable that in his 32 years of life, my son never once had a cross word, profane, or even an impolite word for his mother. I am sure he must have felt that urge, but he never acted upon it. More than a little strange, when his tongue was loosened with drugs or alcohol, he remained respectful or at least quiet around me. Some willpower was still at work.

The other remarkable aspect I want to relate about his passage through and out the other side (or is it the tunnel) of addiction is the fact that he was, as a young man, completely himself again after recovery. His sweetness, gentleness, wry sense of humor, and empathy for others had fully evolved, but he was the same little boy of his youth as a young man.

After Blaise went through rehab and successfully conquered "his demons" as he called them, he told me that he had hated himself during that period. All of his protestations were attempts to keep from going in so deep he could never climb out again. Only later, did he tell me the drug was the only way to tolerate living with himself, but dependence upon the drug only made his intense self-disgust increase.

I lectured, questioned, listened to him, and waited up at night for my son to make it home, to survive another night, and loudly walk in the front door of the house where he would be safe again.

Home. Safe. Those two words frequently go together for many privileged Americans, yet the concept of safety at home is inherently deceitful. When and where do we truly live in a state of complete freedom from injury, danger, risk, or deprivation? Even during intervals of peace and plenty, how many fatal incidents actually happen in the home? In 2017 alone, 64,795 Americans died of poisoning, most accidental and most at their own addresses. Of course, that figure includes some drug-related poisoning. In that same year, 36,338 died from falls in the home, according to the National Safety Council. My own father fell down his stairs, ending his life. We have not even taken into account shootings, a gun discharged in anger or carelessness. In 2017, 39,773 Americans died by guns, many in their own homes.

Add all those to other accidental deaths and severe injuries that happen in the home. How many wives and children risk injury or death from an abusive member of their family? Still, we cling to that myth that we are safe at home.

***

Listen intently.

One eye open.

Light from headlights slowly move across ceiling.

Car pulling up, door opening and closing,

boots or shoes dropped,

a stumble, then

footfalls on the stairs.

Bedroom door shutting.

Relief.

He's home.

Safe.

***

I spent years waiting to hear those welcome sounds of my son's car or his friend's car arriving, releasing a sigh before allowing myself to fall asleep. How many nights was I fearful and straining for sounds to detect my son was moving about on the floor below? I could not stop his addiction. That was his alone to solve, no matter how much I wanted it. And he finally did.

***

On the night Blaise died, he was home, on the couch in our living room. Then, there was a terrifying cry. Waking at midnight to a scream, I half ran, half leaped down our stairs, then I was standing over my son. Thin lines of vomit flowed from the corners of his mouth and nostrils; otherwise, he looked to be peacefully sleeping. Rachel was sobbing and dialing 911. Dan was suddenly beside me, pulling Blaise the rest of the way off the couch to the rug on the floor, giving orders to do CPR, surprisingly composed. I heard Blaise's head hit the floor. "Mouth to mouth," my husband commanded, as he pushed the heel of his hand to our son's chest. I am certain I hesitated for an instant before placing my mouth over Blaise's and began to blow and count, blow, count. Everything in my being was working hard at something I did not believe in because the instant I saw him lying there, I knew he was gone forever.

In that moment, I understood as I never had before, all the world ends. Each one of us comes to an end.

State Police arrived before the EMTs, bursting in the door, jumping into action, our dog Bogie wildly agitated, whimpering, before running out the open door. Dan ran out after our dog as the police pulled out their kit. Six doses of Narcan went into my son as one flipped couch cushions, looking for drugs. Another yelled at me: "What were you doing? Where were you? What did he use?"

Slow to answer out of shock not confusion, I finally said, "Upstairs, sleeping. He didn't use."

Again, the officer barked orders, "Get a spoon." He yanked Blaise's head back at an angle, and my son's head hit the floor again hard. I retrieved a spoon from the kitchen in a stupor. What use was a spoon?

"Take it out," he said, indicating the vomit in my son's mouth, as I clumsily tried to scoop it out.

"Get back," the officer near Blaise's head said, evidently angry with my feeble efforts.

"What was he taking? What drug?"

"He wasn't."

Dan and Bogie had not yet come back into the house. EMTs arrived, and there was a flurry of efficient, useless movements around the body of my son as six large men moved equipment around, still tossing cushions. At some point during that mad activity, my brain went into a slow crawl, scarcely able to respond to even the most basic order. After the first few commands, I heard almost nothing.

What little came through was Rachel gasping for air. A policeman told me that my mouth to mouth pushed vomit into his lungs, causing aspiration. I killed my son? Dan and Bogie reentered the house just before they loaded our son's body onto a stretcher. Someone yelled for us to follow the ambulance as a host of men left together with my son, the room littered with needles and Narcan paraphernalia. One of the officers grabbed some of the needles from the floor, leaving others. Vomit was on the rug where my son lay, cushions were overturned, a girl was weeping, and I knew in that extended horrifically long stretch of hell that my son had already died. But I could not process his death. It was not possible.

Although they rushed him to the hospital, and we followed, driving further into darkness, sitting in a nearly empty waiting room with Rachel and Dan, then racing off again, following another ambulance to a larger hospital with a higher level of technology, I could feel crashing waves of seismic grief as I moved in and out of shock, even before crying first tears for my son.

I did not descend into actual crying until hours later when a doctor at Upstate Medical said, "He is likely braindead. Do you want to donate his organs? Did he leave instructions?"

Blaise left instructions to donate his organs, but I could not follow his wishes.

Only much later, after talking to the Onondaga County Medical Examiner did I know that my son had experienced an aortic dissection in our living room. His heart had literally ripped apart, his brain and brain stem massively bleeding, all effectively, instantly, violently ending his life: all from the comfort of our couch in the safety of our home.

Eight

Reading Hemingway to My Son

Gathering up memories of Blaise, my arms are full. I hold these moments like an infant, yet am no more able to protect them from disappearing than I was my son. But I will cradle this remembrance and sing it to sleep.

***

Blaise is sick, my 14-year-old son laying on our couch, a cool cloth across his forehead to help bring his fever down. As a teen, he was too old for his mother to keep him company, yet young enough that he still needed her if she comes without asking.

His eyes are glassy from his high temperature, and he cannot even watch television. A pail sits on the floor below him in the event of nausea. He hasn't eaten all morning, so the pail is unnecessary.

"Do you want anything?" I ask, knowing he will say no.

My son shakes his head slowly with pleading eyes. He is that sick.

I have come prepared, thinking about fiction that will engage a teenage boy yet not be too taxing. Hemingway had been sitting on my shelf too long for that author's impatient nature. I am also thinking about how the book might cause Blaise to want to read more on his own, like his sisters. Hemingway was the man's man kind of author, succinct in his phrasing, perfect for the shorter attention span but also powerful, his words packing a punch. "How about I read you a story?"

Blaise almost laughs and moves his head. I am not sure if it is a yes or no.

"You're sick but also bored. It's an interesting story, I promise." I persist. "Ernest Hemingway's 'The Killers' about a boxer, well, at least on the surface, it's about a boxer at the end of his rope." I hesitate, wondering if I should point out the pun on "end of his rope," but wisely choose to let it go. "The main character is Nick Adams, a boy who makes a startling discovery: what one man is willing to accept."

"Boxers?" he asks weakly.

"Boxers," I tempt my son, again.

Never fully or verbally consenting, Blaise did manage to nod in either acceptance or agreement with my assessment. He could see I was not going anywhere, and he was not about to get up and leave.

I started reading:

> 'The door of Henry's lunchroom opened and two men came in. They sat down at the counter.
>
> "What's yours?' George asked them.
>
> "'I don't know," one of the men said. 'What do you want to eat, Al?'
>
> "'I don't know,' said Al. 'I don't know what I want to eat.'
>
> 'Outside it was getting dark. The streetlight came on outside the window. The two men at the counter read the menu. From

the other end of the counter Nick Adams watched them. He had been talking to George when they came in.

"'I'll have a roast pork tenderloin with apple sauce and mashed potatoes,' the first man said.

"'It isn't ready yet.'

Full stop in reading. I suddenly intuited the effect of Hemingway's slow pacing and looked up, asking my son, "Do you want me to stop?"

"No," Blaise said hoarsely. I could tell he meant it.

I continued reading. Well past the first few pages, I knew Blaise was either asleep or into "The Killers." I glanced over and saw my son's eyes were still glistening with fever and wide open in attention.

"'Talk to me, bright boy,' Max said. 'What do you think's going to happen?'

George did not say anything.

"'I'll tell you,' Max said. 'We're going to kill a Swede. Do you know a big Swede named Ole Anderson?'

"'Yes.'

"'He comes here to eat every night, don't he?'"

"Wait. They're not really going to kill that guy, the Swede, are they?" Blaise asked so softly I startled. I, too, had fallen under the spell of Hemingway's words.

"Do you want me to finish?" Good, I thought, he's interested, so I continue with Hemingway's story.

"Just tell me now. Do they kill him?"

"Have to read it. Do you want me to finish?"

Blaise might not have wanted anyone to know his mother read him a story when he was a teenager, even a very sick teenager. Then I realized, he would likely laugh about it later, think it was kind of nice, too.

"Go on then," Blaise says.

I read the ending of the story:

"'It's an awful thing,' Nick said.

'They did not say anything. George reached down for a towel and wiped the counter.

"'I wonder what he did?' Nick said.

"'Double-crossed somebody. That's what they kill them for.'

"'I'm going to get out of this town,' Nick said.

"'Yes,' said George. 'That's a good thing to do.'

"'I can't stand to think about him waiting in the room and knowing he's going to get it. It's too damned awful.'

"'Well,' said George, 'you better not think about it.'"

***

Blaise made a snorting sound. "That's it? The end?"

"Yes, the end," I said.

"Not a page missed?" He was incredulous. "That's how Hemingway ends it? With, 'don't think about it?'"

"I didn't like the ending the first time I read it either."

"You read it twice?"

"Of course."

Blaise almost imperceptibly shrugged. I thought I detected the hint of a smile, too. "Yeah, I get it," he said. "Hemingway wanted us to think about it the way Nick did. Maybe keep thinking about it." Then he turned away and fell into a deep sleep. He never did seek out another Hemingway story on his own, however.

***

"The world breaks every one and afterward many are strong at the broken places," wrote Ernest Hemingway in his novel *A Farewell to Arms*. Although not my favorite author, Hemingway had a knack for pithy, concise truths: "But those that will not break it kills. It kills the very good and the very gentle and the very brave impartially," Hemingway continued. "If you are none of these you can be sure it will kill you too but there will be no special hurry."

Although typically concise and cryptic, here Hemingway expanded on Greek historian Herodotus' words, "Whom the gods love dies young." If the gods loved my son, they certainly had a strange way of showing it, but the world did not break my son although it tried, and he was very good and very gentle and very brave.

I have become hyper aware of those beautiful souls who die too young. Former students, children of colleagues. The world does not spare the good.

What it means to be mortal is clear. No words, not even a metaphor with its ability to do heavy lifting; even a metaphor cannot carry the impact and burden of my son's death. Yet, I write.

***

Why didn't I cripple death?

Why did I do nothing when it came for him?
Why did I let strangers remove his body
from our home?
Why did I watch in silence
rather than launch into primal scream?
Why did I allow him to die?
I held no sway,
no jurisdiction over death.
I held my breath and waited
with churning stomach
for death to catch up to him.
Why did I do nothing
when I had no option?
We love so deeply,
so deeply and impossibly
because we cannot stop
death from coming
because we perish
and must watch

everyone we love
given unto death
until our own.

***

I remember the sense, when Blaise was fourteen, that I was still protecting my son even though he was nearly grown. I thought I was keeping him safe from harm by will power alone. How could I have known this son I loved so would be taken in the night, without my permission, without a single word of farewell?

Nine

His Voice is Missing

I woke one morning trying to remember his voice. Silence inside answered a bird outside our bedroom window.

Everything was too much, an assault on my paralyzed state after Blaise's death. I did not begin to speculate as to how I was protecting myself, cocooned. All was framed around my son's sudden absence.

I was not expecting the entrance of a hard-boiled detective. He knocked and entered before I even approached the door.

"So, what clues did you find?"

"Clues? I've been crying. What do you want of me?"

"Me, again? Me? You certainly talk about yourself a lot. You would think you could find some space to allow your son to speak." Suddenly sympathetic, he drops a stack of papers on my desk. Pages sprawl as if independently taking on the task of covering entire surface. "What about these?"

In the discombobulated pile are the beginnings of a screenplay. "Where did you find this?"

"On your computer. You might want to organize your files."

"But, I," I said, starting to get defensive. I drop the pretense and read the pages in front of me. "There are only a handful of pages. What am I going to do with so little?"

"Six pages of his voice, not yours, you might want to remember."

"You're right. His voice." I pick up the first of his pages. Title reads, "Swipe Left."

"And?"

"Some kind of ironic or absurdist commentary about dating in the tech age. Funny but not snark." I read more. "Very funny. His humor, not mine."

Detective nods. "A start," he says before getting ready to leave, pulling up collar of his trench coat in anticipation of the cold. "Anything else you notice?"

Rereading the scene, I say, "Yes. Loneliness, too. I feel both loneliness and comic absurdity simultaneously in this short scene from a script."

Apparently, I am onto something, but I don't know what exactly. My son left very little writing. I read his script again. With every reading, I feel his vitality. Language is purposely crude, dialogue filled with slang and cursing. It is also extremely funny and poignant. I did not know Blaise could be this funny, satiric, and self-deprecating in clever ways. Maybe I did. I am suddenly unsure. I know nothing about Tinder, and a scary thought, I did not know as much about my son as I believed. I knew he was clever but this entertaining, this talented as a writer out of the gate? He was writing a screenplay? We lived at the same address, and while he once mentioned he was thinking about writing a movie centered on dating, he never said he had created dialogue, completed a scene, worked on something of his own with another writer in the house.

Reading his scene over and over, I wanted more, so much more: his words, his wit, just Blaise. Scanning files and documents, I kept looking for his other words I might have missed.

"He's…" I stopped and looked around, turning to our computer. "There was something else; he could be so funny, satirical."

"And you didn't know that because?" The detective is still around.

"Wait. Maybe I knew that about my son, just he didn't share those things with me."

"Things?"

"I used to be more precise, but the thing about grief is…"

"Forget your lack of precision for a minute. His script? His words? His humor?"

"Okay, all of that. I found something."

"What else? Have you looked in his room lately?" I drop my shoulders in shame. "Too hard to go in his room. All too hard."

"Naturally, so you don't actually want to know what?"

"I do. I want to know more." We head upstairs to Blaise's room, curiosity overcoming the terror of confronting my grief.

I look at the posters: Frank Sinatra at twenty-two tacked on his door.

"Your son liked Frank Sinatra? Was like Frank Sinatra?" detective asks coolly.

"No, yes, maybe. Not a singer, but my son was cool like a young Frank Sinatra on that poster," I say as I point.

"Telling you what exactly?"

"I don't know." There is no exactness anymore. "What I mean is, I want my son to know I loved him unconditionally. I never cared if he was cool."

"But he cared. He cultivated cool."

Every item in his room speaks of a story. Past floods into present. Movie posters he loved adorn walls and old DVDs are neatly tucked on a shelf below his television, his tastes eclectic. Classic movies, horror movies, comedies. Blaise was savvy and fashionably aware for a young guy who lived in the city even though he, in fact, lived in a rural area. I think he wanted to project that city edge quality. He loved NYC. He selected his clothes and shoes with attention to detail. Look at that sweatshirt, those shoes, his hats. Coolness was also an attitude he carried even when at rest. Being cool was one of the reasons he did not ask for help when he should have. Why it took him so long to acknowledge that Xanax had him. Why he listened but did not fight back.

"You can find what you're looking for, but you have to be open and unafraid of what you discover." This detective in the room voices his disdain for my inaction, but I sense his understanding.

That was the trick. I knew that part of me was nervous about finding out something that would hurt too much.

I hunted for more of his written work. There was little saved on our computer. I know Blaise had a journal he kept through his battle with drugs and alcohol. I believe he destroyed most of those pages at some point. I found a few entries in a closet; remembered one or two he had shared with me in a moment of reaching out to me.

There were only a handful of his descriptions of the struggle. His brutal honesty in his writing caught me off guard because he was too frequently deceptive during those years of seeking relief in drugs.

His writing is also smart and astute. He could have been a writer, I thought, reading his words a second, then a third time. I am falling into a void at the center of his room.

Detective twists his head around as he moves further into Blaise's room. "He knew."

"Knew what?"

"He knew you always loved him. Now, what did you, in point of fact, want to tell him?"

"I didn't let him talk enough. I was always talking, giving too much advice, lecturing." It's my failing, thinking I can talk or write my way out of anything, but I had to face the facts. There is no talking your way out of death. "I don't know how he could have gotten in a word," I say, starting to sob.

"Guilt talking again? C'mon. No feeling sorry for yourself. You came in to find something."

"Yes, no, I don't know."

"Stop. He would be furious with you right now. You must have done something right. He was a pretty amazing guy. You've said so yourself, and there is plenty of evidence."

"I've been feeding his fish."

Detective laughs gruffly. "A little more than that." He does, however, glance at the fish in the tank. "Looks like his little aquarium could use a cleaning if you want those fish to survive much longer."

I examine the blackening water with some amount of shame. "I know. I've never cleaned the tank before." I didn't pay much attention to his fish until that moment. "The aquarium was his thing. I don't even remember when he got it. I don't know how to clean one without killing the fish."

"You can learn."

"But he's gone." This is too much to bear, I decide. I'm going to ask the detective to leave.

"I see all kinds of evidence of him. Stop with your self-pity."

I nod then add, "I am trying. I read his painful words about addiction, about how he didn't like himself during that time. "I read that he found a way through. He had forgiven himself."

"Where did you find that?"

"In a journal and on our computer. Actually, my daughter Nicole found some of his words on his Facebook page."

"So, you weren't Facebook 'friends' with your son?" Detective laughs.

"No. I tried to give him space."

"And?"

"And his journal entries and posts are honest and raw, tough to read, to know what he went through, like reliving that hard, hard hour, day, months, knots in the gut, sleepless nights, worry, fear a dominant theme."

"But that is not where he ended, is it?"

"No. He conquered his addictions. It is so unfair. I want to scream."

"Go ahead. It won't change anything, but it's a start to honesty." He tips his hat to me and then to Blaise as if he can still see him.

After the detective exits, I start thinking about the impossibility of giving my son's voice expression in my work. He was reluctant to share himself on the page, often expressing in just a clipped phrase just what he was doing.

Once, I asked Blaise if he wanted to write a book with me, from the diverse perspectives of the son going through recovery from addiction and mother as witness and unknowing "enabler."

Blaise shook his head slowly, but said, "I don't know. Maybe someday. Not yet." I knew it was still too raw for him, too hard to go back down a dark pathway that he had worked so very hard to exit.

"But you've conquered it," I said to my son, almost pleading.

"You never beat addiction," he reminded me. "You just go to battle every day and keep trying to win another day."

More than hard to kick an addiction once it grabs hold, the drug won't relinquish you without ripping something away.

During my son's too short of a life, he was brave many times but never more so than when he faced himself and his addiction.

Although he was not one to go on about his courage, he left words for his friends. On his Facebook post that my daughter Nicole shared with me, Blaise wrote in slang to his "peeps."

> "This will be the last time I update y'all on this ting. It seems like people don't care as much the longer you are sober and that's great. I'd rather have them saying, 'oh, so, I guess he does wanna live to see 40,' as opposed to, 'wow, shocking, I won't hold my breath.' I'm happy. People have accepted me back into their lives and establishments. Thanks to my support system. It should have been way harder than this, but because of you guys, it was possible. Y'all know who you are, you wanted to see me succeed. I can count the ill wishes on one hand. Appreciate you guys, and if you are struggling with addiction, just know it is possible to get your life back. It's possible to be happy again. It's never too late 'til it is. DM if you struggling. Peep that money saved, not an exaggeration. Now back2 the funny. 2 years 7 hours. 42 minutes. Drug/alcohol free."

His words, not mine. I am so grateful to Nicole for sharing her brother's words. He loved to be clever on Facebook and Instagram, but his rare, raw post helped ease my own pain. His words, "I'm happy…It's possible to be happy again" were two of the best sentences I have ever read in all of my full life and extensive literary readings.

Marfan syndrome, be damned. My son took all the syndrome unfairly dished out and was able to write, "I'm happy," even with a failing heart and a stomach full of tumors. He had found himself and joy.

***

Words from the medical examiner have stayed with me as she described Blaise's enlarged heart ripped apart, multitudinous tumors growing in his stomach, his kidneys, invading his lungs. Cancer jumping on him because he was so immune compromised by Marfan syndrome. I knew on the day of his death when his heart exploded after sending warning signals for years, on that day his stomach hurt, his head hurt, a brain stem bleed already starting, on his last day, Blaise hauled chunks of wood, told jokes and laughed with his uncle Steve and the rest of the Dafoe Trees crew. When Blaise laughed, his pitch was higher, given over to joy.

He came home, said he was tired but took a call from a friend who was feeling depressed, and he went out to pick her up to cheer her. He took Rachel out for dinner, then came home again and flopped on the couch before falling asleep. He thought he might have had a touch of food poisoning he told Rachel. On that last day of his life and so many others of his shortened days, my son was incredibly strong and brave, kind, full of laughter, faced not his "demons" as he thought, but the full weight of physical decomposition. Stood up to death, laughed, loved, and fell into the deepest sleep undisturbed even by dreams.

My son could have wrapped up my entire book with his one short, social media post I quoted from in this chapter. In his few words, honesty and forgiveness of himself, as well as others, were pride of accomplishment, a genuine offer to help others in trouble, gratitude for another chance with his friends and for the gift of life. Again, a hand extended for others who needed help.

Near the end of his life, Blaise was coming into his own, seeking knowledge in ways he had not appreciated while in college. He was reading and absorbing at a high level. "Did *The New Yorker* come yet? Where is this month's *Atlantic* magazine?" Our son had the luxury of rediscovering himself much later than is typical, and that delayed development offered a richness to his experiences.

Every day, he was involved with helping other people, much of which I only learned long after the fact. Every day, he was learning who he could be and how he wanted to carry on in the world. He was on his way. The young man he had become was a good, thoughtful, smart, remarkable man. I wanted him to find out where those discoveries would lead him.

There is more to tell, I want to say to my son. I do not know if he would shake his head or laugh. Yet he liked my writing, particularly my poetry. I would ask him what he thought about a piece of my writing, and his expression, no, that expressive smile of his and those tender eyes always gave me volumes.

***

It is the evening of July 4, 2019. After a day-long rain, clouds begin to disperse just before 9:30 pm. Dan and I head down to the boat to watch the fireworks over the lake. I forgot a blanket but decide it is not really needed.

"C'mon, Blaise. We don't want to miss the fireworks," I call out to my son. He is waiting on the porch, phone in hand, for his friends who are late. I see his dark figure in shadow against the house lights.

I'm already in the front when Blaise unties the pontoon boat and pushes us off. Dan backs us out amidst whirring, shrieking, screaming fireworks, ash and sparks dropping all around us, some landing on the canopy above us. Little hisses can be heard as hot sparks hit the water.

"They couldn't make it," Blaise says as he goes to the back near the motor and sits down.

"What happened?"

"Nick had to work late," he says, clearly disappointed, but he does not hold onto disappointment.

"Sorry," I say, but secretly glad to have our son to ourselves, the first in years that our boat was not overloaded with family and friends and friends of friends. One summer, I was sure the Sheriff in his boat tour around the lake was going to stop and fine us for being overloaded, passengers on every seat, on the floor of the pontoon, in deck chairs brought on board, and our dog sitting up on the area over the motor.

Our daughters could not make it that last year with Blaise. I missed Colette and Nicole that evening, missed our grandsons' excitement, wonder, and their slight fear as they tucked their heads against their moms with the bursts of light and retort of after-shocks. The year before, Enzo, not yet five, was having none of those noisy fireworks he so disliked.

But I was also secretly thrilled to have our son with Dan and me, just the three of us out on the lake.

Watching the fireworks over the lake was a ritual. When we first moved to Little York Lake all those years ago, we bought a row boat from the previous owners of our house. That little boat was the only one we had. That first 4th of July celebration in our new house, Dan and I put a lifejacket on our one-year-old daughter Colette, took out several flashlights and set them up on the rowboat. We went out past the dock to watch the fireworks unobstructed. Colette opened her eyes wide. She had a wool hat on to cover her ears from loud sounds. After a few minutes, I looked down at my baby in my arms and saw she had fallen asleep. Smoke filled the dense air but dissipated quickly.

From those early days of July 4th celebrations, we expanded to bigger boats and more visitors. Someone was always late in arriving for the show. Someone had to go for another beer run. Someone had to go to the bathroom right at the last moment we were to undock. It was always a complicated matter of logistics getting everyone to the boat, on the boat, in lifejackets and launched before the fireworks started, but not the last year we watched them with Blaise.

The simplicity of just the three of us hopping on and moving out over the water was almost too wonderful. Blaise was still texting in the back as Dan glided our boat into place near the middle of the lake. We were positioned in such a way that the fireworks seemed directly over our heads.

"Sorry your friends couldn't make it," I said.

"No big deal," Blaise answered after a minute, as the first explosion and colored lights hit the now darkened sky. He tucked his cell phone in the deep pocket of his baggy sweat pants. I could not see him very well, and I turned back to the park area from where the fireworks were launched. Boom, boom, boom. Then a high-pitched whistling sound stirred as a light display whirled in the air above. Bursts of light and sound came closely on top of one another. I could not help smiling like a kid again. I have always loved this particular fireworks' display on Little York Lake since we moved into our house, and I was a new mother. Only once, did we miss the Dwyer Memorial Park 4th of July commemoration.

Blaise and Dan are quiet, taking in the display. I was supremely happy. Father and son are often quiet together, a mutual love and understanding between them. I stopped wondering what they were thinking, stopped worrying that Blaise might be upset about missing his friends, stopped worrying about everything, and just allowed myself to watch and listen, to just be, a rarity. Nothing but sensory experience. Loud whistles and clapping from the shore around the lake as an appreciative audience in this hamlet reacted to particular aerial displays.

With a final, glorious burst of multiple rockets going off simultaneously, the sky was lit up with so many illuminations, we could see everything as if in broad daylight for fractions of a second, then were dropped back into darkness. Echoes of ripped air continued booming for seconds longer. It was concussive. I waited for a moment before standing.

"It was the best fireworks we've ever had," said Blaise, appreciation in his voice. He, too, was standing.

We compared and talked over our favorites, slowly made our way back to the dock. Someone turned on a radio blasting Ray Charles' rendition of "America, the Beautiful." The three of us are clapping along with others on shore. Lights everywhere turned the night into day. From his aspect, his face, I could tell Blaise was happy. This is all we have, I thought. We have moments. I wanted to say, it is enough, but it is never enough. We always want more of pure joy.

I did not know then but found out later that Blaise videoed the fireworks finale and sent the clip to his sisters. Nicole told me Blaise knew how much she hated to miss them. In those moments on the boat when I thought Blaise did not care; he was thinking about how much the light display meant to his sisters and was diligently recording that celebration.

Private firework displays were still going off along the shoreline as we headed back. Odors of burning wood, sulfur, and potassium nitrate from spent rockets hung long in the air. Ashes fell over us as we walked back to our house.

Ten

A Boy and His Dog

"Whatever you do, do not bring a dog home for Christmas!" I am certain of my unconditional words to every member of my family. We had previously and tragically lost a young dog, just seven months old, to accidental poisoning. The pretty Golden Retriever pup drank antifreeze from a puddle on the side of the road during one of his walks. Released from the vet who was sure our dog would recover just fine; we were startled to find Quincy dead in the morning. He never let out a yelp or cry during the night to alert us to his peril.

The awfulness of losing a dog that way, the stress of work and the holidays convinced me that introducing a new animal into our family was not going to work for me that year.

My mother, ailing with Alzheimer's disease, would be at the gathering at our house. My younger sister Phyllis drove in and went to pick up mom from the nursing care facility down the road. Expecting a houseful of people and added layers of pressure, I laid down the law on bringing no animals into the mix. With the holiday season, I knew everyone was thinking about getting a puppy, but I was not ready to go through all of it again.

At ten minutes after nine at night, Blaise walked in the door with his plaid shirt jacket pulled over a bulge on his chest. Widely grinning, Blaise also looked a little nervous, his face red, eyes twinkling. Of course! I knew immediately.

"Tell me you don't have a puppy under your coat."

Opening one flap of his jacket, Blaise lifted a black pup with one hand and shrugged, unable to stop smiling. The puppy fit inside the palm of his hand.

"Oh, no. What have you got?" The little black form was nearly still and appeared to be a kitten or miniature bear.

"She said her father was going to kill them all," he told us, setting the pup on the rug in our entrance as everyone gathered around that Christmas Eve. Hearing adoring coos and ahhs, within seconds, I knew my battle had been lost, and the pup would become part of our family. Oh, what am I in for, I wondered?

Blaise disappeared for an instant then brought down a big green, worn blanket and made a nest for the puppy. So tiny, it was entirely lost in the folds.

"He'll never survive," said Dan, taking a look at the size of the pup.

"Yes, he will. He's a tough little guy, aren't you," said Blaise as he set out a dish of water. The puppy didn't drink at first. We got out an old baby bottle from the cupboard. Even that nipple was too large for the puppy's mouth. Finger-feeding was adopted within a few minutes and apparently worked.

The pup, named Bogart or Bogie by Blaise within the first hour, appeared blind as well as weak. His eyelids turned inward, and I was thinking about sizable vet costs when we woke the next morning and saw Bogie inching around on his blanket on Christmas morning.

"I can't have him peeing everywhere," I said unhappily.

"You won't even be able to tell," Blaise answered, but he made a dog pen out of cardboard. "He's gonna be all right. You'll see," said Blaise as he fed the determined-to-live puppy.

Bogie did something for us all during his first Christmas. I was, initially, unaware of the extent of the gift: he made us focus on something other than losses, my mother's worsening Alzheimer's disease, my father's recent death, and the death of my brother. Things fall apart. Bogie drew our attention and kept it through days of holiday festivities, expanding the dinner table, overlapping talking by our large extended family. We all wanted the little pup to make it. He brought us even closer.

Preparing for a trip to the vet's, I steeled myself for the doctor to explain the procedure for putting down a dog. Instead, I returned home with Blaise and Bogie. In fact, the vet explained that Bogie's temporary blindness was a trait of Shar-Peis (one of three breeds our mutt had inherited from his mixed parentage) because their eyelids turned inwards for weeks (entropion). Bogie was filled with worms, naturally, the vet informed me, but worms could be gotten rid of fairly easily, and our little runt of a dog would most likely live a long, healthy life.

Bogie did. We seldom had to make trips to the veterinarian for Bogie after that initial flurry of activity, other than annual vaccinations.

When we got home from his first vet adventure, Bogie stretched his tiny black body out on Blaise's chest, looking for all the world like a contented kitten, on the couch where the two of them fell into well-deserved sleep after the stressful trip to the vets.

"What breed of dog is he?" People would ask us as we set out on walks in the neighborhood.

"Mixed parentage," did not seem to satisfy anyone, so I took to answering, "He's a purebred mutt."

It did not take long for Bogie to earn his way into everyone's heart. Even our neighbors grew to love him.

Genetically, Bogie was mostly black lab with a couple of other breeds mixed into his gene pool. What he lacked in pedigree, however, he more than made up for in character and sweetness. He was not simply sweet; he was smart and clever. Within no time, he had learned to sit, stay, shake hand/paw, lay down, and roll over. He was such a quick learner, I thought we might teach him circus tricks if anyone made the effort.

Bogie's endearing gesture of laying his head against your head as if for a kiss was almost human in aspect. Because he remained small for an extended period, he easily fit on Blaise's or Dan's lap or chest. Surprisingly, he later grew to be a medium-sized dog but always thought of himself as small, climbing up, half falling off a lap for the rest of his eleven years of life.

Once we had all gotten deeply attached to him, Bogie decided that being a puppy meant destruction, and he topped all other dogs we had over the years in that category, all within a six-month period. The real torpedo was the day he was locked in the kitchen with baby gates when Nicole, Adam, Dan, Blaise, and I went searching for reception venues for Nicole's and Adam's wedding. Bogie decided that the gate was simply impossible to get through, but a wall would give way eventually. Our little mutt clawed, dug, and chewed his way into wallboard in a half-dozen places in the kitchen before we reached home. I don't actually remember the words I used upon the discovery, but I'm certain Blaise took the brunt of it.

"He'll grow out of it, Mom," Blaise said, and Bogie did, never really destroying much of anything after that initial span of kitchen wall carnage.

During his entire life, Bogie never had to go to a kennel or be boarded. Someone was always home with him to keep company. Blaise being home and watching Bogie and our house gave Dan and me a comfort level and freedom we had not known before because we always had dogs, even before we got married.

It is not to say we did not still worry about our son sometimes but not out of fear of his returning to drugs or alcohol. Dan often said he was concerned that Blaise was so gentle. Dan knows how hard the world is. Although he loved Blaise for exactly who he was, father worried his son would be hurt. We knew; however, Bogie was safe with Blaise.

Bogie more than paid us back. Blaise curled up with Bogie when he was down, so often it would be impossible to count. And when Bernie Madoff made the decision to steal hardworking people's pension money, Bogie was there to comfort Dan. My husband was particularly distraught, not so much with the money we had personally lost, but the money stolen from pension fund investments he was administering. I had never seen my husband so despondent up to that point. He worried about those other families, and Bogie climbed up on his lap and laid his soft head against Dan's cheek. Their long walks became longer with Bogie offering the best ears for listening.

As Blaise attempted to quit using drugs or alcohol and failed in his earlier efforts, Bogie sat by him, protectively or stretched out over him. "No one is touching my master," he seemed to say.

Once, when Dan and I were on vacation, Bogie was out with Blaise and suddenly took off chasing some small animal. Blaise waited for him to return, but Bogie did not. After walking up and down the street along the lake road, Blaise went back to the house and called "911" because if you lose your best dog friend, it is truly an emergency. The helpful emergency responder suggested he call the area animal shelters and SPCA. After driving to every single one of them in the wider area, Blaise found Bogie in an animal shelter in a little town seven miles away. At the shelter, they told Blaise a woman had brought our dog to them.

"Where did she find him?" Blaise asked in gratitude.

"On Mountainview Drive."

"What? That's where we live." Blaise was not too happy that someone had immediately picked up our dog within sight of our house and driven off with him. Yet, he was also grateful to get him back. For years afterward, we all laughed about Blaise's 911 call.

Although I had been determined not to let a dog on our beds, Bogie snuck onto Blaise's bed or onto Dan and my bed every night, laying his head across your legs. But, his favorite place to be was on the boat with Blaise. Climbing up on the back seat, he would ride with his ears flapping in the wind, checking out wildlife and human activity around the lake. His second favored spot on the boat was the front, with door of the pontoon boat open, so he could watch for fish, his head bent down. More than once, I thought he was about to dive after a big fish he spotted. Instead, he merely barked, too smart for that leaping action.

Everyone around Little York knew Bogie even if they did not know the human companions of the dog. If any of us said the word "boat," Bogie raced to the lake door, quivering with excitement. It was always too long a wait over the winters before he could be out on the water with Blaise or Dan again.

Hot summer days, Blaise would come home from work or between jobs, change into his swim shorts, and grab a towel, Bogie bouncing around him, knowing exactly where the two of them were heading. Out to the water! Leaping with joy, Bogie loved his summers as much as he loved the young man who saved his life..

Blaise took Bogie with him everywhere, so Bogie always expected he would be going along for the ride when he saw the car keys brought out by any of us. He learned to be a decent passenger but made wet nose prints on the windows of the car and still wanted to climb into the front seat with the driver.

Bogie walked in that long line of dogs as man's best friend, endlessly loyal, good-tempered, sweet and attuned to human companions.

I recently read about a man named Christian Lewis who, after walking 8,700 miles of British coastline, holed up on the remote Scottish Shetland island of Hildasay to wait out "shelter in place" orders. While the rest of the world struggled to maintain a distance of six-feet or more from the next person during the novel coronavirus pandemic, Lewis continued his long walks. His only mate, Jet, is a stray dog who followed him then became Lewis' dog.

Lewis podcasts about his journey and talks about his dog as a comfort. Before Christian Lewis began his trek, he admitted he was struggling with mental health, deeply anxious. He decided to direct that anxiety into this nearly endless walk (over two years) and raise money for Ssafa, an organization that helps those who were in the armed forces. Creating a funding mechanism for Ssafa made sense to Lewis because he said he had been helped by that same organization. How Lewis manages to survive in the harsh climate of the Shetland island is partially explained by his training as an elite member of the British Army.

In reading the CNN story about Lewis and his dog Jet, written by Tamara Hardingham-Gill and videoed by Temujin Doran, I thought about how much comfort Jet provided Lewis. I also thought about how much comfort Bogie provided Blaise during his most anxious moments. "There's something very spiritual about it," Lewis said of his isolation from other people and his physical journey as he petted his loyal dog.

There were long nights in which I am certain my son felt utterly alone with the exception of his dog. Blaise, too, walked miles to exorcise what he thought was his anxiety. If only we had known it was his heart. In a short video Blaise made of himself and Bogie before my son's death, the camera shows Bogie resting on a blanket in the library. Blaise's large hand is on his dog's head, gently stroking. "Did I tell you how much I love you, today?" Blaise asks, the twinkle in his eyes evident. Bogie does not move his head but his eyes look up, and there is no other way to describe that gaze other than "lovingly." Then Blaise ruffles his little dog's chin and laughs.

Only a couple of days before Blaise's death, my son asked me to take a photo of him holding Bogie.

"Why?" I wondered what the picture was for, but Blaise shrugged as if the purpose was not important.

He picked up Bogie with one hand and arm, lifting our 65-pound dog to his chest, laughing as he did so. Bogie allowed such foolishness, and I took the picture.

"Come on, tell me what this is for?" I asked.

"Remember that photo you took of me holding Niki's dog Penny?"

I nodded, my daughter's pup joining the family only a month earlier.

"Well, that picture got a lot of likes on Facebook and Instagram. Apparently, Bogie was jealous; 'traitorous,' his words, not mine, so I told him we'd put up this photo."

We were both laughing then as Bogie reluctantly submitted to the humiliation of hanging in the air, suspended over one strong arm of his young master's.

Bogie was there for weddings, both of our daughters' great celebrations and for the funerals of both of my parents, the terribly sad funeral of my brother, of the funerals of both of Dan's parents. He was there for every 4th of July picnic when victuals and family overflowed. When Colette and Dave got married, we worried that all of the commotion in the after party at our house would be problematic with our young dog, but Bogie got along with everyone. He mingled with people and other dogs easily, liking pretty much every person and dog who came his way except for a big bloodhound and one very big black lab who lived down the street from us.

For several years, the bloodhound would pass by, baying in that low howl of his to which Bogie would respond with a high-pitched bark.

***

Eleven years after Blaise brought him home, tucked in his jacket, Bogie moped around the house searching for his master. For so many years, Bogie had met us at the door when we arrived home. After Blaise's death, more often than not, Bogie would not be at the door when Dan and I came home. He would be waiting up in Blaise's bedroom.

On the evening of calling hours for Blaise, Bogie broke open a lump on his neck, scratching at it in nervousness.

The lump turned out to be cancer. Dan asked Bogie to hang on for a while. "You can't leave yet," said Dan. "Just wait a while for us. Give us another six months." The trauma of our son's death colored everything, but Bogie missed Blaise, too.

American poet Jane Kenyon wrote about a dog's understanding of melancholy in her poem "Going Away." I read her poem again recently, considering how much Bogie instinctively understood our melancholy. Sometimes, during the middle of the day, Bogie would suddenly get up from his comfortable spot in front of the stove, climb the stairs slowly, and go into Blaise's room. Then, he would howl in mournful tones before returning to us downstairs or we would go up to get him. He sorrowed for Blaise's absence in a way I had never experienced in a dog before, and I knew Kenyon was right.

Occasionally, near the end of his life, Bogie would climb down from the day bed at the foot of our bed in the middle of the night and go into Blaise's room again. I often wondered if our dog believed he had just missed Blaise, and his friend was coming and going unnoticed. If only he could catch him before Blaise left again.

After Bogie's lump and cancerous mass were removed, our dog seemed to perk up briefly, making it through the holidays.

"Sometimes love does not have the most honorable beginnings, and the endings, the endings will break you in half," wrote American writer Ann Patchett in her essay "Dog Without End," first appearing in *Vogue* magazine and later incorporated in her non-fiction collection *This Is the Story of a Happy Marriage*. "It's everything in between we live for," Patchett added.

Everything in between was what Bogie gave us, gave my son.

Nearly six months after Blaise's death, Bogie passed away. We were crying and driving him to the vets, knowing he was too sick to move. Dan had been carrying him outside each morning and night, but we could not let him go. Finally, Bogie simply would not move at all. Dan got the car keys. Bogie picked up his head with an alertness we had not seen in days. Dan lifted him to the car seat where he lay on a blanket. On the way to the vets, our sweet, little black dog shuddered, jerked his head twice, then died in our car. He spared us having to put him down.

I heard Chris Stapleton's song "Maggie's Song" and the lyrics, "I can tell you right now/ That a dog has a soul," and started crying again.

I often called Blaise when I meant Bogie or started to say Bogie when I was calling for Blaise. Young man and his dog were attached in a way that defies categorization. Even now, when I am walking down Mountainview Drive, I sometimes catch out of the corner of my eye, a tall young man walking across the open fields and a little black dog a pace or two ahead of him.

I want to believe Bogie heard Blaise calling him and finally went off to be with his buddy. Bogie ultimately let us go rather than the other way around.

Eleven

An Irish Wake

Both Dan and I come from big families. My husband has ten siblings, all still with us in the world. I had five siblings, my younger brother Emerson, Jr. tragically died too soon. We had aunts and uncles, numerous cousins, and then there were all of the in-laws. When we married, our two combined families were like a hamlet in size and complexity. Dan's mother was Irish in ancestry, and my mother was half Irish. When we celebrated, our gatherings were raucous, occasionally fractious, and spilled out over boundaries.

Before Blaise's death, Dan and I had both lost our parents, my brother, nearly lost two of Dan's brothers, lost a nephew, all of our aunts and uncles, and several cousins. Funerals are never easy or even bearable, but we had been through so much we thought we could handle anything until the death of our son.

Calling hours for Blaise go on forever, but I was in some other zone in which my physical body seemed separated from my emotional state. My mind felt gutted, and I was stationed in some darkened room somehow alone while we greeted hundreds of people.

At some point, I felt Dan's presence beside me and my daughters and sons-in-law to my left, but we were all still isolated by grief. There were more people in the adjacent room, we were told later, people who never made it into the reception room because it was so crowded. I tried to recognize each person who came through the line and thanked him or her for coming, but at some point, I sensed I had nothing left for anyone.

Yet, I remain grateful and astonished at the kindness and goodness of people who came that evening. Their sadness was evident and, strangely, warmed my heart. Many traveled long distances to say their good-byes to Blaise and offer us their condolences. Ben Connery and his wife Helen traveled all the way from Dallas, Texas. Alena Turturro, Vin Turturro, and Nick Triolo drove up the four hours from New York City. Kyle and Miah Newton came all the way from Virginia Beach, Virginia. Phyllis Avery, Gary, Emily, and Matt Weiner traveled from Plymouth, Michigan. Ethan Weiner flew half-way round the world from Prague. Dianne Avery and Beni Levi flew in from Brooklyn, Michigan. Michael and Lauren Avery drove from Boston. Lisa and Larry drove down from Albany. Dan's college friends Mark Clearihue, George Bartlett, John Bryden, Stan Dickson, and Marty Madeira came from all over, including Canada, Florida, and Massachusetts.

My former teaching colleagues Barb Crossett, Cindy Hlywa, Lisa McDougal, Tess McKenney, Joy Casey-Kelleher, Carmel McColgan, and Joe Musolino, among others, traveled south from the Syracuse area to be there for us. Even some of my former students, including Liv McKelvey, Emer Stack and Steve Cecconi, sisters Katherine and Grace Babcock, and Cole Greabell were present to witness and give comfort. My niece Kassie Taylor took an Uber from Cornell University. Janet Cain drove by herself from South Hampton, Massachusetts. Allyson and Tim Coffin drove down from Cumberland, Maine. Dom and Rita Cusano drove up from Maryland. Shea Dawson flew in, along with his parents Maureen and Michael Dawson, from Billings, Montana, to name just a handful of the hundreds of people who were there for us, there to say good-bye to Blaise. He would have been overwhelmed and amazed.

Blaise's best buddies from high school and work passed through our receiving line. His past girlfriends and friends who are girls were in attendance. I do not know all the intimacies of my son's life with various women he dated and loved, but I know he was still friends with them. He did not share details, but I am aware he never seemed to harbor resentments or anger toward a girl or woman. He forgave and was forgiven readily by those who really knew him.

As the evening wore on, I did not recognize one of his former, serious girlfriends as she moved through our line. Her hair is now cut stylishly short. She was crying hard. I was trying to hold it together. I hugged her. Only after a multitude of other people passed by me did I realize I had hugged Kim. She is still beautiful but looks more sophisticated than when they dated. I try not to think about what might have been for my son if they had stayed together because I was still standing and thanking an endless line of people for coming to my son's calling hours.

My God, I thought, I could not believe why I was standing there. How could I be in a line receiving people for my son's funeral? If I attempted to fully take it in, I would collapse. I smiled through tears at the wonderful people who had come to pay their respects.

Blaise would have been proud of his family and surprised at the number of people who came to honor him. I did not realize how many friends he had or how many lives he had affected. Blaise's absence was acutely felt. My son was, indeed, well loved.

Joan Didion in her memoir about her husband's death wrote of the ritual we perform subsequent to death: "We have no way of knowing that the funeral itself will be anodyne, a kind of narcotic regression in which we are wrapped in the care of others and the gravity and meaning of the occasion."

While I agree with Didion in large measure, there is also something bizarre about our rituals around death. As the calling hours came to a close, the funeral director reentered the room. "Your family now has a few minutes to yourselves. I'm closing off the calling hours," he said before exiting.

We turned to look at Blaise one last time, his long body stretched out in that coffin. We were certain his feet must have been pushed up. Suddenly, one of Blaise's former coaches came into the room, breathless. He had just come from practice, running football drills, he told us. Then he proceeded to describe his practice, the length of runs, and details of which I dismissed before they were fully out of his mouth. Coach talked about his favorite players, those "little hustle guys, you know, the 5-foot-8-inch ones who work harder than everyone else." I tried to listen to what the coach was telling us, but I kept thinking about the impossibility of the fact that our son was 6-foot 5-inches and this coach was around 5-foot 6-inches.

Did this well-intentioned, obviously kind man not intuit the implication of his words? Coach continued, relating anecdotes about coaching conferences he had attended and the near universal agreement that football coaches all wanted those hustle, smaller players on their teams. Anecdote after anecdote followed when the funeral director came back in finally and told us it was time for everyone to leave. The coach, being ushered out, turned his head to remind us, "don't forget, Cortland game tomorrow!" That particular "tomorrow" was the day we were burying Blaise.

Moments after the coach left, my husband, daughters, and sons-in-law formed a small circle, and we all started cry-laughing, the kind of near hysterical laugh that turns into another emotion. What else was there to do? Laugh or cry, and we laughed until tears flowed over our cheeks.

"At least, he came," said Colette at length. That was thoughtful of him."

"Yes," we all agreed, knowing the coach meant well. Coach came. He was one of only a handful of Blaise's coaches, including his basketball coach Mr. Mack, to bear witness. Two of Blaise's elementary school teachers came, including his favorites, his kindergarten teacher Diana Moreland and fifth-grade teacher Mrs. Oechsle. I do not recall his high school teachers coming. But his football coach remembered one of his players, a player who caught four passes for 76 yards in one game, too easily, perhaps seemingly without hustle, just long graceful strides down the field, one long arm extended, long fingers pulling a football out of thin air like magic.

After calling hours for Blaise, family and some friends gathered at our house on that endless night. Family told stories, drank, and cried; laughter flowed through crowded rooms. Food and alcohol were everywhere, covering every surface. I did feel as if I had been drugged at one point in the long evening, almost numb as people hugged me, offered drinks, spilled drinks, talked and talked and talked.

At first, the hugs and stories were comforting, but as the night wore on, I felt myself shrinking, falling into an abyss. Laughter and tongues loosened by alcohol became harder to bear. At one juncture, I stood between two of my many sisters-in-law as they cried and laughed, squeezing me between them. They wanted to share funny anecdotes to comfort. I love them both but wanted only to escape, almost as if I could outrun and hide from grief and the idea of an Irish wake for my son. My son. My God, how was that possible?

There were stories from when Blaise was a little boy and a tale about his younger cousin biting him. "Stupid, baby," little Blaise said, refraining from striking back. One after another, then overlapping, family stories flowed over the rooms. The laughter came from fond remembrances and good, shared memories. Well-intentioned narratives, but it was suddenly terrible for me to hear laughter. Smells of liquor, food left out too long, too many people in rooms, noise level too high. I only wanted to see my son.

Panic washed over my face as I fled up the stairs with my sister Phyllis Ann coming up behind me. My retreat felt inhospitable, unkind, even cowardly, but I no longer cared what anyone thought about me. I was spent, had used up all the strength I had in reserve to get through calling hours. All those good people, and I could only think about my son. Even when we are not alone, we may feel terribly alone.

Finally, in the relative quiet of my upstairs bedroom, I cried, and my sister allowed me to blubber without comment. I then started talking quietly, things I wanted to say about Blaise, but there was no laughter, just little moments. Phyllis Ann's gift to me that night was as comforting witness, as sister, as friend. I will never forget her generosity. I got to talk and say how much I loved my son without a single funny anecdote to lighten the mood or lessen the pain in response.

I finally came back down the stairs to rejoin family and friends. Rooms full of people wandered into and out of the kitchen and living room, every chair with an occupant. Stories of Blaise moved through the air. At one crescendo of noise, our sweet little mutt had scratched and broken open a small bump on his neck. Instantly, we were in another crisis as blood gushed from our dog's wound. Within minutes, the dining room looked like a crime scene, blood spatter along walls and across the carpet. Without me acknowledging the movement, our house was cleared quickly.

Dan tried dealing with this new crisis as quietly as he could, trying to corral Bogie and stop the bleeding. In spite of his ingenuity, blood continued spattering. Dan had used everything from masking tape to wrapping a towel around our dog's neck, but Bogie kept shaking free, more blood flying, towels drenched. It did not seem possible that such a small wound could produce so much gore. Everyone remaining in our house jumped up and back. What kind of nightmare had we entered, I wondered? One from which there was no awakening, no stepping away or slowing down.

Although his wife Lauren and baby Endl had gone back to my sister-in-law's house for the night, my nephew Michael, a veterinarian, was still, thankfully, at our house. He stepped into the fray. Using a crazy mixture of old rags, a strip of towel, and duct tape, Michael was able to get a temporary bandage on Bogie which held in place and stem the flow of blood for a little while.

Then Dan, my sister Phyllis, and I set out into the blackest night to find a vet clinic still open, one that could treat a profusely bleeding dog. During the car ride, Bogie sat very still. Still, blood slowly soaked through the rags. Turned down by one clinic over the phone, we raced in the opposite direction for another emergency clinic. Fortunately, they took our dog in, offered some medication, partially rebandaged Bogie's head and neck, not fully removing the old bandage because Michael's ingenious device was holding. Even the clinic's vet was nervous about exposing the spurting wound again.

Bogie's gushing injury did clear out our house, however, and when we returned late that night, it was finally quiet.

We were able to schedule our dog into surgery at a different clinic several weeks later where a mass was removed from his neck. We got the call only a few days after that: cancer, a blood cancer, hemangiosarcoma. The cancerous tumor was excised, but the vet who operated could not be sure the cancer was contained. How was this possible we lost Blaise and were going to lose Bogie?

During this period, I was almost entirely unaware of passing days. Scrubbing the rug where Bogie bled again, I finally realized the stains would persist. I had enough trouble going back into our living room where Blaise died, avoiding even looking into the large room for a time. Now the dining room felt off limits. My niece came over and cleaned the area where Blaise had died.

When I finally called a carpet cleaner, his kindness surprised me. I asked to have the dining room rug cleaned and a spot in the living room. "A spot?" he asked.

I hesitated. I was not going to explain, but then I found myself saying, "Yes, this area is where my son died."

He looked at me but said nothing, then nodded, setting to work.

I went into the library, tucking my head and concentrated on writing. Sometime later, I looked up to see him cleaning the entrance rugs, and he confessed to having washed the entire living room's wall-to-wall carpeting, for no extra pay. "I just had to finish it all," he said. Another example of people expressing kindness and compassion.

Twelve

When Food Marches In

In the beginning, after the funeral, I could not eat. Even the idea of food made me nauseous, but lasagna marched in the door, followed by a pan of baked chicken. A tin of macaroni and cheese was already sitting on the kitchen table waiting to be noticed. More mac and cheese muscled past the first dish. Cookies wrapped in open foil were growing stale on top of a pile of unused plates in the dining room and another bag of cookies delivered earlier was calling out for an airing. A potato-cheese casserole, still warm, propped itself up on the counter near the toaster. Three inches of counter space remained in any direction.

Two pizzas arrived unannounced, one set atop the other. Expansive bowls of green salads took over a table in the library, competing with one another. More food—casseroles, bags of chips, pots of soup, bowls of salad walked in tentatively as my stomach churned. I tried to clear the table, an impossible task because there was no counter room or refrigerator space available, and a squabble broke out between contending dishes.

"Someone eat," I want to yell, and finally other people started eating. More guests arrived with more food.

My stomach continued to growl, unable to seek relief and unwilling to take in nutrition.

Under other circumstances, I would have loved to down everything that people brought to us, but all of it, even the most tempting dishes had lost their appeal for me. Clashing smells in the kitchen began to further sicken me.

People had been so kind, and I felt so ungrateful for not eating, but I could not. Guilt again. Guilt for not eating what had been kindly provided. Guilt on top of guilt for what I could not name. No, I knew. I was alive and my son was not.

In the aftermath of Blaise's death, generous and kind neighbors and friends brought us well wishes, condolences, and much food. I knew it was important to eat, but it was not possible. The idea of eating seemed like some unfamiliar custom rather than life-sustaining. I was cognizant of the goodwill, but it was difficult to articulate why I could not taste any of the dishes brought to us. I remember picking up a sandwich, forcing myself to open my mouth and take a bite. Everything in my mouth tasted foul. I threw the perfectly good sandwich into the garbage can. We were surrounded by home cooking, and I could not begin to appreciate any of it. I wrapped and tried storing some food items for a few days until even the stuffed freezer stank.

Finally, I threw out molding bread. Everything had turned. A day or two more passed. A week or more went by, and all the food finally disappeared, the last of a casserole, starting to turn black on a back shelf is cleaned out of the refrigerator.

Only then, did I begin to feel as if I could digest food. All is silent. All is empty.

***

When Blaise was in the hospital, hooked to breathing machines, Dan and I walked over to a nearby hotel to get something to eat after our daughters arrived and told us to get some rest and food. I recognized I should be hungry. My husband and I ordered, waited for the food to be served, then stared at the presentation. The impossibility of eating anything surfaced. After a couple of futile attempts, we finally had the food wrapped up, thinking we would eat later. When later arrived, we eventually threw the carefully wrapped, strong-smelling dinners in the trash. What a waste, I thought, then, what a waste: our son gone.

No additional food knocks on our door late at night. Finally, I settle into hunger and want. Hunger and emptiness.

At some point that remains indistinct, I began eating again, and I did not stop. While this might seem to be progress in the "stages of grieving," I did not find overeating helpful. In the six months after my son's death, I gained a great deal of weight without awareness, until I was getting dressed one morning and noticed that everything that I tried on was too tight. My jeans had to be someone else's. In those six months, I had gone from nausea over any food to an inability to stop eating. I knew if I had ever started serious drinking that I would have become an instant alcoholic.

***

"The connection between food and mourning runs deep," wrote Amelia Nierenberg in the October 28, 2019 issue of *The New York Times*, Food section: "In almost every culture or within traditions, a community brings dishes to the survivors in the weeks or months after a death. But for a spouse, accustomed to sharing every meal with a partner, the grieving can go on long afterward, renewed constantly by the rhythms of shopping, cooking, and eating... 'It's almost like the sixth stage of grief is cooking alone,' said Jill Cohen, a grief counselor in New York, referring to the now-disputed theory of the Five Stages of Grief," added Nierenberg.

If we stop trying to force our emotional upheaval into stages, we might come closer to the experience. Because Blaise lived at home, we frequently ate supper or dinner together. I often gave him a choice of dinner options, which made Dan laugh. "Are you cooking just for Blaise?" he would ask, or "Is this a restaurant you're running?" But I remember Blaise was always appreciative of my home cooking.

"Meatloaf or meatballs?" I would yell to my son.

"Meatloaf," he would say, settling on the couch after work or between his day and night jobs. Although Italian food was his favorite, once he started working in a pizza shop, he was less likely to ask for Italian dishes at home. I also did not have the skills of his friend Nick's mother Isabelle Caruso who served him some "mean pasta" dishes.

When I cook something Blaise once loved to eat, I struggle. My macaroni and cheese dish was one of his favorites, and it is one of mine, but I start to prepare the dish and think of him. Everything is a trigger, as they say. Food which should be comforting is not particularly comforting. Food has become, rather, obsession, a need to seek comfort. Food breaks up my day. I have second helpings even when I'm not hungry anymore.

For months after Blaise's death, Dan and I would look at each other across the table and the space where her son sat. Nothing went down well.

I think about Blaise never having second helpings no matter how much he liked a particular dish. At the time, I thought he was simply watching his weight even though he was already lean. Only after his death did I begin to think about tumors in his stomach and wonder how he worked to sustain himself for so impossibly long. On the last night of his life, he told the young woman he was with that he thought he had food poisoning and decided to sleep it off.

***

Opening a drawer in my kitchen, I am confronted with numerous boxes of organic teas: Yogi Green tea, Komucha tea, organic chamomile, Yogi-Bedtime, Organic Gas Relief tea, Rose Hibiscus, DeTox tea, Healthy Cleansing tea, all purchased by my son. I had forgotten that his tea was all still there. I do not drink organic or green tea despite the health benefits but was reminded of how hard Blaise worked to regain and maintain his health after recovery from drug addiction. Of course, he could not know that no amount of organic anything could reduce the tumors in his organs, or stop the tissues of his heart from pulling apart. Just looking at his drawer-full of teas made me want to collapse and weep.

After a prolonged period of time, I notice that I have started to drink his teas, test each one out. With every tea bag I select, I think about how Blaise worked at being healthy in his last few years. I imagine how the herbal tea will connect me to him even though I know it is not logical. I suddenly remember him urging me to try out one of the "healthy" teas.

"It will make you feel better," he says, but at the time, I paid no heed to his words.

Dan and I are not alone in experiencing these triggers. When we call for a pizza, Blaise's friends in the pizza shop always say hello and start to talk about missing him. "Oh, Blaise's mom. He always made me laugh. He made me like working here."

I have often wondered about their conversations in the pizza shop after we hang up the phone. What stories about my son area are they sharing with one another? I want to call them back and ask if they would mind repeating their anecdotes, but I resist. I am trying not to do anything too crazy. Plus, I always think about how Blaise would have viewed my actions.

"Oh, no, Mom, don't call them unless you are ordering a pizza. Get the thin crust, too. It's better."

Someone in the background at the pizza shop yells while I am still on the phone, "Blaiser, yeah, he always made work fun."

When the pizza delivery guy comes to the door, he undercharges us, so that we have to tip large enough to make up the difference.

Hunger and want, the hunger I cannot fill, I begin to understand is the necessity of replenishing the spirit after terrible loss; the want created by permanent absence of my son. All the gourmet food in the world cannot make up for this want. All the other wonderful sons in the world cannot make up for his loss.

Thirteen

Death and Birth in that Disorder

Waking too early every morning since September 30, 2019, my conscious mind sees the scene again: Blaise is half off, half on the couch in our living room, not breathing. He looks peaceful except for those thin streams of vomit coming from the corners of his mouth and nose. There was no surrender; death took him in his sleep, the attack so sudden, so merciless, there was not even a final sigh. He did not yell or cry out in pain. His brows are not pinched in death. Only much later do I think about how peaceful he looked in those last moments I was with him.

I do not want to see this scene again but continue to revisit his death before I am aware of the new day. My eyes open suddenly with a flutter, my heart racing as I work to dispel my son's death from the center of my vision. A counselor suggested taking hold of the scene as if in my hands and moving it to the side, out of my direct line. I practiced this technique, and sometimes it works.

Our hours together on this earth are limited, yet we often treat each other as if we are all immortal and will be around another thousand years. If Blaise could be in this world one more day, he would undoubtedly want to spend it with friends. Because I love him, I would have to let him go off with Nick or Jesse or Alena even on that one final day, but first, I would give him an embarrassingly huge hug and remind him that I love him infinitely. He would likely smile and tell me he knows.

The night before his funeral, Colette, Nicole, and I struggled with which clothes to pick out for Blaise. We sat on his bed, pulled shirts, ties, pants from his closet and set them out: nothing seemed to be right. I wanted my son to be wearing a nice dress shirt, tie, and suit jacket. His sisters were adamantly opposed. "He would not want to be wearing this!" They were, of course, right. He knew how to dress well but preferred casual clothes.

Then we all cried again. Nicole pulled a jacket from his closet, one with a black sheen that read fashionable "rap" and decided Blaise would have chosen that jacket. Of course, it did not go with a dress shirt and tie. We negotiated with one another. The cruel absurdity of the moment that we were even choosing his clothes for him hit us hard. "He would have hated all this," said Colette.

"What do you have me wearing?" said Nicole in mock horror, imitating her brother's voice. We laughed and cried again.

"He always liked to look good," said Colette. "He had style and cool."

"But he could put on anything and look great," added Nicole. We knew this was true.

We sat in his room for a span, going back and forth over his clothes. At last, I gave way to my daughters' opinions, and we settled on the shiny black jacket. We thought it was brand new, and I had never seen him wear it before. My daughters gave in to me, permitting a dress shirt and tie. I remembered when Blaise came home one afternoon with that pink tie. I knew he liked it. Then we took out his never-worn, shiny black Jordan athletic shoes and all nodded our heads. Instant decision. That we knew: he would agree with us on the choice of shoes. Strangely enough, the combination of colors and styles looked really good together, and we settled on an outfit for him.

I still wonder if my son would have laughed at our choices, but he was kind and indulgent and probably would have said, "It really doesn't matter, Mom. I'm not going anywhere."

***

It is June 27, 1987, and a midwife calmly tells me to go take a warm shower in the birthing room at Cortland Memorial Hospital. "I promise, the shower will help relax muscles, making everything easier." I still recall how good that shower felt, but my son was not yet ready to be born. I was sixteen hours in labor but much more prepared for the physical ordeal of childbirth than when I had my first daughter Colette. After an easy birth with my second daughter Nicole, I foolishly thought a third child would also be a relatively easy delivery. Blaise had other ideas.

When Blaise was born, he was perfectly formed with a large, round head, beautiful eyes, long, strong limbs and body. His head circumference was 21 inches, the real difficulty in getting him out. With his full head of dark hair and at nearly ten pounds, he looked much older than a newborn. Then he made an unusual noise when he entered the world which sounded like a surprised, "oh." The sound startled adults in the room, but his noise also expressed the surprise of the infant entering the unfamiliar.

The midwife laughed and said, "Congratulations. You just gave birth to a two-month-old baby boy." His first vocalization was likely the release of a gas bubble. However, it certainly sounded like he was already talking to us. Blaise did not seem fragile. In fact, he was so healthy and easy to care for that I thought, this is the baby I could have given birth to at home without any help. He cried, or rather, yelled only when he was hungry, and he was instantly hungry!

When you hold your infant in that first moment after birth, bring him to your face, breathe in sweet scent of newborn, you feel tremendous optimism followed quickly by fear. As anxious as you have ever felt because you are suddenly and acutely aware the world is not good enough for this new little being.

Youngest of my three children, Blaise was held a lot and was a very contented baby, seldom restless. I remember not wanting to ever put him down, summer months passing with my infant son sleeping or waking on my chest as birds flew down to the porch from pines around us, curious to see this new entry into their domain. I recall well those warm days of glorious summer, not wanting to do anything at all except hold my son. My daughters adored their little brother instantly, taking turns holding him, talking softly to him. All experienced again. I did not think I was afraid when I held my son, yet fears prickled at the back of my neck whenever I would set him down.

***

"When we talk about mortality, we are talking about our children," Joan Didion wrote after the death of her daughter Quintana Roo in *Blue Nights*. A commonly held belief in our culture is that children represent our immortality, our future. When our child is taken away forever, we lose that sense of future, of optimism and aspiration, at least for a period of time, perhaps never to regain it.

My earliest brush with this alarm came as a child myself when I read the Brothers Grimm's tale the *Pied Piper of Hamelin*, story born out of ghastly legend, out of natural fears for survival of the human race. In this horrifying story, not a children's tale at all, the Pied Piper is employed by the townspeople to rid the community of rats, perhaps the plague. When the Hamelin villagers don't pay their debt, the Piper leads all the children away, presumably to the same fate as that of the rats. I recall adults trying to soften the blow, my mother saying the children were returned later when the townspeople learned their lesson. I intuited the truth. There would be no return. Without children, there is no beyond.

***

We outgrow our childhood terrors only to rediscover them. Time condensed into an impossible density, not stretched out luminously before us. We are drilled in the concept of timelines, trying to remember dates as paramount, long before cause and effect in history. Our lives portrayed in a line beginning with birth and ending in death as if all of life is a progression to the inevitable, the culmination of everything: death. Only years later do we begin to question those simplified teachings. Time not linear at all, simultaneously past and present, an interconnected web of lines in which a song precedes a moment in which we relive or reexperience the sensations of another moment in this tangled web that comprises our lives.

Yes, we cannot alter the past, but we do alter the future, continuously reshaping a nonexistent shape with choice. What frame will you choose to view the now moment? Rather than try to wrap our minds around non-linear time and such difficult concepts as event space and event points, it is simply easier, less honest perhaps, to view our lives in linear progression.

To simplify explaining the very complex, I detect odors of an apple pie baking, and I am instantly sensing my mother's presence, see her dark hair curled at the ends, the oven mitt on her hand as she takes a pie out of the oven fifty years ago. She is wearing an apron given to her by her mother that smells clean and fresh. I am waiting for a piece of that pie that is still bubbling out of the vents in the baked dough, drops spilling on the oven floor. "Too hot yet," she says.

Event points may occur and reoccur at any moment, and I exist in that juncture. Why does this matter? Because my son is still present in my life when I hear him laugh again at an episode of Seinfeld in perpetual reruns when it comes on the television. When I see one of his friends in town, Blaise is nodding his head in greeting with me. When a basketball game comes up on the television, I see him sprawled out on the couch behind me, just out of sight. He is forever in my event spaces. I am trained on those chance moments.

Our circumstances were a little different than for some American families. Although my two beautiful daughters had gone off to college then law school and were now practicing law in Washington, D.C., my son stayed home with us in Little York. Not the son who would come home for the holidays, seldom seen, Blaise lived with us for all but a few years during college. He briefly moved into an apartment with friends but moved back during his battle with addiction. Even after he had gone past addiction, Blaise stayed in our home on the shores of Little York Lake. I had often wondered if it was contentment, love of the lake, that light on ever-changing waters, the security of home, or unexplored pain that caused him to stay. Dan and I, however, had come to love and depend on his presence in our daily lives. It may sound unusual, but our son made our lives far richer, the last few years of his life being especially sweet.

As excited as Blaise was to drive to New York City to visit friends, he always seemed relieved and happy to come home. His dog Bogie was waiting. The lake was waiting. Although he was drawn to big city life, Blaise was a country boy at heart, forever creating an internal tension he disguised well.

***

Words are never enough

They scarcely tell the journey
of one lone honey bee separated

from his hive, disoriented, poisoned,
and mad. They barely relate the tale
of air filled with floating pollens
from an elm, white down attached
to infinitesimally small seedlings
swimming on unseen currents, sunlight
causing them to appear as spring snow.

Not nearly enough to express shadow
across sunlit mountain. Not enough
for a single distressed bird calling,
let alone the cacophony of whistles,
chirps, tweets, warbles, and trills
of songbirds telling potential mates,
"I am here. I am alive at this location."

Not nearly enough for the magnitude
of loss of a son. Yet his presence
whispers across the pages, emerges
from the faraway look in his father's eyes,
from his nephews' quick questions,
from his sisters' warm embrace to say,
"I was here. I was alive. I was loved."

**

Returning to the time before and after his birth again and again, I remember sitting on the floor in the hallway of our house under construction, my daughter Colette in school. Nicole had fallen asleep on the couch. Immensely heavy and pregnant, I had not physically fallen but fallen into weeping. No one could hear, so it was okay to let down my composed mother guard and just cry. I was nervous about having a third child. Dan was still working on high power lines away from home during the week and sometimes on weekends, as well. We knew we needed a bigger house than the little camp on the lake we had moved into scarcely a year after our first daughter's birth.

Living the midst of a construction project, however, is not ideal at any time, but much less so when you are nine months pregnant, working and rearing two young daughters. I do not remember what led to the momentary despair, but I distinctly recall sitting down on the bare floor and weeping one afternoon.

How foolish, I think now. How naïve not to know. How fortunate I was. How very lucky that busy young mother was. If only I could have recognized that our lives are finite and precious. I could be that young woman again, awaiting the birth of her son or holding my infant after his birth and realize the glory of those days as I experienced them.

Fourteen

In the Loud Room

For an endless season after my son's death, everything was too loud. People talking appeared to be shouting. Laughter entered my brain as if coming through a megaphone. In many ways, the noise level of the world hit me like an assault, and I was continually trying to find cover. Everything, every voice and vibration, came in with a vengeance. Even other people I love seemed to be shouting instead of conversing.

After the funeral, friends and family descended on our house, drank, and told stories about their love for Blaise. All were invited and welcomed, but I quickly began to wish I could hide. Sometimes, the stories they told were funny and their laughter raucous. At one point in the evening (and I have no idea what the clock indicated because chronology was lost for me),

I was suddenly angry with all of them, wanted to shout, "Get out. Get out all of you." Of course, they were telling stories of good times with Blaise, humorous incidents that happened, but good-humored roaring, mirth, even loud chuckling was unbearable. Wisely, I said nothing and retreated.

For months after his death, I could not watch television or a movie. Even the dialogue felt invasive. The idea of entertainment became insufferable, and I am not sure why except I found the world too loud and indifferent. I knew my feeling was not logical. Instinctively, I sensed I had to protect myself from things as benign as a TV show. Violence was likely to turn up on the television unexpectedly. Blaise's dad was hurting immensely, too, and neither one of us talked much for a while.

What words made any difference? But we were there to hold each other. The house had grown not just still but ceased to acknowledge movements after all the visitors and family left. Any noise made was echoed. What is the word for the level below unbearable? Only our dog Bogie's quiet presence was heard in his nails clicking on the tile in the kitchen, but he, too, was disappearing before our eyes.

I had coffee with my British-American friend, Jane Hall, who suggested I try watching *Great Canal Journeys* on BBC when I mentioned my issue with noise and inability to even watch television. I vaguely heard her but remembered her advice later.

From a few minutes into the first episode of the canal show, I was soothed. The show is about an elderly couple of married actors, Timothy West and Prunella Scales, slowly navigating the 21-mile journey on the Kennet and Avon canals and later through Bristol, England. Watching these "actors of a certain vintage," my panic buried itself as I fell into their slower rhythms. During the canal tour with Tim and Pru, I sat in the back of the boat navigating those waterways with those amazing actors.

Touring the canals paradoxically made me feel both numb and receptive to this other pace of life. The gentleness with which Timothy treated Prunella's mental lapses, due to her progressive dementia, was also soothing. Pru's voice was quieting and tender. Even when Tim occasionally bumped into the side wall of a canal lock, during the most dramatic moments of the show, there was no catastrophe.

"Cast off, please," says Tim to start each episode.

"Aye, aye, Sir," Prunella responds as they begin the next canal journey. They are soft-spoken and witty in the sweetest way.

Pru's most common expression, when viewing the sights they pass, is "magic." I smile when she says it again and again, feeling her magic, her wonder gradually seeping into my immense sadness. A belief in magic has been missing in me for a long time. "Here I am sailing up the Nile in a fully rigged ship, amazing," Pru narrates. Of course, their voyages end. All voyages must end.

"As we head to the final curtain call," Tim narrates, playing with language in a Shakespearean way, using metaphors and puns.

Tim and Pru are aware of the closeness of their inevitable deaths due to their advanced age. Pru is a few years older than her husband. That is the way it should be, I think, sad for their ends but thrilled they have had it all, such a lifetime of adventure, wonder, and lasting love.

I ran through every episode of every season of their trips along waterways, gently lifted not from sorrow but pulled from utter despair. When Pru began to express wonder and joy at the sights along the River Nile, I could feel myself returning to curiosity with her, a quality that had been absent.

Their adventures do not, will not, continue indefinitely, I know. *Great Canal Journeys* is in several respects a metaphor for our journey through life. As they finally docked the last of their long boats, I wanted to climb on board. I knew I was not yet done.

"What happens, next?" Pru asks. Tim lets viewers know their time together is now very limited. Their life spans closing. Rather than frighten, his continual reminder of natural death is a comfort. All of our adventures will end. However, as long as we are able, like Pru, we might take in a few more sights and sounds, and exclaim, "ah, magic."

This quirk of finding solace in British television is not novel to me, I discovered. In talking with other women who have recently lost a loved one, several of them mentioned watching *Great Canal Journeys*. We marveled at the similar disclosure and wondered why the pacing seemed helpful. I believe the comfort of BBC shows have much to do with the civility of style, the gentleness, and most of all, the lack of gory violence and car chases, blazing gun shots, all too common in American television. Everything on these British shows is moderated and muted. Even their murder mysteries are tempered.

Slowly, I discovered another activity that eased my painful, tortured state: doing 1,000-piece jigsaw puzzles. Over a winter's course, I put together puzzles in the difficult to impossible categories yet found they comforted rather than perplexed. The exercise of watching a work of art come together gradually was engrossing.

I realize that must sound silly to many people, but the shock level of my loss was such that I had to come out of an almost coma-like state. Becoming a dissectologist felt like some form of mild accomplishment at a point when I could barely have a conversation or do a simple task.

A more distant parallel occurred days after arriving home with a newborn baby. Every noise was magnified, unintentionally intrusive on this new, remarkable bond.

In thinking about these muted encounters that comforted, I am back on the front porch holding my infant son. Blaise is sleeping contentedly. Somewhere out on the lake, a fish jumped, but I see only the widening circles of its disappearance beneath the surface, hear water lapping shores. I am beyond happy. My baby son is curled in my arms, and a warm sun streams through leaves, dappling effect across our deck. I innocently have no doubt in my mind that I will always protect him.

Fifteen

Solace at the Art Museum

Why is an art museum a most perfect space to enter into after annihilative grief descends? You need to walk around one awhile without answering. Allow subdued colors, as well as bold ones, from paintings and sculptures to wash over you, be willing to invite in art and listen. Let everything fall away for an indefinite time as another work of art arrives. You have not chosen this art or this grief. It found you.

Turn a corner. You are not waiting for anyone. You are in this amplitude alone but not alone, arc of horizon a splash of red, a black monolith, and the path is in front of you. Your feet find their way to a sculpture of a colossal moth, one wing blue with gold swirls and other muted autumn colors. Body of the moth is an amalgamation of oddities, a man's face at end of insect abdomen that more nearly resembles a tail, green and gold protuberance reaching up and curling in on itself: oh, antennae, you decide. You look at work's title, almost reluctantly, discover this artwork has a name, the *Emperor Moth* by Michael Lucero. It is a gift to the collection from the Everson Board of Trustees. You wonder how the trustees reacted when they confronted this intimidating, ugly-beautiful work. Perhaps the gigantic insect-man-bird should be horrifying, but the sculpture is only intriguing.

You wander, not escaping constructed moth, just losing thread of its tale when you are met with a massive, bright red bulbous sculpture of a figure with a black face, a snarling tiger perpetually launching from head of a woman. You are deeply inquisitive now, find that Vanessa German created this political art piece called *The Boxer*, a mixed media "assemblage," reading on the plaque that Vanessa created, with her response to "the reverberation of systemic, institutionalized racism facing her community." You turn to Vanessa's art and look more closely, now seeing blood red hands, not blobs, semblances of bloody infants, body parts, a red toy gun, scrap and detritus: what looks like a red grenade, and in place of hands, there are red boxing gloves. Already, you feel stronger just in the presence of Vanessa's art. She, symbolic woman beaten by her racist, misogynist culture, is not done, nor defeated. She is fighting back. Or, rather, she is still standing with all her wounds, somehow not only undiminished but magnificent.

Witnessing Vanessa's art, you know you have met another who has experienced tremendous grief, and she has found a way to turn that hurt and pain into art. "Take your pain and make something beautiful." You hear the echo of those words.

In another room, a convoluted tree of silver wire, by artist Kathleen Bloodough, is adorned with ornaments of symbolic women sprites, paradoxically delicate, fragile, yet resilient. You think this tree would provide endless fascination in your living room if only your room was five times larger, and little grandsons would not run into pointed ends.

Churches provide this kind of contemplative space for millions, but for me, I need a space that challenges without providing pat, codified, dictated, and institutionalized "answers."

I need a space where my questions fly up and are met with more questions while the

mystery of life expands in all directions. I need a space in which condemnation of one group or another does not result in burnings, excommunications, wars and atrocities to justify a system of beliefs. That place I am looking for is an art museum. I did not know how much I needed to be in this amplitude until I arrived.

I have visited the National Gallery of Art, East and West Wings, in Washington, D.C., frequently. My daughters live nearby, and I have wandered alone through this museum while waiting for them to finish work and meet me. Benches situated in various rooms allow space for sustained contemplation or prayer. I am not a visual artist but can appreciate the differences in brush strokes, infusion of color and sudden restraint on a canvas. I created a series of poems about the women subjects, and frequently the lovers, of famed male painters. Avoid the tour groups and lectures crowding around one work and pass on into that adjacent room, empty of people, except you.

Perhaps the most stunning art exhibition I ever wandered into was in Florence, Italy in the Accademia Galleria. Everyone rushed through the first hallway to crowd around the magnificent, immense sculpture of David in the Tribune. But Michelangelo's other creations precede the David when you enter the hall. On each side of the fairly narrow space are two of Michelangelo's "prisoners" or "non-finito" sculptures of tortured men trying to free themselves, still half-embedded in the rough marble from which they were created. Standing in that hallway, watching this eternal struggle as crowds hurry by, I am reminded of how art speaks to viewers in layers of meaning, how these four, the Atlas, Bearded One, Young One, and Awakening One, suggest latent power, imprisonment, external and internal conflict, man's endless predicament from birth.

Looking at my photographs of Michelangelo's four statues recently, I am reminded of the great labors of my son in attempting to free himself from, yes, addiction, but far more, from the impossible demands of an afflicted body, from pain to transcendence: from the affliction of Marfan syndrome (which neither he nor anyone else knew he carried) into a young man who went about his day quietly doing good deeds.

The neighboring, magnificent *Gallerie degli* Uffizi or Uffizi Gallery in Florence was another sphere to become lost in contemplation. Long hallways with art on the ceilings, walls, and sculptures in the center seemed an entire cosmos. One surprise led to another until we reached the roof that overlooks Brunelleschi's famous Duomo. Standing on that museum roof and seeing sunlight gleam across the city, I felt at peace, crowds disappearing, as if only Dan and I were taking in all of that magnificence.

Even a scaled down museum, such as the Schweinfurth Memorial Art Center found in Auburn, New York, offers solace and intimate discovery. I walked through white-walled rooms in Auburn where art that questions, art that disturbs, art that transcends even death, stops me. I wrote about one such work. There was nothing simple about the exercise or the photograph, however, a gorgeous archival print that nearly spanned the length of a gallery wall in one of the exhibition rooms. As soon as I stood before it, I knew I would be writing in response to the experience.

***

Parallel Delivery on Limits of Sight

A poem already written in the title
of a panoramic photograph by Jamie Young:
"My Mother Sees Her Hill for the Last Time."
I stop, unsure of where to go
from that place of perfect articulation
both with inkjet photo and caption.

I allow myself to be pulled in,
stand at center of an archival, otherworldly
print, suggestive, as my eyes follow paths
of ghostly hillside and trees
walking away from this earth, seeing
moss-covered rocks and knotted lives.

Descending hill in transparency is not choice,
just as dying is not choice for old growth trees
as they become ancient souls
from the perspective of earthly existence.

Each side of this narrow view on gallery wall,
shot by and from an intelligent lens,
rises from outer edges of my iris:
a parallel delivery on the limits of sight.

Her art at once photograph and metaphor
for paradoxical limitations
within wide-angle expanse of her mother's life,
our mother's lives, our own lives, the whole
of what it means to be temporal,
moving in mist through new shoots of forest.

Studying painters and researching their subjects are interests I only discovered much later in life. I have come to find art, seek it out, be present and listen below the surface. Paintings have inspired the creation of art in other mediums and links between ideas, generated new concepts, and unintentionally, perhaps, assuaged grief for hours. Why, I wondered, did it comfort me to think about this other woman, a photographer, documenting loss of her mother through a landscape? Was it partially because I knew my son would not be alone in death?

There was another loving mother walking away between old trees who might guide him.

***

Artist and professor Emerita, Celeste Roberge created a 4,000-lb. sculpture, titled "Rising Cairn," that has touched a cultural, collective nerve, connecting with millions via the Internet during the novel coronavirus pandemic. Although Roberge claims to have had a different intent in mind than woman weighed down by grief, it is what is felt. Artist bent and twisted metal wire into the shape of a crouching person, filling the form with various-sized stones. Roberge's work took on symbolism through the eyes of those who have suffered. Art and our reactions to it are malleable, bending to our emotional state as readily as to our intellect.

Musing on Roberge's disposition of stones inside metal contours, I recalled a poem I wrote after my brother's death. Before choosing a stone to mark my son's grave, I return to that earlier composition. My art, too, feels malleable, and I add a few lines. These lines, too, were inspired by another artist.

***

Returning to That Mineral State

Something about a stone, a stone, a stone—
when my nephew placed
little colored rocks on marbled
gravestone that marked where my brother lay,
it wasn't a tradition I knew,
but one that was comforting,
so, I continued to bring him white quartz
and red-veined granite from shores
near our cabin, where I found myself
searching for stones then thinking
of the past when we kids smashed shale slabs,
peering inside mysteries,

and we pressed fingers into indentations
feeling ridges left by shells
harboring ancient lives, and it seemed
when I was young, that a stone could talk.

II

Carrying a smooth, black pebble
for luck, I rubbed it long, seeing again
my brother watching me skimming
a stone across lakes, opposing forces holding it
seemingly forever on the surface of water.

III

I find I fit inside a W.S. Merwin stone poem,
recognizing Beckett and Shakespeare
and Kenyon who gave her dog a stone rather
than a bone, and Wilfred Wilson Gibson
who sought out stones,
and Margo Berdeshevsky
whose book *Between Soul and Stone*
resides in this density.
Turning it over and over in my palm—
this stone could take our worry,
mark our dead, record our time—
slips and skips across open water,
until all that is left
is a stone, a stone, a stone.

***

Hush of it: expanse in which conversation is muted if
caught at all, even museum walls with their confrontation of ideas
suggest quiet deliberation, even meditation. Quietude in the way

that gentle mother rabbit says, "Hush," to her restless kit in Margaret Wise Brown's children's book *Good Night Moon*. Mother rabbit and her creator offer a hush that comforts, allows worlds to fall away in a tiny painting, a room, even one inhabited by monsters and wonders.

***

It is a lesser-known fact that the very beautiful author of *Good Night Moon* was not an old lady at all but 42-years young when she died in her sleep from an undetected brain tumor.

"Goodnight noises everywhere."

Sixteen

Journeys

On the calm lake, we paddled. With strokes out of sync, my eight-year-old son and I made up for our lack of team coordination with exaggerated flourish. Turning my head to look back at little Blaise, I recognized I was ridiculously happy. Mouth of the river was a distance away with bridge underpass awaiting. As we entered cave-like, concrete domain, I overworked my right hand, and we hit a side of the culvert, wobbling but not overturning our canoe.

"Close one," I heard behind me.

Mold covers top of the culvert that seems much longer than it actually is. Condensation forms on the roof and drips on us like fetid rain.

"Eww, gross," Blaise laughed. "I think I swallowed it."

Nodding, I duck and hear a large, wet drop plop on my back rather than my head. As we exited the culvert, Goodale Lake opened before us, the small, 50-acre body of water that feeds into Upper Little York. A few ducks gathered at far side near tall grasses. You would not take a powerboat over this shallow water, only a canoe or kayak.

"Turtle," Blaise said, pointing. I saw only ripples displaced. "Painted turtle?"

He shook his head. "A snapper."

Living on a lake in the country, children quickly learn to distinguish wildlife. When my son was around five, he and his sisters spotted a huge snapping turtle crossing the road, heading for water. They ran inside and told us. Dan gave them an education in staying clear of large snapping turtles.

"They could take your finger off if you're not careful," Dan said, gently nudging the turtle across the road with a long, thick tree branch. Going up to their grandfather's farm was also a treat, where we might see deer, fox, and the occasional coyote. As a result, even as a five-year-old, Blaise knew his wildlife.

Continuing on our journey, I leaned out over the canoe slightly, worried about flipping my little boy even in this shallow water, but I was unable to spot the turtle that had quickly buried itself in muck at the bottom. Goodale Lake is a turtle and panfish haven.

Although Blaise had just turned eight at the time of our canoe trip, I took a chance without thinking about risks and climbed into that narrow boat with him. It was not a common occurrence. Far from an expert in a canoe, I scarcely ever went out on the lake in one. I was fairly young, however, and still in that mode of believing in near invincibility. Mother and son made our way across Upper Little York Lake and then Goodale with relative ease, only lapping water against aluminum, splashing of a few mallards, and rumbling rush of cars and trucks on an overpass could be heard.

I thought about all the times I wished they had built this highway along the hillside rather than right through the center of this beautiful valley, cutting through the heart of a glacial lake system. Semi-trucks and double trailers shake the earth on their way through this idyll.

Blaise was quiet, as was typical. We didn't talk much until we reached mouth of the West Branch of the Tioughnioga River that fed into Goodale. I don't remember exactly what we said at that moment, just recall a sudden quiet chattering as we entered river. We were excited by the journey in front of us, narrowing of stream, sudden splashes of hidden river creatures. A muskrat or beaver slid beneath our canoe where river was suddenly deeper.

"Right under us," Blaise said excitedly. Our canoe wobbled. We sat very still, stopped paddling.

"Saw him," I responded, not quite sure what I actually saw. I knew beaver had established along this part of the river, however, their telltale markings of cut trees on either side.

After leaving relative domesticity of small lakes, the West Branch felt wild, like uncharted territory, with houses, farms, cars all concealed by dense brush, trees, and weed overgrowth. We could have been hundreds of miles away at our camp in the wilds of Quebec.

"Just like early explorers," I said in muted tone.

A great blue heron startled us or, rather, we startled the bird, as it unfolded its prehistoric wings and took flight, lifted out of that cavern of dark trees and fast-moving water. "Heron," I remarked. Somehow, our paddles fell into sync in a way they had not over Upper Little York, as we glided up river swiftly, much surer of our oars than when we pushed off from our dock.

"Fox, fox," you said excitedly, as we rounded a bend, only its tail briefly visible before it disappeared completely, your finger pointing in its direction. I was not certain of what I saw but believed you as you appeared sure of what you had witnessed. We were advanced scouts. Slippery trout odors filled the air around us; soft soil crumbled at the banks; rains on leaves that hung over dynamic river, water filtered to brave explorers. We breathed in nature. In those moments, we were transported to another place.

I worried a bit that we might come across a coyote since they had re-established in this area. Dense brush along the river would have given them sufficient cover. More signs of beaver as we moved north past freshly cut tree limbs floating. I pointed to downed trees, and you nodded. We had an unspoken agreement that quiet was needed for surprise. Tranquil, strangely exciting, our journey seemed almost mythic from the point of view of our little boat in moving water surrounded by bending trees that blocked out civilization only a stone's throw away.

I thought of Thoreau who went to live at Walden Pond, not far from Boston, where the great Transcendentalist wrote *Walden*. In his own words, he went to, "live deliberately, to front only the essential facts of life, and see if I could not learn what it had to teach, and not, when I came to die, discover that I had not lived."

How far upriver would we venture, I wondered? I, too, wanted to live deliberately and see what the river had to teach us.

At a sharp bend, the Tioughnioga deepened suddenly, and we hung suspended, looking into darkness with glints of silver below us, river teeming with trout. "Oh! Big trout," you said.

"Who would have thought?" I answered.

"There's so many," you said, pitch of your voice a little higher from excitement. The trout were so packed together, we could have reached down and caught one with our hands. Then we put our paddles back in the water and headed north.

A few more strokes up river, everything changed. From dream-like, gentle movements to bursts as our paddles struck surface, our awkward movements relentlessly exposed our fears. We had surprised a group of heifers that broke through their fence. Whether out of curiosity or some other instinct, heifers charged us. Trampling tall Brome grasses at the edge of banks and plunging into the river, heifers snorted then stopped for an instant, looking directly at us.

Everything shifted into slow motion. Whether they were sizing us up or reacting to surprise, they went with curious instinct and quickly moved into the water toward us. They were much faster than I had anticipated, and I felt my heart beating. We tried paddling backwards. In that suddenly shallow part of the river, heifers and bullocks were gaining.

You were silent, looking for your mother's direction and protection. "We're getting out of here," I yelled, hoping to scare the clamoring animals from slamming into us.

Making an instantaneous decision, I hopped out, nearly tipping our canoe over. The gravel bottom made it easy to gain footing. We both had to get out of the canoe and lift it over a few rocks before climbing back in and working hard to get free, huffing young bulls almost upon us. Hot breath on our backs. I am not sure what they would have done had those heifers and bullocks run into us. They are not normally deadly or dangerous, but their rushing bulk and weight presented a threat. I could see us getting badly hurt in the commotion of charging bodies. However unintended, I was suddenly responsible for putting my little boy in danger. Guilt washed over me mixed with relief after we were free.

You glanced at me with a look that said, "Is that what you planned?" Then you, too, suppressed a smile. We made it, of course, and started laughing out loud once back on the pond. How strange, I thought, my angst from close encounter with some young bulls. I was immensely grateful for our narrow escape. Luck was with us that time.

As I write the scene, I'm back in our aluminum canoe with my brave little boy again. I can no longer hear his eight-year-old voice, but I see his face and feel his moods. He must have thought his mother was a little crazy, but he never criticized me. He never even mentioned our semi-dangerous encounter to his dad. That was left to me.

"It was fun," he said in answer to his father's questions.

Only a child, he was a confident explorer, nothing in his healthy aspect, calm voice, or beautiful face betrayed his heart's early warnings, the peril that awaited.

Not all of my son's journeys had such adventurous unfolding, and I found I was less effective at protecting him than that day in the canoe all those years ago. The years of his dive into alcohol abuse and drugs were far more perilous. Even that menace, however, did not approach the unknown threat of his heart.

*****

Blaise still appears to me suddenly. His death has not stopped me seeing him. I was reading and then paused. Sitting in an old leather chair with a broken foot rest, I had been reading an Ann Patchett essay about escaping daily, busy life with her too many visitors. Patchett flew across the country to Los Angeles to hole up in The Hotel Bel-Air where she would write in contemplative, uninterrupted peace.

I tried to picture myself flying across the country to my reserved rooms in this old Hollywood glamour hotel to write. My smile is ironic as I think about how much time and quiet I have in my house now. We have lived with "shelter in place" orders due to the COVID-19 outbreak. It has been too quiet. Now, with Blaise gone, silence has become eerie, and I long for his footsteps, the quick "hi, heading to work. Love you."

When I look up from Patchett's anthology of essays, I momentarily see Blaise standing in the dining room, collecting his wallet and keys, as he had so many times before. His back is turned to me. He turns his head slightly. We don't speak, but the fractions of a second image of him is so real. He asks for nothing. Within a blink of my eyes, he is gone again. Light ever changing as the sun works its way through cloud cover to produce sparkling undulations across the lake, reflecting through windows, wavering images along walls of my house. Tricks of light. All part of this disappearing act.

Gulls in the distance take off from the water, not in unison but haphazardly. They appear as scattered leaves that have left their colors behind in damp earth, leaves already half-decomposed, turning into leaf mold, but caught in sudden updrafts, whirling overhead. Gulls turned to leaves, leaves turn to regret. How I perceive the world is now colored by loss of my son.

Even a good life full of love, satisfying work, and relative comfort is too hard a journey sometimes.

***

Years after our canoe trip up river, Blaise mastered the kayak and went out on long excursions alone. I never asked him what he saw on those trips, and he never shared his experiences over the water. One day, he came back from his outing in the kayak, and he was soaking wet. I assumed he went swimming, but I never saw him use the kayak after that day. I wondered what had happened, but when I asked, Blaise would just shake his head and say, "Nothing." He would offer that little half smile of his that said, "mystery."

I found out from a good friend of mine that her a daughter-in-law's mother drowned using a kayak. Mother and daughter were out together when tragedy happened, and the daughter was thrown out of the kayak that continued on down the rapidly moving river. The image of this woman trapped beneath the kayak was one I could not get out of my head. I have wondered several times since that day if Blaise had scared himself in our kayak, unable to right it readily on some occasion. How close had he come to drowning in our lake? I did not know but could sense a flicker of worry in his eyes when I mentioned the kayak.

I asked him once much later why he didn't take the kayak out anymore, and he just shook his head slowly. Interpret, as you wish, he seemed to say.

There are so many things I want to ask my son, but I am no longer able to do so. I tried to refrain from questioning him too often to avoid being the annoying mother. I actually worked at not bothering him because I was afraid my questions would feel like an inquisition. Of course, now, I wish I had asked him every question. I wish I had pressed for more answers. I wish most of all that I had hugged him on that last day.

Although Blaise lived at home, there was always a feeling that he was about to set off on a voyage, but his boat remains tied to the shore. For all his desire, he could not untether that skiff. His life was finite and shortened, but the enigma of my son, of his longings, his many loves, and the great love he evoked in others, these seem infinite.

Seventeen

"Some Days, I'm Six"

Nothing is right now. "Things fall apart." That line has come to me many times over the years, ever since I first read the phrase in Yeats' poem, and then later was surprised to see it again in Chinua Achebe's novel title. Yes, I think, so very true. The nature of nature.

A colleague mentioned that it would be impossible for a reader to follow a non-chronological narrative such as I proposed before the writing of my memoir, the difficult telling of this story of the most terrible loss of our son Blaise Martin. I gave considerable thought to the problems presented for readers but knew that my life experience was, indeed, anachronistic. Things do not feel flung apart chronologically.

My grandson Enzo, a very intelligent seven-year-old, recently asked his mother, "Do you ever feel like you're one? Sometimes, I'm one years old and some days, Mom, I'm six." This innocent question and statement go directly to the heart of how we perceive, how we experience our lives. One moment, we are sitting on a boat basking in the sun and the next, we are in the middle of a traffic jam with honking horns and cursing drivers, but the moment on the water comes back to us. We can hear the water lapping, feel the sun on our warm skin, taste humid air. Even at his young age, my grandson appreciated the fact we are moving along these looping threads of time that double back on us within an instant.

My daughter Colette answered Enzo, "I don't feel like I'm one, but some days, I feel like I'm a teenager." When my daughter related this story, I had to laugh because I still think of my very young looking, successful daughter as a teenager, half expecting her to again take the mound in a softball game. Of course, I still feel myself pacing along the sidelines, nervous over every pitch she delivers. I don't tell her that I still think of her as that age.

Even for a six or seven-year-old, it is not impossible to follow an anachronistic ordering of existence; we see our past impact our present every day. It is what memory is made of, all those moments we do not simply recall but reexperience through sparks from another lived flash.

Deep breath. Blaise is two and marching toward our front door with his sister Nicole, a seven-year-old. Nicole is so patient and such a good big sister. Wearing yellow backpacks stuffed with blue and pink pajamas, t-shirts, and crackers for the road, they set out for, "New York City," Nicole says confidently. Her little brother has adopted the attitude: fearless adventurer ready for the trail. When they reach the door, two-year-old Blaise turns and waits for his sister to unlock it. Even though he is tall for a toddler, we have child-proof knobs on the handle.

His mom and Colette are laughing at the gates. They know something the toddler does not yet know: he can't actually go to NYC without an adult along. When Nicole turns and tells him they cannot really go, little Blaise lets out a forlorn howl of despair. He was ready and believed. Disappointment was earth-shaking.

Deep breath. Blaise is four and sitting across the table in a coffee shop that has long since closed down. I'm having my morning cup after dropping off Colette and Nicole at school. Stirring his cup of hot chocolate, Blaise appears as if he is just another urbanite on the way to work, having an espresso before heading out. From the moment of his birth, Blaise looked older than he was. In front of me are pages of a work project I am intensely studying, making corrections in the margins. My son does not interrupt. We often go long periods together without talking but comfortable in each other's company. Without appearing to do so, Blaise studies people coming and going, listens to what they are saying, watching their body language that expresses stress or anger, excitement or boredom. There is not a drop of chocolate on his clothes or across his mouth. He is very neat for a four-year-old.

When we get home, he asks a couple of questions before I set up my boards to do the layout for an issue of a client's newsletter I am producing.

"Why do you think that woman was sad?"

"What woman?" I have no idea what he is talking about. He shrugs. "No, what woman are you talking about?"

"Where we get coffee. Her head was down. She looked at me, and I could tell."

"I have no idea, honey." I realize my quiet little boy is taking in everything while I'm busy working. He is studying how the world works, the manner in which people express joy or sorrow.

Deep breath. Coming out of the cabin, I looked through the camera lens and snapped a couple of photos of my father Emerson, Sr. and Blaise when he was five. The two of them are wading in the sparkling waters of Lac Yser, moving slowly as my dad held his grandson's hand, their feet digging into the soft sand at the bottom. My dad did not splash his grandson or dunk him.

Gradually moving into deeper water, they swam, letting out happy yelps from the shock of cold lake. After a few minutes, they came back across the white sand, dried off, and went inside for a nap on the pull-out couch on the porch. The only sound in that quiet cabin was my dad's snoring. Half an hour later, I took another photo of them sleeping, my little son's long legs tanned and curved with young muscle, his hand and long fingers draped over my dad's chest that moved up and down in dreamless sleep. I snap another photo. It is a scene I revisit many times.

Both are gone now. Emerson, Sr. in a terrible fall down the stairs while caring for my mother ailing with Alzheimer's disease, and Blaise to this rare, fatal syndrome twenty-eight years after exploring the lake shore fronting my dad's fishing camp in Quebec.

Deep breath. I was not with my grandsons and daughter as they explored a stream in Silver Spring, Maryland because of the pandemic "shelter in place" orders. Nicole sent me photos of my grandsons standing ankle deep in the water close to their home. Three little boys walk in the crick that runs into the city where it widens, passing through suburban communities on its way.

My grandson Owen in red sneakers, thoroughly wet, water mark halfway up his pant legs, is very still in this photo. Nearly always in motion, this stillness is a rarity. He is balanced on slippery river rocks, gazing out pensively. He looks wiser than his five, almost six, years on that warm spring afternoon. I know without asking that Owen had been running through the water, checking under rocks for salamanders and tadpoles. He is a bundle of energy and full of questions about the nature of things.

Then Owen's sweet mother asks her little boy to listen to the peaceful river. I can hear my daughter's soothing voice as she tells me this anecdote. Nicole has the kind of voice that comforts, one you want to hear at any time.

My daughter and I are texting late one night recently, after my grandsons are finally fast asleep. Our texts read like conversation, not abbreviated with typical text slang but full sentences with punctuation. That is what you get with a mother who taught English and writes and an articulate daughter who responds in kind. It is raining again in New York, but I hear Nicole through her texts as the evening rain creates surrounding rhythm for the music of her words.

Nicole wrote that she said to her sons, "What do you think the river is saying?"

Owen responded, "I think it's saying it is Blaise, and it loves us."

She texted, "I hadn't mentioned Blaise, so it surprised me."

Owen's cousin Enzo said, "Yeah, I hear him, too. This is a happy time and sad time. I'm happy because I can hear Blaise and sad because I wish I could see him."

"It was a beautiful moment," Nicole texted.

Of course, Blaise is the river. Blaise is also now the rain and the trees' rustling leaves, the rain falling outside my window as a I write.

I don't want my little grandsons ever to be sad, but it is also comforting to me to realize they, too, are thinking about Blaise.

Water has throughout human history been imbued with restorative powers, with life and resurrection. We emerge from water as in the embryonic sac. Water is life-sustaining in that we must drink water to survive. Water is also a symbol of multiple levels of consciousness; what lies beneath. But, as in T.S. Eliot's poem *The Waste Land*, water is a dual symbol, also connoting death through drowning. Even in death, however, the body is washed. Water baptizes, water purifies. Seeing through Owen's eyes, I, too, see my son in the streams, the lakes, water all around.

Blaise always seemed so connected to water even in ways that the rest of us have forgotten from our time in the womb. I cannot look out over Little York Lake without seeing my son.

I am not a believer in ghosts, but I know in that moment while my grandson Owen stood on those rounded slippery stones, looking out, Blaise had become the river. Blaise Martin rippled and flowed, speaking to his little nephews.

I knew at the moment of Owen's comment about Blaise as the river, as I have known before, Dan and I are not alone in our grieving, in missing larger than life Blaise Martin. His sisters ache for him, his nephews see and hear him in the rivers. His brothers-in-law miss his friendship. His friends feel a little jump in their hearts at any one of a thousand prompts in which their buddy, their brother is with them again at unexpected moments.

Eighteen

Man of Few Words

There ought to be one chapter shorter than all the others, one chapter just to reflect Blaise as a young man of few words.

"You can stop there, Mom." I hear him saying. "Finished."

"You mean, stop writing after one sentence?"

"It's plenty." He turns away and leaps up the stairs so quickly I'm not sure if he skipped the stairs altogether and simply appeared on the landing.

Certainly, part of the puzzlement of my son is that so much remains unspoken. He communicated but sparsely, frequently through movements and gestures, his expressive eyes, a language beneath the spoken one. The source of his power to command your attention was not in what he said, but suspended silences in which he transmitted intelligence, fears, longing, joy, anxiety with a quick movement or contemplative smile. I am certain that held within my son's lengthy periods of quiet, there was a need to just breath, a need, as French author Nathalie Sarraute wrote in *Tropisms*, "to move about a bit, without knowing where ...then come back home, sit down on the edge of the bed, and once more, wait, curled up, motionless."

Beneath everyday human exchanges, a great deal of meaninglessness is tossed into the exchanges between people. I always had the feeling that Blaise held a bit of contempt for such inanities. I have only felt this way around a few people in my life, but my son was one of them. It is also possible that Blaise had for so long held his thoughts and emotions hidden from view, during his secretive years of using drugs, he had perfected leaving them below the surface. But he was a quiet little boy, too. Of course, the problem arose when his silence was misinterpreted as needs that may not have been there.

Aware that I offer a portrait of my son skewed solely through my eyes, I have to admit that Blaise talked much more with his friends and sisters. He loved to make them laugh, and I know he could be silly with them. I do have remembrances of a language Blaise and his great friend Nick Triolo made up, consisting entirely of ridiculous sounding nonwords. Occasionally, I would pass by him when he was younger and on the phone with Nick. I would suddenly hear a weird noise coming from my son followed by laughter.

"What was that about?" I could not help asking.

"Nothing, nothing," Blaise would smile. "Just talking with Trio."

But with his Dad and me, Blaise could get serious, discussing the state of the world, upset about corruption in politics, indignant about various kinds of injustice, particularly racial injustice in our country. He listened well, too. Between conversations with his father, watching historical documentaries, and his readings in the last few years of his life, Blaise gave himself the education he did not acquire in college. This education happened after his hard climb out of addiction.

Because of the years Blaise was abusing Xanax, in particular, I worried about him without knowing the exact problem he faced or the extent of it. Even after my son successfully went through rehab and was doing well, I continued to worry. All that time gave me a hard-to-break habit of fear and worry. I recall an afternoon when my concerns spilled out, and I questioned him in a manner that may have come across like an accusation, "Are you depressed?" There were many instances when I felt his disquieting presence without him saying anything. I had been reading about a rise in suicides among young men. The fear surfaced.

Pulling his boots on, then his coat, Blaise shook his head, 'I'm not depressed. I'm anxious. Anxiety and depression are not the same, Mom. I am not suicidal." I understood he was carrying a weight, a weight I was not ever able to remove or help shoulder. None of us really understood where that weight came from or the actual form. From where did the anxiety emerge?

Keeping spoken words minimal, we too often accepted the sparseness of his words. From my perspective, Blaise's life for a long time seemed smaller than I thought it should be. With his room dark, almost cave-like, most of the time, Blaise appeared comfortable in his little bedroom even when he could have opted to move his things into one of the larger guest rooms, once his sisters moved to the Washington, D.C. area. I never knew if he just like the enclosed space of his room or did not want to make his sisters feel as if he was moving into one of their spaces. If I brought up the idea of changing rooms, he always said he was fine where he was.

Once I said to him, "You can have our room, your dad's and mine, someday. It is the largest."

"Don't talk like that," Blaise responded, clearly upset. "I don't ever want your room, and you're always going to be around."

He refused to continue the abbreviated conversation I tried to have about his future or our eventual passing.

Yet, his agitation, the sense of restraint, remained a part of the experience of being around him. While I could read more into it, his disquiet may have been as simple as wanting to escape a prying mother.

Deep breath. To state that Blaise was a quiet child is inadequate. During a terrible rain storm in the summer month before he turned three, I had to stop our softball practice and take my children home. For a number of years, I coached my daughters' recreation league softball teams. That afternoon, I had one extra child with me because the little girl's mother could not come to the ballfield until later that day. So, I set off for home in a driving rain with four children in the car. Lightning and thunder crackled around us, inspiring "ohs," "wow," and a couple of frightened screeches from my daughters' young teammate. When we reached the house, strong winds bent upper branches of trees and blew refuse down the road, rolling garbage cans. We hurried inside and dried off with every clean towel I could find. We watched as wind strengthened and blew our canoe across the lawn, then our fence fell flat, the entire length of it blown down.

"Okay, kids. We're going to go into our cellar just in case this wind gets any stronger," I said, trying to maintain an even, calming tone.

The little girl from our softball team started to cry. My three children, including nearly three-year old Blaise took their cues from me and could see I was still okay with the situation. I opened the trap door in our living room, and we descended the ladder stairs into the cellar with one flashlight. As we made our way down, we could hear a terrific rumble and reverberation, a thud worthy of an explosion above us. We felt our way to my photo darkroom with that flashlight. I set Blaise on the counter where recently developed film strips hung all around his head. I did not want my little boy on the damp floor, but I also wondered if he would pull down all the hanging developed film. He did not. The girls stood together in a small circle. I suggested we tell stories to allay the fears of our young visitor. She continued to cry at every loud crack from outside. The storm produced the greatest number of close lightning strikes I could recall. I expected the power to go out at any moment, but we had our flashlight. Then the lights went out.

I remember trying to reassure this little girl, hugging her as her mom would have done. I stopped thinking about my children temporarily because they were so quiet, not crying, staying still. A half-hour later, the violent storm had blown through, and we all climbed back up the stairs to the living room. After closing the trap door and replacing a corner of the rug to cover the door, I turned to see our huge elm tree brought down by a sheer wind. The tree came to rest against our front door, its leaves covering our lakeside windows almost completely. The damage to our yard was astounding, roots of giant elm standing straight up in the air nearly twenty feet, pulling the soil and a large chunk of our lawn with it. We could not have gotten out the lake door if we tried.

The child's mother came to pick her up a couple of hours later. My little softball player had cried much of the afternoon, only coaxed down from hysteria with much attention and kind words from my daughters. What surprised me was not that my two daughters, ages 10 and 8, had taken the storm so well, but that my two-year-old son seemed perfectly at ease with the situation, not being held by his mom in the dark room, with the crashing of thunder and trees above us.

That night, I listed events of the scenario in my head: we rushed from the field where lighting was striking, drove through torrential rain with a little girl crying hysterically until we calmed her down for a few moments, ran to the house in a downpour getting soaked, dried roughly, then descended into a pitch-black cellar with only one dim light, and Blaise never screamed or let out a yell. He did not pull down the strips of film around his head, either. The incident was not isolated. Blaise was, quite simply, an easy-going, sweet little boy who seldom, if ever, cried. He accepted altered situations and unpleasant surprises with seeming ease. He was to need that quality more and more as time passed.

***

Those character traits from his childhood returned to Blaise as an adult. My son's last few years were very generous ones. There was something even heroic in Blaise's gestures near the end of his life. His expressive eyes still occasionally showed fear or confusion, but they also offered love and joy. He was exceedingly generous during that time.

A man of few words, but they were astute, perceptive, political, thoughtful ones. If he could read what I have written, he would very likely want to edit here. "You should add something," he might say.

"About your interest in rap music?" I ask.

"About racism and bigotry in our country. You should say something about how our history is based upon a racist structure that is still hurting everyone in this country today."

I long wondered how and why my son seemed to identify with young black men in America, but I also found his assessments to be accurate, and sometimes more astute than my own. On several occasions, I would find him fuming or in a deep well over the death of a young rapper or the wrongful shooting of a black youth by a white policeman. He was acutely attuned to injustices in our culture in ways I never fully understood. In that, he took racial injustice personally, not as some abstract concept of right and wrong but as the wound he felt that could not heal.

Blaise was the one who brought home a stack of Impeach Trump decals. One morning, after his coffee, he positioned Resistance/Impeach Trump decals on our cars then offered them to friends and friends of friends. Although he had never read John O'Donahue to my knowledge, I thought of O'Donahue's words in *Anam Cara* about how we view others who are in trouble, who lack political power, who are economically disadvantaged: "Part of understanding the notion of Justice is to recognize the disproportions among which we live...it takes an awful lot of living with the powerless to really understand what it is like to be powerless, to have your voice, thoughts, ideas and concerns count for very little. We, who have been given much, whose voices can be heard, have a great duty and responsibility to make our voices heard with absolute integrity for those who are powerless."

Blaise seemed to embody that concern and responsibility. He never gave up on trying to help his friends see that politics mattered in everyone's life: "Some of my friends say they don't care about politics, but I want to tell them, our politics are who we are."

He was politically aware, well read in terms of the fraught state of our nation. He was moral and compassionate.

To honor his precision and succinctness, I offer my poem.

***

When I can't find words

When I can't find words,
I mark the page in long strokes
followed by short constructs,
looking for meaning in unintended
patterns like the woman who found
the face of Christ in a peach pit.
We're predisposed to ordering chaos,
something, anything on the head of a pin.

Let a word lift as vehicle for the tenor
who is still singing in an empty room.

At our ending, is life itself
illusory? Last breaths most real
to the dying? Whole of human thought
no more intricate than a spider's web
from blind eye of an atom?

Silence follows questions
follows endings follows
beginnings in which a word
shapes itself into a question.

***

A number of years ago, Blaise came down the stairs with a pink tie with tiny blue dots loosely draped around his neck. "Can you help me with this?"

Dan was away at an annual golf tournament with his college friends, and Blaise had never bothered to learn how to tie a tie since he so seldom wore one. When he did have to wear a tie, he always took one of Dan's premade to pull over his head and tighten.

"Of course," I said, flattered that he asked me, but as soon as I started to fold a length of the tie over itself, I realized I did not really know what I was doing. After a fumbling attempt, Blaise shook his head. We both laughed. Then, I said, "Let's look it up on the Internet."

We did, and Blaise learned to tie his tie quite perfectly; such a small gesture, such an unexpected little failure and success. I only later thought about how our lives are made up of these slight adjusted movements, unexpected requests, and the perfect knot.

That was the tie I chose for him at his end.

Deep breath. The Beard. A whole chapter could be written about Blaise's beard, that dark mass of largely untrimmed curly growth extending well below his chin to his chest. Full beards have a mystique all their own, a symbolism dependent upon the type and style, as well as their own characterization.

I did not like my son's beard when he first grew it out fully. I finally, tentatively, asked him, "Have you thought about trimming your beard?"

Giving me that sidelong glance, Blaise hesitated, then said, "I started growing it out fully when I got sober."

I nodded. "So, the beard is kind of a symbol of sobriety?"

Blaise tilted his head to the side as if to say I was close. "Maybe I'll cut it in the future but not yet," he said. No, the beard was staying, having seen him through drug and alcohol addiction recovery. Its importance was no longer lost on me.

Reading a bit more about men's facial hair, I discovered that a full beard symbolizes not only power and masculinity but self-restraint and patience.

Carolyn Day, in a historical essay "Darwin's Beard and George Eliot's Hands" for the March 14, 2018 issue of *Public Books* online, wrote, "To explain why Darwin's beard mattered, Hughes provides a cultural history of facial hair, focusing on its varied meanings in the 19th century. Before the mid-century, beards had an unsavory connotation and 'were for men with something to hide.' After the Crimean War, however, the beard became a marker of virility associated with returning war veterans. Inspired by 'the sight of these hairy heroes,' a number of prominent Victorians welcomed the fashion, which allowed them to hide those features they found embarrassing.'"

Beard styles and symbolism have probably been through as many evolutionary versions as Darwin's study of our species, but Blaise's beard was not grown to hide his face, a very handsome one. If anything, it seemed a shame that part of his face was hidden by a sprawling beard. But that beard became a touchstone for my son. It was the point from which he could say, "I have left addiction. I am comfortable in my own skin again." It also said, "I don't care what others think."

I grew to love even the beard my son grew. As I previously related, his beard is what I saw in my dream while I was in the hospital. That beard was distinct, unique like Blaise.

***

For me, Blaise's quiet presence was always a gift. Unlike my son, I came in from the opposite shore where words are anxious to find expression. Blaise's sisters and his close friends knew his humor, his clever wit, did not find him nearly as quiet as his parents did. For his mother and father, however, he reserved his most unadorned self, and he was beautiful.

Nineteen

He Rolled His Eyes

Blaise is in the room with me at this moment, looking over my shoulder and reading this text. I feel his presence. He smirks and shrugs his shoulders. Maybe rolls his eyes. "I'm no saint, Mom. Don't write that." He is shaking his head a bit, too.

A word is needed about how expressive Blaise's eyes were. You could read sorrow, compassion, disdain, anger, joy, or fear in his eyes alone. If you practice, you can read these expressions in most people's eyes, but you did not have to be particularly adept at it to read my son's moods through his eyes. He could have been an actor. Although his face might be still, his eyes betrayed or conveyed everything.

I am not sure Blaise would recognize himself in my recollections and the images I have tried to recreate of moments in our lives. He was much funnier than I have shared. He was also more attuned to satire and skepticism than I have written. Yet he retained a boyish innocence and sweetness in manhood, qualities that were apparent but not necessarily ones he wanted to project. He might be annoyed or embarrassed at the words "innocence and sweetness," but anyone who knew him well would agree. Not innocent of experience but innocence in the sense of believing anything is possible.

Although he went through years of doubt and fears during his twenties, he came through that hard time and was fully present, fully himself the last three years of his shortened life. I know he practiced being clever with his Facebook posts and with his friends, but at home, he did not have to entertain. Near the end of his life, I could see him ready to spread out and take on new adventures again. His dad and I knew he might have thought about leaving, but something held him back. For a long time, I speculated the factor keeping him at home was concern he would return to using drugs. With more information, I have come to believe he knew something was wrong with his body, not his mind. His instincts for self-preservation were exactly right, more accurate that he knew. "No kidding," I can imagine him saying now.

***

Every parent who has ever attended a teacher conference knows this feeling: you go into the meeting expecting mild or exuberant praise for your amazing child. You think about how you will temper flattery offered by the teacher but secretly long to hear those words. Then your child's teacher adjusts some papers on her desk. She looks up at you as if you have greatly inconvenienced her at a critical moment. She speaks with exasperation and what comes out is not praise or understanding or kindness. You reel before gaining your footing and adjust your stance to one of protection for your son.

At a parent-teacher conference I attended for Blaise when he was in seventh grade, the first of his teachers complained about him. He had excellent grades on his report card. What was the problem? I don't remember everything she said, but I heard the edge of anger in her voice. Shocked at first, I recovered quickly to ask what he was doing that upset her, and she said, "He rolls his eyes." I knew what this meant. Blaise was not showing her proper respect. As a twelve-year-old, he was already indicating his disdain with someone or something. He never complained about his teachers at home, but I knew the look and understood it.

Parents of most bright children will likely find that scene familiar. At a certain point, smart kids have figured out that school no longer holds treasures and new exploration for them. They become bored and restless unless someone decides to challenge them. You know it is the system, but you are still embarrassed for the failures of your child, of yourself, and of that teacher. Why did he have to roll his eyes? And why is that somehow humiliating?

Many years later, after Blaise had successfully gone through rehab, he told me, "I don't think I had a good attention span in school. Maybe I had ADHD or something." When he stated that, I thought he was simply wrong, even making an excuse for not being more consistently successful academically.

Only after his death, after I found out my son had Marfan syndrome, I began looking into the problems associated with that syndrome. I should not have been shocked to find out that some studies of individuals with Marfan's have shown an association with "increased susceptibility to Attention Deficit Hyperactivity Disorder," according to the American Society of Human Genetics. While there are other studies that show no direct correlation, I have thought about how your attention might be diverted by strange happenings in your body. If you are not feeling right, it is difficult to concentrate. I have no idea of how you might be distracted by unfamiliar and sudden aches in your back and legs, how you might wonder about stretch marks on your shoulders when you are not lifting weights, how it might feel to have your tissues pulling apart, not in growth.

So many of the issues my son had intuited turned out to have a causal origin and were not "all in his head" as he, and everyone else, thought. With Marfan's, the heart, joints, bones, tissues, and eyes are all affected. I could not remember the last time Blaise had an eye test. Although he did not complain of eye problems, he did not grumble about much of anything. Compared to his chest pains, he must have thought a little trouble seeing was really no big deal.

Research into this connective disorder shows there is typically, "swelling of the membrane that surrounds the brain and spinal cord. This is called dural ectasia, and many people with Marfan syndrome have it. Dural ectasia may cause low back and leg pain, abdominal pain, and headaches," according to OrthoInfo, the American Academy of Orthopedic Surgeons online website. Although he did not cry out in pain nor seldom complained, Blaise occasionally stated matter-of-factly that he had a headache, that he had lower back pain, that his legs, his abdomen hurt. Because he worked out so hard and was always involved in athletics, everyone assumed these mild symptoms were strains as a result of stretching his muscles and ligaments in sports or from dehydration. I continually reminded him to drink more water. He would look at me with exasperation. Only now have I discovered that my son's body was giving off every signal of the danger. His body was shouting, "help," and no one was listening. Not one physician, or friend or family member, not a single teacher or coach heard his need because he was too quiet about it, and "he rolled his eyes."

Blaise's restlessness and anxiety were not due to his personality but an enlarged aorta. Remembering those days of his relative struggles in school, in comparison to his sisters' ease with academic excellence, I also realize that my son helped me to be a better teacher and, perhaps, a better parent. I knew in a very personal way that not every bright student comes into a classroom ready to learn. The care I gave my non-academically inclined students made a difference in their lives. I am not guessing at this outcome but have heard directly, over the years, from many of my former students who have thanked me for this attention when they did not want to, or could not, pay attention.

"I should have been a lawyer," Blaise once said after he came home, distraught and drunk. Although I heard the drink talking, I knew he was deeply disappointed in himself in a way I could not help. I understood he believed his inability to follow in the path his highly successful sisters had taken was failure. He was far harder on himself than any of his teachers or coaches could have been, and they were hard on him, or they were indifferent.

Blaise had to find self-respect alone, and he finally did, only after following a perilous path. Like climbing out of mine shafts, Blaise slowly worked his way to the surface, determined never to go back down. He became far more generous and thoughtful after he left addiction behind, but he retained his skepticism and some degree of cynicism. Yes, he still rolled his eyes occasionally.

I know exactly why Blaise offered that gesture of distain as a seventh grader. At the time, I was upset with my son in that he caused his teacher's criticism. I wondered if I might have rolled my eyes in that classroom?

What does it mean to question authority? To regard an authority figure not as the answer but simply as a messenger? Later, I realized how proud I was, and still am, of my son. Challenging authority, questioning whether something is true or false regardless of the status of the figure pronouncing the statements, these are things I consciously worked to give my son.

He could never have been the member of a cult. Once you have embraced doubt, you cannot go back to closing all the windows and doors. Be the one seeking, not the one pretending to have all the answers. He absorbed those lessons, perhaps too well for some on his journey.

Lack of bigotry, accuracy, intelligence, curiosity, and distain for ignorance are qualities that Blaise demanded of himself and expected of others. He demonstrated those qualities as a teen and fully in his last years. As he said once, "I want my nephews to be proud of me."

There occur moments each day when I descend into illogical anger.

***

Until the Furies Have Left

To all those weary from our sadness,
let bemoaning mothers say what's permissible
in bereavement is more than sorrowing in solitude.
Store away the platitudes and ready-made
"thoughts and prayers" banality for those
who care less than mourning mothers.
When we, who have lost our sons and daughters,
lament, we will cry out for the unnatural return
of our children, abducted like Persephone.
Mothers suddenly leaping into fury,
punishing ourselves fiercely like the Erinyes,
snake-like hair writhing in our grief.

Let us who long for beautiful son or daughter
scream and shout, moan and gnash our teeth,
pull away rocks until fingers bleed in breaking.
Allow us to dig deeper into rage,
raving until those wild and violent winds
lift and bear us away.

It is not the dead, but the grieving
who refuse our children going gently
into that good, black night.

Twenty

Imperfect Perfect

"Don't pretend I was anything close to perfect." I can hear exasperation in Blaise's voice. He was right but missing the point. During the end of high school and deep into his twenties, Blaise used drugs and definitely over imbibed in alcohol, dipping his feet in at first then leaping without checking water's depth. Reckless and out of control at moments, he did things he regretted. A lot of things. There were even a few he did not remember doing.

I could hardly believe the young man who was so gentle and kind could get so crazy when he was drinking or using drugs, but he did. He was not alone in this behavior, however, which is neither excuse nor meant to ameliorate his actions, just a statement of fact. I went to bed many nights during those years, and they were years when I did not know what might happen. I also did not know how to prevent it.

Around midnight, when Blaise was in high school, a State Policeman woke me up with a phone call. I had been asleep, but the ringing phone at that hour was enough to make my heart leap. I answered to the stern voice of a policeman, and my mouth opened. I tried to calm my racing heart and brain. For an instant, I thought I was being told Blaise was dead. "Your son has been in an accident." Then the policeman added after a pause that felt like eternity, "He's alive. You will need to come pick him up and arrange for a tow for your vehicle." I scarcely remember what he said after he told me Blaise was okay. I woke Dan, who swore out of fear and anger, that our son had gotten in a car crash.

When we arrived on the scene, the sight was stunning and surreal. Police lights like fireworks. Our Ford Bronco totaled, in such twisted metal shape, it looked more like an abstract sculpture than car. Blaise was nervous but stood there, on the verge of tears, but fine, physically untouched. He was with a friend who was being escorted to the trooper's car, put in the back. I could hardly understand what was happening. I wanted to help his friend out of the police car.

"There must be some mistake," I wanted to say but was silent.

We listened to a lecture from a NY State Trooper, and after taking personal items from our wrecked car, we took Blaise home. We had to arrange for our vehicle to be towed. Everything was so unnatural that I had trouble comprehending why Blaise was not being arrested, too. It was our car, but Blaise's friend was driving.

Years later, one of Blaise's friends told us there were several other boys in our car with them. They were taking one of the boys back to his house after all had been drinking together. Someone decided on the driver who had the least to drink. How they landed on that kid is difficult to imagine since he was clearly as drunk as the rest of them. They had all obviously erred in judgement many times over. Fortunately, the other boys had been dropped off before the accident, miraculously escaping injury. Blaise and the driver were left standing there when the police arrived.

I remember the feeling of panic spasms that went through me, seeing our mangled vehicle and knowing how close my son came to losing his life in high school. How close he and his friend driving came to being gone too young. When we emptied our car, we found Blaise's lacrosse helmet. Two huge dents were clear, and I thought about the level of force it took to make those incisions. If only teenagers would decide they are not immortal because they are not. Although Blaise could often be thoughtful and sweet on occasion during those years, he was also on the edge of losing his life more than once. I was not unaware, but as he got older, it became harder to restrict him or know precisely what he was doing. To be honest, he was very good at masking. I was not entirely oblivious to the fact he was drinking, but I kept telling myself that he would "grow out of it." He would get through it, that poorly defined "it" as youthful urges, lack of perspective, and recklessness. Still, I lectured, forbid his use of the car for periods of time. Dan once threw away his phone. Blaise never defended himself of argued.

One afternoon, the mother of two of Blaise's high school teammates stopped me in a coffee shop. She asked if we could sit down and talk. I complied. I could see from her somber face and determination that she was about to tell me something I did not want to hear. Then she proceeded to say my son was an alcoholic, and she and other parents thought I should do something about it. "There are some things you should know," she said with an air of what felt like feigned sympathy although it may have been genuine on her part. "Your son is an alcoholic, and everybody knows it except for you." I was not unaware my son was drinking. There was the ostracizing remark: "I have to tell you, several of the mothers have been talking, and we don't want him influencing our sons."

I thanked her for the information but could feel blood rushing to my head. When I questioned my son later that afternoon, he admitted to having been to a party where everyone was drinking, including the two sons of the mother who had given me the lecture. Over the years, more information came from other young men about their activities when younger. Blaise was not influencing any of them. They came to drink and party on their own. I did not resent the woman for telling me that my son was drinking, but her assumption that I was a fool for not knowing what my son was doing when she was unaware of the risky behaviors of her own sons.

While Blaise engaged in some wrong-headed acts in high school, it was only much later that he fell into drug addiction. It is not a question of blame but understanding why so many seek this route. Yes, there is something called individual responsibility. We all need to take stock of our actions, but as a culture, we fail to fully examine our own part in why so many young men, particularly those in the athlete culture, use drugs and alcohol. Parents, teachers, coaches, and society are also failing them. "Just say no," is not effective. Punishments for some and not others are ineffective, as there are none better at detecting hypocrisy and injustice than teenagers. Knowing their coaches hit the bar after work then lectured about not drinking just does not cut it.

During the time I was teaching English in high school, the mother of a Skaneateles student came before the senior prom for a full-school event, actually a warning. This grieving, brave mother came to talk about her lost son. The young man had been killed driving in the car with his friend. Both boys had been drinking after celebrating a lacrosse game win. Only the passenger died. The driver, an 18-year-old senior, went to state prison. The two in the destroyed car had been best friends. I sat in the audience and listened to high school boys snickering at the anguished mother's words, emotion in her voice enough to cause me to quiver. Those boys in our auditorium seats still believed they were invincible. I knew that no matter how many times someone bravely stood up and said, "Stop drinking and driving. It will kill you," young people and adults will continue to drink and drive. Clearly, lectures, words, pamphlets, educational meetings are not enough. We live in a culture that promotes and celebrates drinking at the same time we deal out harsh punishments for imbibing.

Part of the issue is the air of invincibility young people carry with them as flawed armor. Part of the problem is we are a society that drinks and drinks to excess. We drink "socially" for nearly every occasion. We drink with friends and strangers. How many teachers and coaches I know meet at the local bar after work? We are asking our children to do something adults do not do. Deputies, sheriffs, police officers, and judges are also stopped for drinking and driving, but once their identity is known by the arresting officer, that privileged citizen is almost always released without a ticket unless someone happens to die.

While that brave mother from Skaneateles was standing in our school auditorium and pouring her heart out in the hopes of saving at least one young person, I suddenly realized that my son had played lacrosse against her son only a couple of days before her son's death. I also knew that death in a car crash could have been my son. I have had time to reflect on the male athlete culture, both the joys and dangers of it. Our culture generally treats male athletes very well, raising them to heroic status almost, yet the moment one of them makes the inevitable mistake, we are ready to destroy.

There was more than one occasion I could have lost Blaise to drugs and or to alcohol. But, somehow, he survived. Perhaps the most bitter irony is that he finally conquered his addiction and had become thoughtful, responsible, and considerate, and then his life was taken.

After beating the considerable odds and leaving addiction behind, Blaise became the designated driver for his friends who continued to drink. More than once, he actually drove a bus for them, dropping off wedding reception guests at their houses or apartments. One night when he got home after taking a few drunken friends to their homes, Blaise told me that he was surprised how idiotic people sounded when they were drinking. He knew he had once been in their shoes, and he showed compassion. Once Blaise finally stepped away from his addictions, clarity of thought and purpose returned, but something else happened, as well. He became remarkably kinder, performing small acts of kindness everywhere. Only after his death did I discover some of these generous acts and thought about the ways Blaise had come to another type of grace.

When Blaise played basketball (a sport he never should have played if we had known about his enlarged heart), he moved with such minimal overt effort that it sometimes appeared he had not moved at all. He blocked a shot at one end of the court, then in the next instant, pulled up for a jump shot at the other end. Because he was tall and his movements so quick, he seemed not to "hustle," one of those words that coaches love. Blaise played sports like he was born to play them. Yet, with his heart, he never should have played any sports.

Deep breath. End of the game, with the 5th and 6th grade basketball mini-season on the line, I call a time-out. I ended up coaching a group of young boys more or less by default because Dan was working away from home, but found I was enjoying it immensely. "Mikey, bring the ball down the court and pass to either Blaise or Matt, whichever one is open. We have 12 seconds to get a shot off, so whoever gets the pass, pivot and shoot," I said as the red-faced, out-of-breath boys nodded earnestly.

Our team was down by one point. We were playing the first-place team in the league and not expected to win.

Blaise caught the inbound high pass from Mikey and drove the lane, getting hammered by opposing team players on the way up. The referee called the foul, and Blaise went to the line. He released the ball, and it circled the rim endlessly before dropping out. I called our team's last time-out.

"Okay," I said as if I knew exactly what I was doing. "Miss the second foul shot on purpose, hit the front of the rim. It will bounce toward you. Grab the rebound and sink the shot." Everyone nodded again as if this was a good plan, and I was not asking something ridiculous of a 5th grader in his first taste of organized basketball.

Blaise went to the free-throw line and launched the ball. Bouncing hard against the front of the rim, the ball careened into my son's hands, and he tossed it up without catching it, no time left. Swish. End of season. Our team erupted in cheers, laughter, and a pile of clapping bodies hugging and falling in a heap on the court.

Glorious not for its importance of anything but its improbability and splendid attainment. That moment was what I would call the best in sports. Those kids laughing and hugging in a bond.

Looking back, I am still amazed that our young team understood exactly what was needed to bring them to victory. At the time, I was irrationally certain my tall, fifth-grade son would put that ball through the net just as planned. Perfect proficiency in a moment. That is the glory of sports.

Blaise's great friend Nick Caruso sent me a clip from an old video tape of them playing football. In the short segment, Blaise is seen making a long run, a great one-handed catch and further run down the field. You can hear the fans and announcer in the background. The lights are shining on the dark grass. Promise of glory hangs in the air all over again. Those scenes are what makes sports so enticing.

Deep breath. Every recollection now carries additional weight, portent, foreshadowing. His shoulder pops out of joint.

It has happened before. Once, Blaise dove into his Aunt Theresa's pool, and his shoulder came out of joint again. She ran to her computer to look up how to push it back into the socket. Successful. After that, Blaise learned to force the bone back into position. Why did we not know these episodes he experienced were symptomatic of MFS?

***

At eight or nine years old, Blaise started collecting basketball cards, not baseball but basketball. The opening lines in Allan Gurganus' story, "The Wish for a Good Young Country Doctor" in *The New Yorker* reminded me of Blaise: "Most kids lose or break their toys. I curated mine." While Blaise did not exactly curate his toys, he was careful with them, never breaking any. Once he stopped playing with a toy, he boxed it and neatly stacked the box in his closet. Later, he kept the collectables unopened. He said he was saving them for his nephews when they were old enough.

Before one of our grandsons' visits, Blaise got out a carton from his old collection of toys for his nephews to play with. Most of the toys were in pristine condition. His cards, however, remained tucked away. There were foil-wrapped cards that could contain a surprise, and he struck gold a few times, getting a piece of the hard court and a bit of fabric from an NBA player's jersey. Whenever he got money for a gift or had earned points for chores when he was a kid, Blaise was off to the basketball card shop where the potential for something amazing hung in suspense. Over the years, he had acquired a substantial collection.

I remembered my own brothers' collection of baseball cards. Emerson, Jr. and Bob had original Mickey Mantle, Roger Maris, and other greats' rookie cards. My mother sold them all one day in a yard sale while my brothers were in college. She got next to nothing for them, unaware of their worth.

I was surprised Blaise never tried to sell his cards on eBay during the period of time he was addicted to drugs. Those cards meant enough that they stayed put. I think he wanted to give them to his nephews when they got old enough to appreciate them.

One afternoon before my grandson Truman's birthday, Blaise asked if we could buy some cards or a bubblehead sports figure for Truman, Owen, and Enzo.

We pulled into the parking lot and saw a sign out front, "Closing for Good." We went inside, and Blaise talked to the owner who remembered Blaise from those years he was one of the owner's best customers. I watched them chat as if old friends. When Blaise asked him why he was closing shop, the sports memorabilia store owner told us that someone had broken his door and robbed him. The merchant was tired of the fight, he said. He gave Blaise a really good deal on a Starting Lineup Allen Iverson resin figure wearing his Georgetown University basketball jersey.

As we got in the car, Blaise looked unusually down. "He practically gave away that Iverson," he said.

"You should be happy about that," I responded, misreading the intent behind his words.

"He's a good guy. Who would someone steal from him like that? Who would do that?" He scarcely talked all the way home, his newly purchased figures tucked on the seat with him. Those resin figures were intended to start the next generation on a search for the best sports collectibles.

I realized our visits to the sports collectible store all those years ago had made a deep and lasting impression, one of joy for both of us. I knew Blaise was hurting for the store owner and for losses less well-defined.

I do not know if the store owner was a good man or not. Looking back on that afternoon, I remembered something my father often said: "People are basically good." I probably tried reasoning with my dad about that unlikelihood, but he was firm in his conviction until near the end of his life. After my mother's diagnosis of Alzheimer's disease and his own continued struggle recovering from a stroke, my dad's clients and friends abandoned my parents. It was just too hard for them to remain patient with my mother's strange reactions as a result of the disease. I said something about one of his friends, and Dad responded, "He went to another lawyer. All those years, I took care of his business for nothing, and then when he had an estate to settle, he goes to someone else." I saw the terrible hurt in his eyes, heard it in his voice. I knew he would not continue to tell me that, "most people are basically good."

My father's defeated look of disappointment and the realization of how cruel and petty many people are stayed with me. I saw it again in Blaise's much younger eyes as we drove away from the closing memorabilia shop. Blaise, however, continued to forgive those who wronged or hurt him. During the last years of his life, it was as if my son was on a secret mission to do as much good through little gestures and kindnesses as he could.

Twenty-One

Grief Stays to Open the New Year

Reading lovely messages of good cheer from people excited about the New Year, about resolutions, and long passages of what a wonderful year 2019 was for them, I turned away from social media for an extended time.

Here is a small note about grief: it separates you, places you on a deserted island, even as it is, perhaps, a most universal human emotion, love being the one binding both. Acclaimed writer V.S. Naipaul, who passed away in 2018, wrote a wonderful essay on grief just printed in *The New Yorker* magazine. I quote from the article below because Naipaul's essay lies at the heart of the plane where I found myself standing on the eve of the New Year.

"We are never finished with grief. It is part of the fabric of living. It is always waiting to happen. Love makes memories and life precious; the grief that comes to us is proportionate to that love and is inescapable. This grief has its own exigencies."

Considering Naipaul's words, I felt not peace, nor happiness, nor hope, rather, a sense of awe. How much I loved my son Blaise is, indeed, proportionate to insurmountable grief that has come and continues to arrive in waves. How fortunate I was to have loved so well so fine a boy and young man.

Resolutions flutter like hopeful butterflies on Facebook. All this before knowledge of COVID-19 which would alter everything and everyone's perspective. But at the beginning of January 2020, bloggers and Facebook posts decry weight gain and resolve to lose twenty pounds, read more, save money, improve their romantic relationships, get a better job, go back to school, take an interest in world events, all before it is too late which it is, because world events have already reshaped every resolution as they are being made.

"I am going to lose fifty pounds" becomes within three months after the onset of COVID-19, "I am going to find toilet paper and wear a mask, not see my friends and many members of my family."

Every New Year's resolution has an implicit "future" embedded within it. And what does future mean exactly? Not the dictionary definition in which future is abstract, time that is yet to be. Future is the continual unfolding of the imagined instant after our present, out of thin air, like a magic trick. Yet we live each day with implied promise of future. How could we possibly go about our lives without this promise? Why take any action if there is to be no "next?" Yet, we all face that reality where a next no longer exists.

So many of our decisions and behaviors as human beings, and particularly as parents, relate to this theoretical contract with the future. We try to prepare our children to meet that unknown in a thousand little ways, from exhorting them to brush their teeth so they do not one day lose a "permanent" tooth to studying in school, so they may one day be successful in college and then in some career. Until our children leave home, we approach that threshold which we all assume will open into a good destination of some kind.

Blaise arrived at a threshold, the other side of which is entirely unknown by anyone, despite religious dogma. We simply do not have either empirical or scientific proof; we do not know. Knowing is not the same thing as believing. Plenty of people believe in all kinds of imaginings of an afterlife, some of which include pearly gates or a thousand virgins bizarrely offering themselves (since apparently, heaven for some comes at the expense of hell for others), but no one knows exactly what lies in the "undiscovered country," as William Shakespeare called it, or if anything exists at all.

After my son's death, my contract with the future was torn up and discarded. Reading those New Year's resolutions had been incredibly painful. Although aware that many people will open the door and find solid footing in the next moment, I found it difficult to move or imagine.

***

Hope for Water Bears

At furthest edges of human destruction,
past the reach of cruel, manipulative politics
played out in bombed out cities, hateful racism,
misogyny, xenophobia, homophobia; close to atrocities
committed on women and children; beneath war drones,
past boundaries in a gun-fueled, nuclear-threatened,
man-altered world of the starving and desperate sinking
into utter hopelessness; we have the calm of the water bear,
the most indestructible species on our planet.

This little, eight-legged micro-animal
is believed to have survived cataclysm and will withstand
our own apocalyptic endings—take your pick—
likely surviving everything, really, except an extinguished sun.

"Moss piglets," or Tardigrade,
if you want to get scientific with naming, but it's likely
water bears don't care much for nomenclature,
human intervention in world affairs, wars, lies, hate.
They aren't very strong, but they can endure
a trip into outer space on the skin of a rocket ship
and back into our fiery atmosphere.
Only around 10 billion years of drawing in water
and lasting through dehydration in their desiccation state,
reminiscent of hibernation,
water bears are all about coming through.
No food or water for thirty years? They endure.

Not terribly attractive, water bears resemble
an Idaho potato gone soft, sprouting tiny claws.
Or looking like miniature moles with rhino hide,
they have long, sunken slits where eyes would be
but are not likely to care about
our estimation of their beauty
as they burrow in the lowest parts of seas
or attach to highest mountains.

If we only speak of humanities' love,
of our art, music, quest for knowledge,
we might mistakenly pity the water bear.

Twenty-Two

"Strangeness in My Mind"

Turkish novelist and Nobel Prize winner Orhan Pamuk wrote a number of story anthologies and novels, one of which is titled *A Strangeness in My Mind*. A curious and apt phrase. After Blaise's death, I recalled that title as I experienced a profound sense of separation from our culture, people around me, even, and at times, from family, feeling almost unrecognizable to myself. Pamuk drew his title from a phrase in the English poet William Wordsworth's poem "The Prelude." When everything becomes abnormal, there ceases to be "normal." I imagine this phrase describes the experience of many who have gone through a deep and lasting trauma.

For those surviving the novel coronavirus' COVID-19 pandemic, a strangeness of mind applies to the lack of "normalcy" in daily acts, in entire regions, cultures, countries, the world.

I'm trying to remember a day when I truly experienced a complete sense of wellness since my son died. There must have been a handful at least in the last several months after recovering from pneumonia and sepsis. I was deathly ill for several days and finally hospitalized with extremely low oxygen levels and very high white blood cell count. My fevers were sporadic, not constant, but it was an illness from which I initially thought I might not recover. I was still reeling from Blaise's death.

Only much later did I look back on that illness and wonder if I, too, had COVID-19 before any physician in New York State was actively looking for it? My double pneumonia came upon me in January, and as early as two months later, talk about COVID-19 was heard everywhere. After the fact, physicians and patients began to recognize symptoms and realize they probably had the virus before it was known. Only from a perspective of distance have I viewed my illness differently. I was certainly the most ill I had ever been, and I had many of the symptoms of COVID-19 I later discovered. But no one was testing for COVID-19 in Upstate New York at that point in time. If I did have it, no one else around me got very sick. Dan had what he thought was a bad cold. My daughter, too, but they recovered quickly. My youngest grandson Luca had a fever that kept spiking. He bounced back finally.

Still, I wonder. I am grateful for surviving but also continue to agonize over the fact I lived and my son died. In some respects, being physically ill mirrored my emotional state.

I again saw the scene of Blaise in another hospital in those last hours after he was declared dead, but we could not give up his body. Reexperiencing those concerned nurses coming in to check for my son's non-existent vitals, not relinquishing at that point because he was young, and of course, there must be hope. Over and over, his death scene replayed until I heard again my daughter Nicole describing the boat Blaise was floating on with warm sun on his tanned back. She was softly telling him it was okay to leave, indirectly telling his sister Colette, his father Dan, and me that it was time to let his body go. We did. I am certain of very little in this cruel, chaotic world, yet I feel Blaise heard his sister, too, even if his hearing contradicts my understanding of science.

In the midst of reliving those seconds turned hours with my family in another hospital, a nurse came into my designated room. She needed more blood for another lab test; my veins rebelling. She said my vein doors were shutting, so I watched as she tried again in another position with no luck, an angry-looking fresh bruise setting up along my arms, others on my hands. Feeling guilty and seeing evidence of tears on my face, she said, "I'm sorry. Are you in terrible pain?"

"No. Yes, not physical pain. I miss my son." I told her that I had lost my son recently.

She immediately told me about losing two of her brothers. "My mother had nine children." Then she said, "This is my nephew's son," showing a photo of a little boy on her phone. "He had leukemia. He was five, no, only four, not yet his birthday when he died."

All the grieving women, still isolated even when talking to one another. I do not believe I fell asleep that first night in the hospital. I thought about that five-year-old child and his mother and father, about their awful journey and how powerless most of us are in this vast world. I did not stop thinking about my son.

After a couple of days running through a gamut of antibiotics, my body started responding positively, my low oxygen levels coming closer to normal, my white blood cell count returning to typical range, infection defeated. There were moments in the hospital when I thought I might join my son sooner than I had expected. I was not afraid of dying. I was not thinking of any afterlife. I just thought, if this is my end, then I will know that, too. At some point, I slept and dreamed.

In a dream, I was looking for my son, when out of the corner of my eye, I could see the wiry construct of his big dark beard next to my face. I woke, the feeling of having been with him powerful and lasting.

A short time after I had physically recovered from pneumonia, news of the novel coronavirus, COVID-19, or SARS-CoV-2 (more precisely) began to reach the wider population, but only as far-away news. Initial reports of the pandemic were downplayed by the White House. This is not an essay on our lack of Federal leadership at a critical time, nor one on our lack of government preparedness, but a quick assessment of how an entire country went from obliviousness about a pandemic to rising panic and altered lives.

How this pandemic relates to telling the story about my son and my grief begins from two divergent paths. First, the shutdown of businesses to help keep the virus from spreading at the same exponential rate impacted me and my family outside of the typical avenues. We could not get the delivery of the gravestone marking Blaise's place of burial due to business closures or temporary shuttering. Tall, black granite was ordered within a short time after Blaise's death, yet it would sit in a warehouse nearly a year. It was an unusual stone, and Dan and I thought our son would have liked it.

Seeing only the rough, overturned ground at his gravesite had been awful enough that I was not able to go there very often at first. I thought seeing his headstone would help in the smallest way. Then, even my son's monument was on hold.

A short time later, so many thousands of people were unable even to mourn the loss of a family member with a public funeral or calling hours.

The pandemic altered my view of the world once again. This explanation requires more than a few words. Instead of feeling isolated and outside the rest of humanity in my grief, I suddenly awoke to a world, a country in panic, in mourning for their losses, a country in fear and terrible uncertainty, a people disconnected from their previous lives and far more anxious, even experiencing symptoms of psychosis. People lost their jobs, were isolated in their homes away from the homes of friends and relatives. The elderly in nursing facilities were forbidden visits to try to stop the spread of the virus to the most physically vulnerable. It did not work. Thousands of nursing home inhabitants died of COVID-19.

Suddenly, everyone's identity was hidden behind literal masks, and we were all told not to touch our faces. I ached for the country, for the people of the world, but, strangely, I gradually began to feel as if I was part of that world, part of our society again. A most terrible pandemic reconnected me to the larger whole.

"The virus will not have a chance against us," Trump said before the nation during the early weeks of news about COVID-19. One state governor and then another asked people to remain at home and isolated. COVID-19 cases went from a documented handful in our country to 100,000 seemingly overnight as testing kits began to become available, although still not nearly enough. People were dying, some of their deaths hidden for political reasons. While a majority of state residents complied with a handful of governor guidelines, leadership messages were often in conflict with one another; messages from the White House disconnected from facts.

Suddenly, as COVID-19 spread and began taking its toll, people all over the country entered a traumatized state, physically and psychically separated, unnerved, alarmed. "Don't touch your face, wash your hands, wash every touchable surface, stay in your homes, don't go to work, don't go to school, stay back six feet from other people." California Governor Newsom, then governors of New York, Connecticut, and New Jersey ordered stay at home guidelines, with several more northern states following suit in an attempt to stop the rapid spread of the novel coronavirus particular strain of COVID-19. The country's divide became more pronounced as too many political leaders used the pandemic as a wedge.

Just like that, much of America was standing at a station where they began grieving as they counted losses, missing people, routines, income, and any kind of normalcy even as the idea of imminent death pushed its way to the front of the bus.

Americans, in particular, have long been experts at attempting to deny the reality of the approach of their own deaths. Suddenly, COVID-19 made death the topic of the day and night. Instead of worrying about trying to get ahead, striving to get a raise in pay, to be accepted into a prestigious college, to be accepted on a team, Americans were trying to stay alive. For all of our technological superiority, we were reduced once again to the fate of every living creature: attempting to ward off impending death for as long as possible.

The United States of America was remarkably underprepared, remarkably inept, and perversely hindering our own efforts to combat this deadly virus. It struck me that the emotional turmoil I experienced over my son's death seemed universal. Loss and fear are, indeed, experienced by us all, although in the moments of our great losses, we continue to feel most alone. Our grieving has caused other problems, with people falling ill to stresses on the heart or unable to ward off other diseases attacking immune-compromised bodies, and many descending into more severe mental illnesses.

Considering how grief affects the body, particularly the immune system, I was not surprised to read research findings on the topic everywhere. In an article in the September 11, 2014 issue of the *Atlantic*, titled "Understanding How Grief Weakens the Body," Cari Romm discussed studies conducted at the University of Birmingham's School of Sport, Exercise, and Rehabilitation Studies about how different age groups are impacted by grief. In her review, Romm quoted Anna Phillips, professor of behavioral medicine: "'Even though [members of] the bereaved younger group were equally as psychologically affected, we didn't see the physiological changes that you see in the older group,' Phillips said, a difference the researchers attribute to age-related hormone fluctuations. The effects of the stress hormone cortisol, which weakens the immune system, are balanced by a hormone called DHEA, which bolsters the effectiveness of neutrophils. But around age 30, a person's DHEA levels start to drop, leaving their immune system more vulnerable to cortisol's influence in times of stress. A prolonged emotional response to something like a death, then, may leave someone of advanced age more prone to infection."

In other words, the fact I am of an advanced age plays a role in how my body responded to grief. Mind and body are not separate but intricately interconnected. Restating this important fact, how my mind responded to grief is affected by a number of factors, including my age. Even when I was feeling physically well, my mind felt ill for a much longer extended period. That "strangeness in my mind" is evidence that grief dislocates everything.

***

One year and a half dozen days before this writing in March 2020, Dan and I drove into La Spezia, known as the Gulf of Poets, in Italy. Surrounded by water on three sides, this Italian city is said to have inspired English poet Lord Byron. One year and a dozen days ago, I was gloriously wandering endless hallways of *Le Gallerie Degli Uffizi*, noting the influence of the Medicis on the art of Florence, the great art of the world.

I slowly climbed up white steps on a hillside of the Boboli Gardens in Florence, stopping to take in miraculously beautiful views and to catch my breath. As I took that breather, I texted Blaise to remember to put out the garbage on Thursdays and to visit his aunt Bobbie Jo and help her with any tasks she needed to complete. I was attaching to those texts to my son the glorious photos of our extended trip to Italy.

Italians may have resented tourists but welcomed us anyway for the lifeblood of capital we brought into their beautiful country. As I thought about our intrusions, I looked out between arches on the Ponte Vecchio and considered myself most fortunate, my wonderful husband at my side, remarking on quality and angle of light touching hillsides around the city. I was, in short, supremely happy.

Before boarding a plane destined to land in Rome, Italy, still sitting in JFK airport, Blaise sent me a text: "All's good" as I settled into my small seat next to the window, looking out as a brilliant sun all but blinded me.

Another morning that felt a thousand years from one year ago, I thought about how every village, city, and region we went to on our trip to Italy last year at the time of this writing could be called the Village of Poets, City of Poets, Cave of Poets, Coastline of Poets, the Mountains of Poets for their inspiring vistas. I am also thinking about death. Today, Italy is racked with fear and paralyzed by restrictions to try to slow the killing tide of COVID-19. Italians are not alone in their victimization by this virus, but they were, in the first months, the hardest hit with more Italian deaths from COVID-19 per person than even China. Already, projections were showing the United States' death rate from COVID-19 would surpass that of those countries.

Deep breath. My son is gone, and I have not touched anything in his bedroom except to feed his fish and frog and to open the curtains, letting sunlight into that dark, cool space.

One morning the world awakened to discover a wedding could not take place as planned; graduations would be cancelled; funeral services would be private with no more than immediate family in attendance; favorite bars and restaurants were closed;

attempts to meet the possibility of the loves of their lives through Tinder and Match, Elite and Zoosk, eHarmony and Plenty of Fish had now been rendered useless. In "stay at home" and quarantine, we would, essentially, be meeting no one new for some time.

The world awoke at various times to drastically altered lives, to COVID-19 fears and inconveniences, to disruptions and near collapse of economies, to business closures, to coffee stops shuttered, to rationing of toilet paper for reasons we are all still trying to fathom.

Last October, I was reeling from Blaise's death, feeling separated from the rest of humanity that appeared to go on about their daily business while I curled into a calcareous shell like a mollusk. In that blink of an eye, everything was again altered.

An indifferent world moved at breakneck speed before a novel coronavirus strain hit the shores of the United States of America sometime in January 2020 (perhaps months earlier), crossing borders, boundaries, and artificial walls with ease, finding its way into every social stratum, demonstrating for all that even wealth cannot protect the billionaire and politically advantaged class (although their access to better health care is evident). Within a few weeks, nature in all of her strange variations, indifferent to the case humans have tried to make for supremacy, resumed ruling in chaos and disorder. Human beings were collectively reminded at the same time: we all shatter; we all die.

Deep breath. COVID-19 continues somewhat abated, but one recent morning, the world also awoke to less pollution. Space agencies have reported less nitrogen dioxide in our atmosphere. One morning, Venetians awoke to clear waters in the canals in Venice, to seeing swans, Dolphins, and fish spotted once again in their waters. Venice's famed canals, emptied of human traffic, saw wildlife return and thrive. After only a week without human movements, the canals in Venice were so clear you could see to the bottom, according to residents. Dolphins were playing below.

I read about wild mountain goats roaming deserted streets in Wales. In the waters normally crowded with pleasure boaters and humans, fin whales were seen leaping off the coast of Southern France. Air pollution fell, and fresh clear air filtered over cities. When man pulls back, nature thrives again.

Waking one morning to the image of my son being hugged by his father, sisters, and me while he resisted, I recounted the dream of him in life.

As I write this section, a notice pops up on my computer: the great Americana singer/song writer / musician John Prine has died of complications from COVID-19. "Angel from Montgomery" notes start moving in my head. His lines resonate: "to believe in this living is just a hard way to go," and yes, John, "to believe in this living is just a hard way to go."

While I have no advice to offer on how to treat or survive a pandemic, I do want to observe how in the slightest aperture adjustment, the world can change, my own life drastically altered within that year. Life now altered for all of us with this pandemic. Catastrophe and fear cannot ever be banished, but we can acknowledge our human frailty and be kinder, be more compassionate, be more thoughtful in our responses to each other. Americans have already shown their best and very worst instincts as we begin to deal with COVID-19 in our country. We can each choose to lead with our best instincts and discourage the worst in human nature. In this prolonged critical period, we still have choices.

We can choose our responses to what an indifferent cosmos throws our way. We can choose to be better as Blaise decided to do in his battles with his addiction and then his heart; how he chose thoughtfulness and kindness to others in his responses before his end.

Twenty-Three

What My Brain Refuses to Accept

Vanessa Bryant used a social media Tweet to publicly express her anger at the tragic death of her 13-year-old daughter Gigi and her famous basketball legend husband Kobe Bryant in a helicopter crash: "My brain refuses to accept that both Kobe and Gigi are gone," she wrote. "It's like I'm trying to process Kobe being gone, but my body refuses to accept my Gigi will never come back to me. It feels wrong. Why should I be able to wake up another day when my baby girl isn't able to have that opportunity?! I'm so mad. She had so much life to live," Vanessa wrote.

"I'm so mad" is something I have sensed over and over since my son's death. Anger, denial, and deep pain are so closely aligned they sometimes seem to be the same emotion. There is an unnaturalness to losing your child. We come to accept many great losses in our lives, and some part of our brain gets that life is finite. Yet, our children dying before us is an indecent and abhorrent concept.

Gigi should have outlived both her famous father and mother. She should have played basketball, made strides in the women's movement, proving again and again that women are more than capable of greatness. Of course, she was special, talented, exceptional, and she is dead.

***

Deep breath. Blaise is defending Kobe Bryant, and we are trying to arrive at some understanding. I want my son to see that the young woman in the sexual assault and rape case could have been telling the truth. The subject came up because Bryant was retiring from the NBA, and all things Kobe suddenly resurfaced.

Blaise was adamant in his defense of the NBA star: "She refused to testify. Doesn't that tell you something about her?"

"He apologized later. That tells me something."

"Not an admission of guilt but of poor judgement. He was apologizing to his family and fans for what he put them through. He is no saint, but the story does not add up."

"I'm not saying I always believe the woman, but."

"Much of the time, women are telling the truth about assaults, I know. I just don't buy this one. People were wrong to discount the woman in general, but we're also wrong to think that a woman is always telling the truth. We are all individuals."

"There are, however, societal and sexist patterns we need to be aware of." I recognize that we are on opposing sides partially out of power dynamics between men and women, not just between parent and grown child.

"You don't always have to believe the woman. She might be lying. Too much of what she claimed sounds fishy," he said.

"And you don't always have to believe the man."

"I don't," he said, and I knew he meant it because he had defended women in similar dynamics, in multiple other situations. "I just think Kobe is a bigger target because of his profile, his money. He was 24. He didn't handle it well."

"No, he didn't." We finally agreed that neither of us knew what happened in that hotel room in Colorado.

I recalled my verbal clash with my son when Kobe's plane later went down, and the basketball star and his daughter were killed. From all accounts, Kobe had been a good father and champion of girls since becoming a father. I tried to reconcile those stories with that of a suspected rapist, and I, too, was uncertain. I also thought about the imbalance of power between famous athlete and young woman working in a hotel, between parent and child.

***

Deep breath. Descending into darkness, twenty-four-year-old Blaise is the first to climb down a wooden ladder jutting out from a square hole scarcely large enough to fit his shoulders. I snap a photo of my son disappearing, only one hand, his long arm, and his New York Yankees cap showing above surface of the stone floor. Below are Anasazi ruins of the Spruce Tree House at Mesa Verde National Park. I cannot bring myself to climb down into that mysterious chamber, but I watch my seemingly fearless son descend. I think, he will always remember this. I will always remember this moment. Perhaps he was afraid but didn't appear to be. He was young.

On a family trip out west for my nephew Shea's wedding to Jill, Blaise was our most adventurous explorer. In another photo, my son is all smiles, thumbs up in his shades, Sean John tee-shirt, and cargo shorts, as we gaze in wonder at the Anasazi homes built into clay in another century.

Looking at these photos in which my son seems larger than life, I wonder how he would be gone only eight years later? Not a single one of his gestures foreshadows sorrow, ill health, or his death in these photos. But I was not looking for death in the living. If I had, I never would have appreciated all those moments in which he was "perfectly fine."

In his remarkable novel of imagining and reimagining our histories and the life of Columbia in *Love in the Time of Cholera*,

Gabriel Garcia Marquez wrote the most breath-taking line that resonates each time I think about love for my son: "He was overwhelmed by the belated suspicion that it is life, more than death, that has no limits." Thinking about my son's life, I quietly agree. It is life and our love that are limitless.

Twenty-Four

How Are You?

How many times has someone come up to me since Blaise's death and asked the simple question, "How are you doing?" I cannot count the number of times that question was asked.

I want to respond, "Forever altered. Not dead, I but feel as if I am drowning." Of course, I don't say that. I offer some polite words that will not offend or make others ill-at-ease. C.S. Lewis aptly described this period of grief as feeling like, "being mildly drunk or concussed." In his memoir *A Grief Observed*, Lewis wrote about the well-meaning words of others: "I find it hard to take what anyone says." No matter how kind, too many condolences feel incomplete, dishonest, even abrupt to the grieving.

Before my son's funeral, the minister asked me to send her a statement with which she could introduce the service. "Send me something about Blaise's work, his career," she wrote. I knew immediately that I would not be sending her anything about his work or career plans. Any plans he might have had early on were sidetracked. Agonizing over the introduction to the service, I finally stopped thinking like a writer and just thought about what to say as his mother.

I sent these few words to the woman who opened his funeral: "Blaise is remembered by his many friends and family as 'gentle, kind, funny, clever, and as a tremendously loyal, big man whose heart was enormous.' He had a soft spot for children and animals. He brought extensive knowledge of music, film, television, sports, and politics to any conversation. Blaise Martin was highly intelligent but often quiet. People usually talk about a person's career and their work when someone passes away, but looking back on his life, it is apparent that Blaise Martin's "career" was considering people. Loving them, comforting them, making them laugh, and most of all, listening to them. He was a professional listener."

Joan Didion, in *The Year of Magical Thinking*, wrote: "Grief turns out to be a place none of us know until we reach it." Perhaps that explains why so many people struggle to say the right thing to the grieving. Yet, there are those who manage to say and do exactly the best thing. My friend Judith McGinn called and tentatively asked me one afternoon if it would be all right if she stopped by. When she came, I broke down and just sobbed and talked and sobbed and talked until I was spent. I realized how badly I needed to have a non-family member witness my grief again and allow me the luxury of expanding on how I felt and what I was thinking. Although Judy finally talked, she was extremely generous in letting me lead on that occasion. It was a gesture I will not forget, and one very different from, "Call me if you want." The open-ended invitation remains closed.

Because I knew so well the pain of losing my child, I have become better at helping someone else with grief. A short time after Blaise died, a friend and teaching colleague of mine lost her daughter in a horrific car accident. I could feel her pain down to my bones. I knew letting her and her husband talk, vent, cry was the best thing I could do for them. I listened. Be present.

People grieving do not need cheering up, but rather acknowledgement that after the calling hours, after the funeral, devastation continues. They need the generosity of a friend who is willing to listen, giving advice only when or if asked.

There were friends who sent me books about grieving. This lovely gesture was accepted, allowing me the time to decide whether or not I wanted to read or even consider the advice and under my terms. Another of my friends named Judy sent me pamphlet-sized books about grieving. While certain aspects of the literature were not helpful to me, I could pick and choose what resonated.

Opening *Finding Hope and Healing,* by Kenneth C. Haugk, I appreciated reading the chapter "Share—Don't Compare." For a number of reasons, many people feel compelled to relate all of their painful stories and compare them with yours. Haugk wrote, "Trying to decide whose grief or loss is greater or lesser won't reduce either person's pain." I took this statement as true and accurate of the experience.

If you have never lost someone very close to you, it might be difficult to know what to say and do when confronted with a friend who has. Some people, unwittingly, say remarks that are very hard to take and even unwelcome. Those individuals are not ill-intentioned. A poorly worded comment, however, may do more harm than good to the person in mourning.

There are also people who avoid talking to you because they feel awkward and aren't sure what to say. Everyone who came to my son's calling hours meant well, and their graciousness was appreciated. Honestly, just being present is a kindness. Yet, there were remarks I heard that made my night harder. So here are my suggestions of what helped me and what remarks are less likely to help those grieving:

***

What may or may not be helpful:

I will pray for his soul.

Too many presumptions here. Perhaps that helps the person praying. Such a comment may not be all that helpful to the grieving. It sounds innocuous, but it

is not. I have no evidence there is an afterlife, but if there is, I am certain my son and his soul are perfectly fine.

My aunt died recently. I know just how you feel.

I lost my mother two years ago. I know what you're going through.

My cat died. I still can't stop crying about her.

The grieving person does not need to take on anyone else's grief at that moment. Give her time and space before sharing your burdens and sadness. You probably don't know how the other person feels at that moment either. Everyone grieves at some point in his or her life, and while the emotions involved with loss are universal, how we feel our grief at any one time is unique.

It's good you have two other children.

"The need is for someone to be fully present to the magnitude of loss without trying to point out a silver lining," wrote David Kessler, author of *Finding Meaning: The Sixth Stage of Grief.* There is no silver lining in losing your child. None. Period.

It was his time.

No, it was not. Thirty-two is too young. He was just getting started. Hold that platitude.

I heard he died of an overdose.
Well, he did not. Your gossipy comment is cruel, intrusive, and not relevant.

I just found out the janitor's son died of an overdose, too.
Again, my son did not die of an overdose, and your speculation about a death you know nothing about is not welcome. Please do not compare other deaths to the person grieving at that moment.
I didn't know him at all.
You did not know him? Then say nothing.

God called him up. God wanted him.
Why?
What did he do for a career? What was his job? I heard he was selling pizzas?
How little all of that means in the end.
His struggles are finally over.
All of our struggles will be over soon enough. Life is a struggle. It is not a relief for those grieving.

I think doctors already know about Marfan's. You don't need to educate them.
Well, a host of doctors who saw my son over his thirty-two years could not identify the syndrome in Blaise when he exhibited nearly every symptom. A little help diagnosing rare diseases and syndromes never hurts. Also, giving a "lecture" or admonishment to someone hurting at that juncture is not very helpful.

This must be terrible for you.
Stating the obvious does nothing for anyone. Beyond the obligatory, "yes," what more is there to say in response?

My husband has the worst back pain. This is my second marriage, and I thought we would travel; there are days when he doesn't want to get out of the house or even out of bed. I am in emotional pain, too.
Sharing tales of sadness and difficulty between friends at an appropriate time is fine. However, funerals or calling hours are not the time to express your list of disappointments and grievances in life.

It must be hard. I'm trying to imagine. I lost my dog a few years ago, but I can't image losing my daughter. I just could not handle that.
Don't try to imagine what it feels like to lose a child. If you can't find empathy or the lesser quality of sympathy, simply say, "I am sorry for your terrible loss."

My friend's husband died of heart attack, and then she found Jesus, and she is much happier. Her life is finally full now. You can find Jesus, too. Welcome him in your heart.
As C. S. Lewis wrote in *A Grief Observed*, "Talk to me about the truth of religion, and I'll listen gladly. Talk to me about the duty of religion, and I'll listen submissively. But don't come talking to me about the consolations of religion, or I shall suspect that you don't understand."

Thoughts and prayers.

Keep your meaningless shorthand that has become both obnoxiously political and hollow; learn to say or write a complete sentence.

I'm donating to the Smile Charity because it is something I truly believe in.

That is wonderful if the deceased person also supported that charity or the family asks for donations to that charity in his/her honor. If not, ask what charity the family would like you to support in his/her name?

How are you doing?

Ask this question only if you are prepared to stay awhile and listen. It is not a question to ask in passing.

What is deeply appreciated:

- Anything heartfelt and kind: *I will miss him. Loved his smile.*

- Relate an anecdote about something you did together. These stories about the life of a loved one will be treasured by family.

- Relate something you plan to do or have done in his honor because he or she touched you, and you talked with the deceased about this idea.

- Donate to his/her favorite charity or to a cause you know the person or family supports.

- Talk about the person who has died and share good memories. The person grieving wants to talk and listen to remembrances about the person she/he is missing. Don't avoid the subject of death or the person who has died.

- Most of all, be willing to listen. Listen with intent. Listen patiently. Be fully present in listening. This kind of listening is the most precious gift you can give to those hurting.

***

C.S. Lewis wrote after the death of his wife, "Kind people have said to me, 'She's with God.' In one sense that is most certain. She is, like God, incomprehensible and unimaginable."

I loved Lewis' words. I thought, yes, Blaise is like concepts of God, incomprehensible, and his journey now is unimaginable.

Thank you to all those friends and family who listened.

Twenty-Five

Jealousy Rising

Love Bruce Springsteen as a musician. I don't know him personally, of course. Why do we feel like we know musicians and entertainers through their performances, their activism, and public statements? Bruce's son, Sam Springsteen, was just sworn in as a Jersey City firefighter. Made the national news. My first instinct upon reading about the youngest Springsteen was to smile and feel joy for son, father, and mother. My second less gracious instinct, which followed almost instantaneously, was jealousy.

I will never be able to feel new sources of pride in my son's adventures and accomplishments again. I will not be able to cry with joy at his wedding or hold my imagined granddaughter. This would be the granddaughter whom I am sure I would have met after Blaise found the woman with whom he wanted to have children. I will never see his gentleness with his little daughter. I won't be able to share news of his travels. He will never decide to become a firefighter or anything else.

At first, jealousy arises out of anger from my loss. Then I begin to be jealous out of mourning and ache for Blaise's losses.

All the things he wanted to do, all the people he wanted to interact with, the people he loved and would yet love, share joy, have fun, exchange parenting advice with, mull over the win/loss records of his favorite sports teams, finally get to see the New York Knicks become a dominant basketball team again rather than perpetual bottom dwellers in the NBA, teach his daughter to play softball or lacrosse, or hike up a mountain with her someday.

Jealousy is an ugly and damaging emotion. I don't want any part of it, yet here it is, waiting for me in surprise. "Caught you," Jealousy says with a wicked grin.

One evening before news of the novel coronavirus strain hit airwaves, we had Phil and Janey Connery over to share dinner they brought for us. Dan and I talked as if we had just been released from some prison, and it was one of the first times I had laughed in ages. Before they left, Phil handed us a card from my son's very good friend Ben. Inside was a photo of his baby daughter, Camille James, born on January 19, 2020. This little sweet darling was healthy and perfect, wearing a white bandana with a puffball attached. The sight of Cami (because she already had a nickname) made me smile, and for a long time after Phil and Janey left, I mused about the joy of Ben and Helen as first-time parents. I remembered the excitement and joy of our first born. So many dreams ahead for them, I thought.

The next morning, I set out the photo of Cami and knew how excited Blaise would have been for his friend from childhood. Blaise loved kids. Without warning, I suddenly experienced rising jealousy in me. Why did my son have to die? Why would I never have a granddaughter from his love with another? Why would he never be able to name his child and watch her grow up?

Fortunately, jealousy and self-pity can be short-lived if you work at it, and I banished them temporarily, certain that they would return unexpectedly while I was making dinner, or in the middle of a reading, or upon opening my eyes to the world in the morning. I am aware that jealousy is another face of grief. Today, I pick up Cami's photo and smile, readjusting it next to a photograph of Blaise. He would have journeyed to Texas to meet the addition to Ben's family. Blaise would also be the first in line to sing little Cami to sleep if her family were visiting Upstate New York.

Love Blaise's friends and their families; cherish them. Love for every parent who realizes he or she is fortunate in having a child. Hold onto that love, I tell myself.

***

Deep breath. Dan has been a remarkable comfort during this terrible grief. That is not always the case with grieving parents. The death of a child too frequently separates parents, isolates them even from the solace of one another. I asked Dan how he deals with the loss of our son. He said he does not really deal with it. "When I took Bogie for long walks, I would swear and curse about Blaise dying. I would tell Bogie how unfair it was. Now that Bogie is gone, I walk and curse alone. I'm still angry and will never accept it. I still cannot believe he is not here."

My husband also shared another image with me. He said, "when I go for my walks, I look up to the top of that hillside and focus on that stand of white birch. They remind me of Blaise." A few days ago, he saw deer next to the birch for the first time. He told me about it.

"The birch because of their height?" I asked.

"Because the first time I ever noticed them was after Blaise died."

I don't walk and curse, but I knew exactly what Dan was feeling during those walks. I, too, go on walks and feel again scenes when Blaise was alive. What would he say about his parents on these separate walks of torment? He would not want us to suffer so, but he would recognize how we loved him, love him yet, always will.

Although a very human emotion, jealousy is something I seldom saw Blaise display. If someone was better at doing something than he was, Blaise seemed to take it in stride as the way the world works. Only once did I see him angry over a girl choosing another guy, but he got over it so quickly, it almost did not register. "It's not worth my time," he said, as if he knew his life span was limited. He also seemed to get the idea that jealousy is ultimately self-defeating. Just thinking about him reminds me of my own good fortune in this life.

"You are still lucky, Mom," he would say.

I am vividly aware of my love for my four grandsons: darling, smart, active little boys. Blaise would not want me to stop loving others or to stop feeling joy for other people's good fortunes. I have to recognize my own wonders: beautiful, smart, and thoughtful daughters; loving sons-in-law; sweet grandsons; intelligent, kind friends. And a husband who is also my best friend. Slowly I realize jealousy is not anger but longing, the longing for something or someone we cannot have. I let jealousy go but hold onto grief. I'm still a work in progress, I need to tell my son.

Even now, I will talk with people who ask me what my son did for a living before he died. Why is that the first question people ask of each other? I suppose those who did not know him are trying to fit him into a category, into a box other than accept the unknowable. He never fit into a category.

Deep breath. Let me be grateful that Sam Springsteen is making his parents proud and living large. I am. Let me be glad that Sam's father still makes music for all of us. Raise a toast to Ben and Helen for the wondrous birth of their daughter Cami. Raise a glass to young love and the endurance of the human race. Sing praises for the successes and victories of our incredible, flawed, talented, intriguing species.

Twenty-Six

Give Sorrow Words

"Give sorrow words; the grief that does not speak knits up the o-er wrought heart and bids it break" (l. 245-246). William Shakespeare's words from (Act IV, scene iii) his tragedy *Macbeth* articulate far better than me the imperative for writing about grief. Writing about the loss of my son allowed me time to reflect, revisit, and relive moments of our lives together. The act of writing about him is, in many respects, my solace. In this undertaking, I often feel as if he is sitting near me, listening to my words, nodding or shaking his head in disagreement. I try to listen for and anticipate his riposte.

"No, that is not right. I would never say that." I hear him now. "Never mind. Don't worry about it. What you wrote is okay. Write what you want, Mom." He was indulgent. Something he might have learned from his mother.

***

A House on Little York Lake is Grieving

A house on Little York Lake is grieving.

All that was good is horribly altered by his loss.
Confronted by his extra-large, colorful Jordans
as we entered, we wept because those shoes
were like boats that held his long feet
when we longed to hold his beautiful hands.

A box, delivered on the day he left our known world,
each selection of coffees ordered just for him;
even the kitchen is now in mourning.

We could not pass his bedroom with Frank Sinatra poster,
without looking for our boy just beyond reaching shadows.
On his bed pillows, impressions left by his head in sleep.

Living room sorrowing while we try to grow used to pain
of seeing where he lay, his music humming as if he still
moves through quietly before slipping away.

Even his boat tied to the dock rocks gently weeping
over his passing. Lake slapping the shore
as if in sorrow he is no longer in this world.

His dog waits by the door somehow knowing,
investigating each room, expectant
until dropping his head as we all do.

Our young man, a Greek god, "like Achilles,"
his sister said, with his vulnerability inescapable and worn even in
his smiles and clever words. Those engaging bright eyes open is all
we asked.

***

How can we accept this death? We understand nothing can stay;
he has left us bereft. It would seem all is desolate in this world

without him. If allowed, he would shake his head slowly, although beyond our sight. If given death's reprieve, he would wrap his long arms around us all and say tonight, "I'm okay. Love you all."

***

Returning to our house in Little York after staying with our daughters in Silver Spring, Maryland following Blaise's death, Dan and I were apprehensive about how we would cope. I was nervous about even the idea of walking in our house. We cried together and separately as we hit Main Street in Homer, well before passing the funeral home. I could hear my breathing and was aware of my heart beating as we pulled in our driveway. The lake was in view, ice melted. I scarcely noticed. I looked at my feet as I moved.

The dread we anticipated upon entering our home never materialized. Instead, the house welcomed us, wrapped us in the love of memories of all of our children. You could hear our collective sigh of relief and sadness mixed with love. We had previously moved Blaise's athletic shoes from the entryway up to his room. Every space spoke of him, and it seemed as if he and our house had been waiting for our return.

Yet I still have incredible sadness going into his bedroom. I enter every day to feed the fish in his aquarium. I say good morning and good night to him. It doesn't feel silly or crazy. I am aware of how it might look but indifferent to others' judgement of how I grieve. His presence is still so very strong there.

Many years ago, when Dan and I moved back to the lake where Dan grew up, a terrible tragedy happened in the neighborhood. A young man shot and killed his ex-girlfriend and then himself standing on the driveway of his mother's home, the house in which he was reared. The woman lived alone because years before, her husband had drowned in the lake when another boater rammed his fishing boat in the dark. For a long time, I would pass that woman's pretty house and wonder how she could continue to live there, bearing all that tragedy.

After returning to the house in which my son died, I think I have some understanding of why that woman did not move. While her house may have held tragedy and unbearable sorrow, it also held all the family's memories of love, of every good moment they had together.

Deep breath. Someone close to me once said about the act of creating a memoir, something I had written after my mother's death from Alzheimer's, "Memoirs are just a writer's mental masturbation." Her comment hurt. I thought about the words and understood that creating from chaos, from words tossed about then crafted into form, did give me some pleasure, as well as solace. Not ecstasy, however, more like a spiritual journey on which language could ease pain, define moments not to be forgotten, and sometimes help in trying to understand the undefinable.

Great British writer Graham Greene wrote, "writing is a form of therapy; sometimes I wonder how all those who do not write, compose, or paint can manage to escape the madness, melancholia, the panic and fear which is inherent in a human situation." Like Greene, writing is all of those things to me, and it is something more. Writing about my experience has been a way of processing, a way to continue to confront and absorb life with my eyes wide open, and my heart still wanting to beat.

"We tell ourselves stories in order to live," Joan Didion wrote in her essay "The White Album" which appeared in two of her collections of essays, a book by the same title and *The Year of Magical Thinking*. I know I, too, write in order to live, in order to survive. I also write because I believe that, sometimes, we have something to share, a story that will help at least one other person in some manner, a story that will truthfully connect us with another or others.

Yet writing is not always about revealing truth. In the act of shaping language, writers are choosing which words, which syllables, which events, which tics, sounds, sunlight or twilight to include and which to exclude. Perhaps the act is not so much seeking truth or producing a lie as securing a vision, a template from which to look at the world.

I also find we are always looking for a way out of the seeming chaos: everyone, "wants to believe there is an initial ciphering, that there is some direction or promise to their days," wrote Quignard in *Roving Shadows*. Although I reject statements such as, "God wanted your son and took him," I still seek answers for this obliterating loss, not just this privation, that most terrible loss of my husband's, Colette's, and Nicole's, that of his friends, and most of all, that of my son's. He could light up any room he entered, and then Blaise was gone.

A while after my son's death, I wrote nothing for a month or two, a long time for me. It was not simply that I could not write; I could barely talk or listen. I know I occupied rooms with other people talking, yet recalled little of the conversations. I sensed my mind had hardened into protective dullness. Then I started with a few lines. I continued. The process of taking words and sculpting them did ease my mind and aching heart, but I thought about my son's bravery and decided to be brave. Nothing could take the pain of losing my son away, but I clicked keys and considered the next word. I was in communion with Blaise in that process. I could hear his voice either encouraging or telling me to back up, delete a passage or bring in something entirely new. Writing this memoir made me feel as if he was with me every step of the way.

Writing is my way of discovering what I think and working from thought formation through to words on a clean sheet of paper. Simon During in the opening of his pedagogical work *Foucault and Literature: Towards a Genealogy of Writing* noted, "Language is, as it were, its own ground." In the act of writing, there were also planned gaps, holes deliberately not to be filled. In the same text, During wrote, "absence as such carries death's traces. If that were not the case, there would be no writing, as writing is to be regarded...[as] the attempt to incorporate absence." I knew I was trying to get at that most terrible absence.

There are no words adequate to express the loss of my son, however. No poem, no fiction, no memoir. All language seems meager in comparison to life. Yet, there were traces of him everywhere in my lines. Writers know the magic trick of taking the smallest details and expanding upon them until a red cardinal on a bare tree limb moves to the universal. When the subject is confronting death; when the subject is the loss of your child, you are already starting out large scale, as if there is no place to go from that devastation.

"Look again," my detective says. I had been unaware of his presence until that moment when I turn and see him taking out a cigarette.

"You have to smoke outside," I tell him.

"Like you told your son."

"Yes." On the coldest days of our long winters, Blaise would step out our door to inhale those tobacco fumes. I could see the tiny red light at night if I glanced out in the dark yard. A tiny detail that brings back my son. Strangely, I even miss him smoking furtively.

I recall Blaise as quiet, reserved rather than disinterested. He could also be clever, quick-witted, talkative, especially with his sisters and friends. Occasionally, when we were in the car together, he would start a conversation about something that bothered or intrigued him. When he did talk while we were driving, it was often about the injustice inherent in our racist society. He seemed to feel this racial divide and oppression viscerally. He took racism personally. I sometimes wondered why a Caucasian male raised in a fairly rural, non-diverse community took racism into his bones with passion and fury. I hoped I had something to do with his goodness and understanding of justice, but I suspect it was an understanding he came to on his own and through experiences he did not share. He would often ask if he could introduce me to some rapper he admired. "Just listen to his words," he would implore, as if my heart would be touched as his had been.

At home, Blaise was more often quiet, but his laugh was infectious. There was no one easier to be around during those times. Silence was also communication that said, "I'm at ease in this moment. Don't break this trust. I know you worry about me. In this time between us, recognize and regard our bond. You don't have to fill the space. Just be." Blaise could be in great fullness of life and communion with another and understanding without comment.

***

Discoveries about my son after his death caused me to want to write again. I wanted to shout to the world about his generous acts, his selflessness after his recovery from addiction, his thoughtfulness and gentleness with others in trouble or need. Writing was, in part, seeking answers and soothing crushed spirit. In fact, once I began writing about my son, I did not want to stop. In the act of writing, I was listening to him, for him, telling others something he could no longer tell.

After nearly completing a book that I hoped would reveal some aspect of a remarkable person, ease my immense sadness, I realize my son is still a mystery to me in certain aspects and will remain so. There were secrets I came to discover after his death, about his kindness and generosity, but there was that gap. I knew his vulnerability as well as his strengths, his sweetness and satirical bite, but there was so much more about him, some of which he was still discovering.

I recall moments in which my big, strong son would slowly turn to me with a look that I did not comprehend. The look was fleeting, hovering between us. "Something is wrong," he appeared to say, "but I'm dealing with it, okay." For years, I thought the fear I detected in him was related to drug use, to his concerns about slipping back. Only after his death, when I stop and watch his face closely again in memory do I finally understand he sensed something else, something beyond our conscious knowledge.

***

You Have No Guide Like Virgil

Sometimes the world's colors are too bright,
and you traverse charcoaled, limited palette of density,
vista or perhaps a seascape if that body of water
is as indeterminate. Foaming, cresting waves
in the distance are nearer than you think
with the partially clouded moon still
above your head, not reflected at your feet
as Dante, the poet, found in unholy descent.

You have no guide like Virgil at your ready
to orient you, lift you as you traverse this achromatic
landscape without purpose of revenge like Hamlet
with his "inky cloak" and "suits of solemn black,"
though your darkness weighs on your shoulders
and shades surround you as intended when,
"all forms, moods, shapes of grief" denote you
as surely as they did Shakespeare's Danish Prince.

Yet, there you are setting out: mystery, rebellion,
fear, questioning immortality in this recognition
of loss, but no cowardice shown on your journey
with shadows as philosophical and as meditative,
yet immediate, as the wounds on your hands, scars
now lost through absorption of visible light. You walk,
knowing there is no predestined path, only suggestion

of horizon, possible break, leading through darkness.
When you lift your weary head with such effort,
you become aware of presence: those who came before you on
this impossible passage—your past in front of you,
before you comprehend how doubt informs.
In process, becoming, even in falling away.

***

Giving sorrow and love words, Blaise's good friend from junior high, Ben Connery, spoke at my son's funeral. I gratefully share the message he offered at that time:

"For those who don't know me, my name is Ben Connery, and I considered Blaise one of my closest and best friends in the world. We became fast friends in 7th grade when we both broke our hands playing football, and then both got cut from the baseball team later that spring. Most lacrosse players won't admit this, but a lot of lacrosse careers start when you get cut from the baseball team, and that's how Blaise and I got started! No matter what, sports brought us together. Whether it was football or lacrosse or playing basketball at the Dafoe's home on Little York Lake, we grew up together. We got to spend a lot of time playing sports, shared a lot of great memories with many of us here in the room today.

"First, I want to express condolences to the Dafoe, Hartnett, and Avery families. Dan, Nancy, Niki, and Coco, I'm so sorry for your loss.

"I live in Dallas now, and yesterday, my wife Helen and I had a flight out at 5:00 am to get home for the services for Blaise. And when we got up to altitude, I kind of opened the window shade and looked out. It was seriously the most beautiful sunrise. The sky was vivid red, orange, and white with light blue and dark navy. And the scene really reminded me of what Blaise would look like incarnated. It even had the colors of his beloved Syracuse Orange, Homer Trojans, New York Knicks and Yankees, and the

New York Giants. I could almost feel Blaise in that moment. It was like a psychedelic trip I was experiencing. The plane began to shake, and I could sense Blaise even more at that moment. I thought maybe it was the lack of sleep, or maybe the plane was going down. I started getting nervous and then, then I remembered. I took my medicinal marijuana THC: CBD oil before my flight to help me "relax." It's decriminalized in Texas. Just don't tell my boss!!

"I did want to share some of my last memories I was fortunate enough to have with Blaise when he and our friend Nick Caruso (and Nick's wife Lainee) came down to visit Helen and me last spring in Dallas. We had a great time. Things had really come full circle, considering Blaise was the designated driver the whole trip. He looked great. We just had the best time. We rode scooters through Dallas, went to a Mavericks' basketball game. He even came and checked out my office. I was so proud to show Blaise off to my friends and colleagues in Dallas.

"By the way, when I took him to my office, he immediately starting hitting on our front desk lady as soon as he walked into the building. He had style and swagger, and he was definitely a ladies' man. She actually asked about Blaise a couple weeks later. He made his mark on people. He's so big, the beard, the name Blaise. He was just such a cool guy.

"At the Mavericks' game, Blaise and I made a friendly lunch bet on the game, and Blaise won the bet. 'Lunch' was somehow negotiated to mean filet mignon, lobster, several sides, and chocolate cake for dessert from five-star steakhouse, Al Biernat's, in Dallas. Cost me about $200 but well worth it for the memories! Blaise's reasoning was, 'well, I don't drink, so you got off cheap!'

"I, like everyone else here, wish we had more memories we could make with Blaise, but I know, like I experienced yesterday on the plane, even if it was induced by my CBD oil, I'll continue to make more memories as Blaise really will live on through me, his friends, and his family, all of you here today. You share the honor and privilege of keeping Blaise alive through memories. I think that is really powerful.

"Again, to the immediate family, I am so incredibly sorry for your loss. Blaise was one of my all-time favorite people, and I loved him very much."

***

Ben had Blaise's friends and family laughing and crying simultaneously. As Ben expressed gratitude for knowing Blaise, I offer my gratitude to Ben Connery for the subtle yet powerful way in which he expressed love for his friend and reminded everyone of Blaise's turn from addiction to responsibility. Blaise would have said it did not matter what other people thought, but it still mattered to me that people knew he had conquered "his demons," as he called drinking and drugs. I am learning to care less about other people's expectations and judgements, but I am not there yet.

Blaise's unknown illnesses made him vulnerable without confirmation of that vulnerability. Not a single doctor followed up on his strange symptoms. Each one looked for what they thought was the obvious. But Blaise instinctively knew something was wrong. That sixth sense drew him closer to home. The undiagnosed, the unspoken, the felt shifts in his body were the reasons he put up with a nagging mother. He wanted more than anything to live, to find his way.

For a brief period after college, Blaise decided to try to become a high-voltage lineman. He entered the apprenticeship program and struggled. Being a lineman was something his father, grandfather, and all of his uncles on the Dafoe side of the family accomplished, every one of them journeymen linemen. One day after successfully climbing a 50-foot pole, on his second attempt, in the training session, Blaise came home and told me, "this isn't for me. I won't survive long in this field." Even though he was strong and athletic, Blaise knew he had his weaknesses, discovering that fear. He wanted to please his father, but he knew he had to be true to himself, as well.

What were his constants? What held him back, I often wondered. None of us knew the constraints under which Blaise was living: with a deadly syndrome that attacked his heart, his tissues, his skin, his eyes, his joints. But he responded not with complaints nor the unfairness of it all. He made life seem effortless when every day was a struggle. He could not be a magician with some trick of light or sleight of hand, but he could respond to the urgency he felt. The most basic of all wants and desires, he answered for himself. He wanted to live. He did live, and then he gave and gave and gave.

Twenty-Seven

Stages of Grief and COVID-19

Psychologists have previously written about and discussed the five stages of grief as if we were on a ladder, climbing up one by one. There is even a chart in which you begin with "loss-hurt" then follow a curve swinging back up to "loss-adjustment." It all sounds so patterned and optimistic. We are always looking for ways to make order out of chaos, but I find the oft-quoted "stages of grief" not to be stages at all. Emotions whirl as chaotically as the world we inhabit.

The Kübler-Ross model is based upon the supposed five stages of grief, as outlined by psychiatrist Elizabeth Kübler-Ross in 1969. Today, most counselors and psychologists will admit the limitations of this model. Herein lies my experiential problem with these various models: nothing is that delineated; nothing is organized or that separated during the intense pain of losing someone you love. There is no curve or model in which resolution arrives, and hope, hope has often taken wing as Emily Dickinson's "thing with feathers."

In fairness to the theory's developer, however, David B. Feldman, Ph.D. points out in an article in the July 7, 2017 issue of *Psychology Today*, "Kubler-Ross didn't originally develop these stages to explain what people go through when they lose a loved one. Instead, she developed them to describe the process *patients* go through as they come to terms with their terminal illnesses." Feldman's article "Why the Five Stages of Grief Are Wrong," explains the theory's shift from patient to patient's family and intimate circle: "The stages—*denial, anger, bargaining, depression*, and *acceptance* were only later applied to grieving friends and family members, who seemed to undergo a similar process after the loss of their loved ones." Yet, any theory that does not address the extended chaotic state of mixed emotions in grieving is not truly representative of what happens to those deeply grieving.

In the midst of my sorrowing for my son, feeling isolated from the whirring world of global news as usual, a pandemic hit the United States of America unaware. Why Americans were so unprepared for this world-wide contagion belongs in another essay of a more political nature, but the fact of its impact could not be separated from my emotional state.

At the first mentions of the novel coronavirus COVID-19 in the U.S., journalists initially took the word of President Trump and repeated his words: "I would view it [COVID-19] as something that just surprised the whole world," he said in a press conference early in March 2020. "Nobody knew there would be a pandemic or epidemic of this proportion." Of course, those claims turned out to be not only misleading, as journalists like to write, but unfortunately for everyone, a lie.

The lack of preparedness in the United States led to a chaotic and often contradictory official response that affected the nation, not only through the number of cases and deaths from COVID-19 but through national angst.

Within another month, as the number of American deaths leaped well beyond White House projections, it was suddenly no longer possible to treat COVID-19 as a "Chinese virus" that was going to quickly disappear as Trump repeatedly informed Americans in February 2020: "It will go away in April." Later in February, Trump said that it would "disappear...like a miracle" long after he had been informed that the novel coronavirus was, at the time, spreading more rapidly.

Almost overnight, Americans were experiencing disorientation, sorrow, fear, confusion, and extreme anxiety, often simultaneously, all emotional states I had been going through for months after losing Blaise.

Even more unfortunate, Trump's words turned Americans against one another into camps that believed in science and those that believed in Trump. And none of it helped the psychological or physical state of living in this country.

There is little question about the veracity of the initial stage of shock, numbness, and denial with great loss, except that these sensations seem to be happening all at once rather than on a progressive spectrum. I have no doubt as to the validity of the identified emotional points in grieving: anger, fear, disorientation, panic, guilt, isolation, depression, "re-entry" troubles, bargaining, altered patterns, loss adjustment. These emotional touchstones are often tucked into five, six, or seven neat categories by psychologists, ending with acceptance and hope. I have yet to find optimism, however, that latecomer. And there is nothing neat or distinct about emotional responses that converge upon one another, doubling back, overlapping, skipping and reversing. I understood why Americans on both sides of the political aisle were living in an ill-defined fear.

Deep breath. Sitting by the fireplace in the living room, I heard a scratching sound, the kind of terrible disquiet a bird makes in attempting escape. Instantly, a scene from years earlier filled the room, Blaise telling his nervous mother he would capture the bird trapped in the fireplace chimney and not hurt it. Bird's claws frantically scored metal then silence fell. Covering the stove opening with a sheet, Blaise carefully opened the stove door. "Just wait," he said. We backed up, and I started to laugh nervously, expectant. Finally, the bird flew into the sheet, and Blaise scooped up the ruffling sheet and carried it outside where he unfolded it. Stunned and blackened by soot, the bird stood momentarily on our porch railing before regaining its senses and flying away.

It was a scene that was repeated a few times over the years until we got a better covering over the flu, so birds could not enter. Only in retrospect do I recall how gentle Blaise was, making sure not to further harm the creature. Over the years, my son had captured a few mice and released then, and covered at least two bats in our house before letting them go outside. He followed a mole from under the Christmas tree, blocking off escape until he released the frightened creature outside.

Coming back to the present, I sip my lukewarm tea, realizing I had been lost in that other time, thinking about how compassionate Blaise could be. That gentleness extended to other animals and children. He was never the uncle who would tease and torture the younger kids for amusement, for a joke.

Months after Blaise's death, I suddenly find myself getting angry, in disbelief, crying as if my son had just died, all the while not accepting what has happened. His death at 32 years will forever be unacceptable.

I do not want to relinquish my love for my son. If I am holding onto grief, perhaps it is by design. I realize I have stopped jumping at the sound of every ambulance passing in the night. Yet, I still hear them and think, "someone loved."

Grief does not so much come in stages as alter the position from which you view yourself and the world.

Twenty-Eight

Slender Thread Between the
Living and the Dead

Arriving at Upstate Medical in a state of panic in which there are
no boundaries, no days, no time, Dan and I never closed our eyes
for twenty-four hours, taking turns holding Blaise's hand. On a
deep level, I knew we had lost our son in our living room, on his
favorite couch, but a flurry of activity, of rough, precise New York
State Police, of busy paramedics, then quickly moving, efficient
nurses, IVs, tubes, monitors, and beeping machines cast a shadow
of doubt. We want to believe that science and technology will save
him, a belief as futile as believing prayer will stop death. But we
prayed and watched the machines attached to our son with a
hypervigilance.

Deception and betrayal are rooted in urgent need. Staring
at those tubes and monitors all hooked to Blaise, I had started to
posit the impossible: all of this technology could somehow save
him. Perhaps the hardest I cried was the moment one of the ICU
doctors implied that Blaise could possibly pull through, drug

masking brain function. In those endless few hours in the ICU with our son, we had moved mercifully from horror to vigil, into to the deepest dark sorrow.

At the first sign of cautious optimism, based on error, I listened intently as doctors and nurses made assumptions that a healthy looking, 32-year young man was in a coma due to drug overdose. Overdosing patients may appear comatose with depressed brain stem reflexes because of the effects of the drug, a doctor was heard saying in some part of my brain still operating. That ridiculous sliver of encouragement that entered was unintentionally cruel. Nearly everyone, except me, believed that Blaise must have somehow returned to drug use. Only because of this miscalculation, persistent resuscitative measures were enacted rather than understood as hopeless and inappropriate. If I had read the statistics on comatose patients, I would not have fallen into even this temporary reverie of hope.

Making that dreaded phone call to Nicole, I could scarcely breathe. I have no recollection of what I explicitly said, but it was something along the lines of, "He's in the hospital. I don't think he is going to make it." I know I could not say, "He is going to die."

Nicole offered to call Colette for me, and I guiltily let her carry that additional burden. My two daughters had hours in the car ahead of them before arriving at the hospital, all the while riding in horrifying uncertainty and fear.

As time passed without our awareness, Dan and I awaited Colette and Nicole who were driving from the D.C. area to be with their brother. We inhabited a kind of suspended state, floating between ridiculous hope and utter despair.

We heard again the conversations between the medical staff: "Well, he's young; he's strong," with extended pause and that was enough to induce the notion that Blaise could return.

Our daughters arrived, and there was wailing and rising fear redoubled; the four of us watchful of any change. During those hallucinatory minutes turned uncountable hours, we left Blaise's side only when nurses ushered us out for a procedure.

When Blaise was taken to get a CAT scan the next morning, Dan went home to check on our dog Bogie, and Colette, Nicole, and I went to the top floor to get something to drink. One of the nurses kindly told us about this quiet coffee shop visited primarily by attending doctors and nurses. I asked Colette and Nicole to go to the hotel room we had rented to get a couple hours of sleep at some point.

A short time after my daughters left, I was heading back down to Blaise's room when I heard, "Code Blue" over the speakers. Immediately, my eyes widened in panic. I thought it had to be for Blaise, then I told myself to calm down, be rationale, as I walked quickly; I reminded myself that Upstate Medical was filled with people in distress, and the likelihood of the Code being for Blaise was slim. As I rounded the corner, a nurse ran toward me.

"It's Blaise," she said.

"Oh, my God. What? What?"

"I tried to reach you." I struggled to say any actual words. My phone volume had been turned down.

I called Dan. Called Colette and Nicole who had just gotten to the hotel only to turn around. Finally, I got out something between hiccupping fits of sobbing, "Come back now. He's coded. They got his heart started again, but."

When the CT scan came back, the reading was as bad as it could be. He had died in our living room as we had suspected. The brainstem bleed showed he had died when his heart broke. In his hospital room, my husband, two daughters and I stood around Blaise's bed, silently at first, and then we wailed. We stroked his hands and forehead. We whispered to him our private words. I stopped pleading for him to come back. I told him his next passage would be easier than his life had been.

I held his fingers in mine and thought, "his fingers are so long, so long and beautiful." He looked perfect, healthy in death. My brain worked hard to maintain some semblance of the real in this hallucinatory state.

The four of us finally let go of that slender thread of hope. That abstract line between the living and the dead had been crossed, and we could find no way back for him. Those moments were more terrible than any experience, any imaginings, any horror I could have conceived. We had moved into another realm, that of the stricken. We were together yet entirely alone with Blaise who was on a lonelier journey yet.

I thought I wanted to stay at his bedside for the rest of my existence. I found it nearly impossible to leave him, but a charge nurse came in and told us that we had four hours with his body. There is a time limit on death and dying in a hospital.

At the moment you are least capable of making decisions, you are required to make myriad ones: choosing a funeral home, arrangements for the body to be picked up from the hospital, a funeral date and time, calling hours date and times, writing the obituary. Who will write the obituary? Whether or not you will have a graveside service? Who is making first notification calls? What cemetery will he be buried in? Burial or cremation? Will there be a viewing with an open casket? Organ donation? What kind of coffin will be chosen? Casket liner colors? Who will be speaking at the funeral? Who is paying for the funeral? How many copies of the death certificate do you need? Do you agree to an autopsy? Will there be flowers at the grave site? Who is taking the flowers after the funeral service? Are you donating the flowers after the service? What kind of note cards will be printed, and what do you want written on these cards? Who is making the selection? How many people will be speaking? Who will direct the speakers if they go on too long? Will everyone who wants to speak be allowed to speak? Who will be directing the funeral? Are clergy involved? If so, from what church, and is everyone's faith represented in some manner? Is there a prayer card; will a selection be chosen? Who will fill out the necessary forms? Is there sufficient time for out-of-town family and friends to attend a funeral? Who is contacting family and friends? Will there be music? If so, what music will be playing in the background during the service? During calling hours? Is there a special charity your son would want people to donate to in his memory? Who are the pall bearers carrying your son's coffin? Will you host and offer refreshments after the calling hours? Where will the gathering of family and friends be held after the funeral? There are decisions to be made about what food to buy and serve. Is there going to be a caterer? Is there going to be alcohol? Are you going to make it through the next five minutes? Oh, God, no. Are you going to let your head fall upon your dead son's chest and weep until they remove you from the hospital?

What clothes will you choose to dress the body of your son? Absolutely inconceivable. All of it. I suddenly realize we had decisions to make which should not have to be made. Is there going to be a slide show or photo boards? Who will be preparing these photographic journeys of his life? Have you purchased a cemetery plot? What will you choose for a headstone? What inscription will be on his stone?

I just wanted to hold Blaise's hand and ask if he could please, please alter this waking nightmare. But, somehow, and I really do not know how, I made those decisions with Dan. We only struggled for a moment in trying to choose a funeral home, then everything after that felt like climbing a mountain, but we found the handholds and toeholds to make it up that cliff.

Driving home from the hospital after Blaise was officially declared deceased, everything filtered in as gray, lifeless. I was suddenly cordoned off from the living, even from color. Crying alone, yet beside my husband in the insulated space of our car, I recall him looking out the driver's window. Crying and driving.

I think I cautioned him about not getting into an accident. He said, "I can cry and drive."

Dan commented on water levels as we passed the lake's dam, wondered out loud how the county had lowered the water level early and remembered only then our boat was still in the water, tied to our dock, stuck in the muck. Everything froze, my mind, like our boat, mired in some other frozen lake, waiting for a thaw.

Two or more indistinct months went by without keen observation, without awareness of a lot except damage and death, the calling hours and the funeral. Every room in our house felt empty. I did not write. I barely read during that period, and what I read, I do not remember. Watching television became an impossibility. I was in a metaphorical fetal position even standing.

Where would memories lead me? To other episodes of fear and panic. I instantly recalled a one-sided conversation with my daughter Colette that had happened nearly four years earlier. On the way home from our camp in Quebec, I called my daughters as soon as we had cellphone reception, after a week of being cut off from outside contact.

Fear detected in my daughter's voice before she told me what had happened, that emotion vibrated all the way through me. Colette and Nicole had driven in the middle of the night from Washington, D.C. to bail their brother out of jail for holding an amount of Xanax over the prescription limit. Blaise had gone into withdrawal, and they got him first to the hospital then waited with him at home for placement in a treatment facility. A kind, very compassionate doctor in the Cortland hospital emergency room worked his magic to get our son a placement, they told us later. What a kind and compassionate man.

"It was the worst moment of our lives yet, somehow, it was so good to be with him, talk all night together," Colette said, later. "We cried and laughed and just held each other."

Colette and Nicole kept vigil as their brother struggled with withdrawal, and he began the first steps of his long, arduous journey out of addiction toward physical redemption.

He entered rehab of his own volition. Turned once to look at his waiting sisters in the car before going through those doors. No turning around anymore. Dan and I were still driving the twelve hours toward home, our quiet car filled with tension and fear.

By the time Dan and I arrived, Blaise was already in the Tully Hill Treatment and Recovery facility. That long, torturous car ride home from Quebec was a kind of Hell, filled with confusion, anger, and, most of all, impotence. There was nothing we could do except drive.

When we reached our house, Colette and Nicole were waiting for us to explain everything that had happened. How they had gotten the call, their middle of the night drive to save their little, big brother. We could not talk to Blaise yet, according to Tully Hill rules. We listened, cried again, got angry, listened some more to the rational, compassionate voices of our two calm daughters who reminded us that this was a beginning, not an ending.

I clearly recall the fear of that night, yet I would give anything now to return to such a night rather than the one we faced later at his death.

During the years of his drug use, Blaise had been secretive, but he was intelligent enough to cover his actions well. I had grown used to his furtive looks, his gestures of dismissal, his rationalizations for odd responses. But after his arrest for drug possession, we finally all found ourselves in a position where deflection no longer worked.

Blaise and I listened as his judgmental lawyer said to me, "you're an enabler." I did not argue with her, thinking it not smart under the circumstances, but the contemptuous remark stuck. I kept going over everything, trying to figure out another way of handling what was happening in our house, to our son and to Dan and me. Only a few years later, did I think about the fact that the lawyer had no children at the time. I imagine it is easier to condemn a parent for indulgence and enabling, whatever that means, if you have never experienced that relationship and fear for your child. I did not allow Blaise to do drugs. Rather, I did not know how to prevent him from going to that dark place.

What I did not say in the lawyer's office was that we could have lost our son many times before (the time he was riding in our Ford Bronco and his friend was driving, flipping our SUV over and over). I could have told her about the afternoon Blaise tried to quit Xanax without help and went into seizures, falling and cutting his head open. I could have told her about that other time he had seizures trying to quit using again, without us knowing about it until a couple of years later. At that time, I did not even know he was using Xanax, thinking he had fallen into alcoholism. Even that drug takes a planned and careful withdrawal. Blaise was not typically stumbling around at home. He looked and talked logically and could trick you into believing he didn't have a problem although I knew there was something deeply wrong.

During the end of his teenage years and early twenties, my son reminded me a little of my wild and wonderful brother Emerson, Jr. who died much too young but lived fully and well and, when he was young, recklessly. My parents could have lost my ten-year-old brother when he hopped on his bike and went straight down a dirt road that was really a forest path and flew over the handlebars into trees; when as a young man he put the waterski tow rope behind his neck; when he was slammed to the mat and suffered a severe concussion and skull fracture at the New York

State wrestling tournament; when he partially ran through a glass door; when and when and when, the times too numerous to count. But my brother survived to go to law school and marry and have a wonderful, beautiful wife and amazing sons. He became a lawyer and respected judge before he died too soon. I imagined my son on a similar path.

Reflecting on my own responses and behaviors during the years Blaise used drugs, I know I worked hard at trying not to annoy my son by constantly lecturing him. Yet, lecture I did. I nagged and left scientific articles about the dangers of drug and alcohol use in his bedroom, on the table in the dining room where he would see them as soon as he walked in the house. I made notes and taped them to his TV and slipped them on top of his pile of clean laundry. I recommended podcasts and documentaries about the risks of alcoholism and addiction. I questioned him every time he came in or went out the door. I wrote lists of counselors and psychiatrists with their phone numbers and left them on his pillow. I called doctors and asked if he or she could take on a young addict. They all said that they could not talk to me without my son's consent since he was an adult. I looked at Blaise's eyes and tried to read where he had been and what he was doing. I was so relentless that Dan had to stop me numerous times.

"Just stop," Dan would say. "He's not listening, so why are you still talking?" Although he was as frustrated as I was, Dan's approach was different.

But I could not stop doing everything I could think of to help Blaise even if it did not work. I did not know exactly what would be successful, but I knew I could not stop trying to reach my son. More than anything else, however, I was fearful. My stomach hurt all the time. I could not sleep at night. To say that I lived with a high level of agitation and anxiety is fact. Yet, to my son's young lawyer, I was nothing more than an "enabler."

Near the end of residential treatment, parents are asked to participate in recovery discussions and lectures. Again, and again, we heard the words "enabling" as if it was as closely linked to addiction as the drug. I felt as if I was walking around with a big, red E branded on my forehead. I felt that shame, then thought about the kind of shame my son carried around every day, all day and night. He later told me that he hated himself during that period of time.

Three of us sat around a table in a large meeting room, other families in tight circles in the rehab facility. There is no laughter in this somber room. Blaise's eyes are bright and clear. I could see thoughts racing across his still face and just a question: can I do this? His words unspoken but stalled and present between us. I could not stop beaming then, so happy to see my son after this long wait, and so relieved to find him whole, smart, alert, and thoughtful. I wanted to reach across the table and bear hug Blaise, but nervous, watchful eyes all around us restrained me.

Then we walked outside, the three of us, Dan and I on either side of our tall son. He was talking quietly but assuredly, telling us about the struggles and pain of others around him, even now sensitive to those who "had it bad," "worse than me," he said. As we walked slowly, I noticed another difference in Blaise, his typical reserve gone. Honest and a little afraid, but terribly brave, he talked. He was finally ready to make that journey no one could make for him. Here we were in what many would think was a terrible place to be, and yet I could not suppress the joy welling inside. Dan and I could feel the difference in him. He was ready.

Going through rehab was transformational for my son, and the journey deepened our relationship. He was done hiding everything from me as we made drives back and forth from Tully Hill counseling sessions, AA meetings, court dates, the gym where he worked out as part of his therapy. Because Blaise had lost his license, and I had just retired from teaching, we were each other's constant traveling companions for a year and a half.

At first, I thought of myself as his teacher, his guide, but I learned that he had to find his place again without this unequal partnership of parent and grown child. He was his own guide now. I learned that if I did not press him, did not push him for disclosures, for answers and commitments, Blaise opened up slowly, revealing himself, his ideas and hopes for his future.

"You're the best mom ever," he said with quiet certainty. "There was nothing you and Dad did that turned me to drugs. I did that on my own. Don't ever blame yourself. I thought of everything to keep it hidden."

"And you're making this work, you're leaving addiction behind on your own, too. Something for which I'm very proud of you."

"Addiction is always with you," Blaise reminded me. "You have to fight it, but the fight gets easier over time. Right now, it's still really, really hard."

To my credit, I did not reach for more that time. The fact he began to believe in his future was astonishingly good, and he opened up while we were driving together.

"I finally figured out that I'm worth this fight," Blaise said. I had longed to hear him say those words.

"How far would you go for me?" asks Ann Patchett in her essay "Love Sustained," first appearing in *Harper's Magazine* in 2006. "Farther than you would ever have thought possible."

How far did I go for my son? The answer is there was no limit, just as there is no limit to my love for him. I wish I could have spared him pain. I wish I could have done something to keep that genetic mutation Marfan syndrome from touching his perfection, kept him from having lymphoma, kept him from experimenting and then falling into drug use. Wanting to protect my son and actually being able to protect him were based upon two very different conditions.

Following Blaise's autopsy, the medical examiner talked at length with me. In her careful descriptions of my son's blown apart heart, the cancer that riddled his organs after jumping on his immune-compromised body, I felt something break open in me. I remembered the "enabler" badge of shame attached to me. At the moment the medical examiner explained MFS to me, I wore "enabler" without shame or regret. I realized I helped enable Blaise to live for as long as he did. "If only I could have enabled Blaise more, for longer," I said out loud. If I eased anything for him at all, I was grateful for my impulse toward indulgence to him. I was also grateful to my son for helping me lose my worries about what other people thought of our circumstances.

After Blaise's death, I discovered something else incredible: while he may have been secretive with his drug use for years, he was also secretive with his talents, his kindness to others, his generosity, his big-hearted gestures. He was not looking for acclaim or reward.

Deep breath. During the middle of the afternoon, I glance into my son's bedroom. I had made and smoothed the bedcover, yet an indentation pushes the cover in waves on each side. I ask Dan, "Have you been sitting on Blaise's bed?"

"I went in there last night before coming to bed. Nothing helps." I agreed.

We try not to cry again. Keeping our son's room as he left it: neat but with clean clothes piled high on his dresser. Dan leaves the room. I wait a moment longer. If only Blaise had not been so concerned about cleanliness. There is no odor of him in the room, no familiar smell.

When I cannot breathe well, I, too, go into Blaise's room and place my head on a pile of his clothes. They feel thin, hollow. He is not there.

Twenty-Nine

Courage, Pain, and Marfan Syndrome

"Want of courage is the last thing to be pardoned by young men, who usually look upon bravery as the chief of all human virtues, and the excuse for every possible fault," wrote the great Russian writer Alexander Pushkin in his short story "The Shot." In this instance, Russians are not so very different from Americans, courage long having been held up as an attribute of ideal man.

For years, we asked, no, demanded Blaise find the courage to conquer his addictions. For years, our son battled what he called "his demons," without knowledge that his every act in trying to stay alive was, indeed, brave.

His decision to leave an apartment with good friends and return to live at home after falling and hitting his head took courage and showed his desire to live. I will never know if his fall was a result of using drugs, trying to get off drugs without a step-down program, or his enlarged heart sending out noticeable warnings.

His return home rather than heading to New York City to make movies with his friends was not out of trepidation of adventure, I have come to believe now that I have more information. His hesitancy was related to a condition of which we were all unaware. What Blaise was attempting to overcome, it is now known, was impossible. He could not heal himself. All of the will power, herbal teas, regular exercise, and good living habits would not change the outcome or stop his impending death.

Although Blaise did not know about his Marfan syndrome, he must have instinctively known something was not right inside. Staying with his parents gave him the best chance for survival, he believed. He instinctively knew that to fight it, whatever that "it" was going wrong with his body, he had to have a starting point. The starting point was home.

When it came time for my few ounces of courage, I found it at length. Would I allow such an invasion of my son's body as an autopsy? At the first mention of the procedure before his death was technically fixed in the hospital, I broke down into hysterical crying. I could not. I would not go there. I think I surprised Dan with my unreasonableness, but he understood. After my son's death, I could not think or reason for a time.

My husband and daughter Colette did not want this invasive procedure done after Blaise was declared dead. When the medical examiner called our house of mourning, Colette told her, "no, no autopsy." I was kept out of the initial discussion because Colette answered the phone, and she and her dad talked it over. The medical examiner, however, called back, and I answered the phone this time. The official pressed, "I think you will want the truth. As a mother, you should know the truth." I agreed fully. I did want to know wherever that answer led. I found at least that bit of courage. If Blaise had returned to drug use, then I would love him no less. "Go ahead. Yes, perform the autopsy," I told her.

None of us knew the pain Blaise was suffering in life until after autopsy. The astute medical examiner told his about his enlarged aorta and the aortic dissection that killed him. She patiently explained how his condition must have been very painful for him. She introduced to us the idea that our son had Marfan syndrome (MFS). She asked about his medical history.

When I said that I did not think anyone in our family had this autosomal dominate connective tissue disorder (learning the information much later), the medical examiner, a physician, explained that sporadic occurrence of MFS happens in 25-30% of cases. It was not enough that my son had a rare genetic disorder, but his case was even rarer in that he was likely one of those outliers in the 25% category.

Further, the medical examiner explained how MFS affects the skeleton, heart, blood vessels, eyes, skin, nervous system, and lungs. She talked about symptoms as I ticked off Blaise's medical history, providing her with details. I put her on speaker phone, so Colette and Dan could listen.

She told us about the Non-Hodgkin's Lymphoma that had attacked Blaise's organs with tumors in nearly every vital organ in his body. "They were in his stomach and had started in his lungs. I'm not sure how he was walking around," she finally said.

Why had everyone missed all the signals of my very sick son? I have had time to think about both what was possible and what made detection so difficult. There were several reasons that contributed to the fact no physician tested or suspected Blaise had Marfan syndrome. First, my son looked tremendously healthy and fit. Secondly, he did not have any facial distortion as happens with a certain percentage of cases of MFS. In fact, Blaise was handsome and well proportioned. The length of his arms and legs did not seem that unusual for a tall man.

Another problem area was Blaise's past addiction. Because my son readily admitted to having been an addict, doctors started at that point and made assumptions that his variety of symptoms were all somehow related to his past struggles with drugs. Because physicians looked for an obvious answer first, no one looked for the obscure answer to his ailments and symptoms.

When Blaise told a doctor that he had chest pain, the assumption was made that Blaise had anxiety as a result of being a former Xanax user. When he complained of red and itchy skin, he was referred to dermatologists who told him he had rosacea based on his past with alcohol. No one was looking at a distressed heart causing reddened skin. When Blaise told his doctors he was fatigued often, they suggested he stop smoking and get more sleep. All reasonable until the puzzle is finally put together.

With so many specialists, fewer and fewer doctors are treating the whole patient, asking their patients for the less typical health experiences. Because Blaise's pathology was complicated with overlapping conditions, a rare genetic syndrome, cancer, and former drug use, physicians went for one diagnosis rather than ask for all of his symptoms to get a better picture of his health.

Only after Blaise left us did I come to know symptoms of MFS, the rare genetic anomaly that comes with a particular set of characteristics. No one recognized these attributes in Blaise in a way that they all fit together: long face; tall, thin build; flexible joints; heart palpitations; chest pain; long arms, fingers, toes; pain in the lower back; unexplained stretch marks on the skin not caused by sudden weight gain or loss; crowded teeth with high palate; dislocation of joints or shoulders coming out of socket; skin reddened face and neck. There are a few striking symptoms of the syndrome that Blaise did not display, including a chest that sinks in or sticks out, scoliosis, and, perhaps, eye problems (at least that we knew of). No one fit his thirteen symptoms into diagnosis of a condition of anything other than a healthy boy and, later, strong young man.

Deep breath. At four, Blaise had to have several baby teeth pulled under general anesthesia in the hospital due to crowding in his mouth. His permanent teeth were coming in at weird angles with no space left. I do not remember exactly what we told him, except that I still feel that panic, recalling the agonizing seconds as they rolled his stretcher away from us into the operating room. Absurdly brave, little Blaise did not cry or whimper, just looked straight out at the world. I was so frightened to have my baby have an operation. Squeezing my eyes shut tight, I prayed. Minutes perceived as hours and time slowed to a crawl. Exhale. He made it through the surgery, and his dad and I hugged him, not wanting to ever let go.

Following the operation, Blaise's teeth and mouth looked perfect, straight, just right. He still had to have braces a few years later. No one mentioned, not the orthopedic surgeon, not his pediatrician, not his dentist, not his orthodontist, that too many teeth and high arched palate in a child's mouth could be symptomatic of anything, let alone a deadly genetic syndrome.

What kind of courage and strength were needed for Blaise to go on about his day living with his enlarged heart sending every desperate signal it could until its aortic dissection? For him to work two jobs, resist the temptation to return to drugs when his organs slowly filled with cancerous tumors?

After our son was gone, we learned of his enormous determination and endurance in fighting to live despite the odds. I wish just one doctor had listened and taken in all of his numerous symptoms before it was too late. They could have operated. I wish we could have saved him. I wish I could have told him how brave he was just in living.

Deep breath. On a family vacation in Virginia Beach, Blaise was body surfing when a surprisingly large wave pulled him under, slamming his face to the sand and broken shells on the ocean floor. When he finally emerged from the water, Blaise's cheekbone, forehead, and eye socket had skin torn away. He picked up his body board and walked the long way up the beach to our rented house. I saw him coming and took his photo from high up on the porch. He looked unconcerned and handsome, strong and invincible. Nothing in his gait suggested he could have drowned moments earlier.

We asked him what happened, and he laughed. There must have been an instant, tossed under the water, shot to the bottom, when he wondered if he would make it back to the surface. If that was the case, he never confessed. How little we knew the ocean was less an adversary than the syndrome he harbored from before birth.

Tolerance for pain is something that runs in our family, but I never realized the extent to which Blaise bore that trait until reflection after his death. We are coming to the first summer that Blaise will not be mowing our lawn. That task was his, and he attacked the lawn in one go. I remember listening to the hum and rasp of the lawn mower choking on grass, spitting out a stone or stick, and when Blaise came inside to get a drink, he would have a gash or two, one on his leg and another near his temple.

"What happened to you?" I would be amazed, smelling the fresh cut grass on his clothes, in his hair and beard.

Indifferent to the cuts, Blaise would typically respond, "I must have caught a tree branch mowing." He brushed it off as nothing. Unless he was gushing blood, he paid little heed to his injuries. Was just curious about them.

Always insisting he clean his wounds, I harped on him to get a band aid. He sometimes laughed but usually obliged his mother's concerns. He injured himself frequently while cutting and chopping up trees for his uncle's tree business. Again, his scraps, gouges, and slices seemed not to concern him overly much. Looking back, he must have thought, everyone lives with constant pain. This cut is nothing.

***

After his death, there were people who told my daughters and me that we were courageous when we stood up, one by one, and spoke about Blaise before those many attending his funeral service. I never felt brave. I felt emptied and moving automatically in the kind of vacuum that looks like strength. Joan Didion wrote in her memoir about losing her husband and daughter: "to others, you may look as though you are holding up well. Because the reality of death has not yet penetrated awareness, survivors can appear to be quite accepting of the loss."

A few days after the first Christmas without my son, Molly called. It was late, nearly midnight. Molly was Blaise's first serious girlfriend in high school. They were passionate and wild and reckless, like many first romances. It ended badly but, somehow, they had found their way to friendship. Molly did not have my cellphone number, and Dan and I were not home. We had gone to stay with my daughter Colette in Silver Spring. Dan was asleep. I was still sitting up in bed in the dark when my phone rang. Molly's voice was barely audible between sobs. She had tried to make it home from Florida for Blaise's calling hours, but car problems on the way delayed her.

I attempted to stay calm and not cry. "I talked to Blaise not along ago," she said. "I wanted to tell you that he was saving his money to pay you back." This was a surprise. I did not think that Blaise had saved any money. He scarcely had a few dollars at any one time during the years of his drug use. Only later, once he had left addiction behind, to find out that my son had saved a considerable amount in a bank account was almost mystifying.

As sad as I was, I wanted to comfort Molly, a young mother just starting out again after leaving Florida. I don't remember what I said to her on the phone but clearly remember what she said to me: "Blaise told me," she said between sobs, "to be as good a mother to my daughter as you were to him."

At that point, I lost my composure. How Molly found my number, why she called at that low moment for me, the fact she called at all when we had never spoken on the phone in all those years, all of it was both strange and wonderful, a flicker of light in such darkness. Then to have my son's words. I wrapped them in my heart.

I have come to fully appreciate the courage, near audacity, it took for my son to live. With MFS, with aching back and joints coming out of place, with skin that itched and reddened with chest pain that ebbed and rushed in over and over, with continual headaches and leg aches, then with severe stomach pain from the cancerous tumors growing inside. Every day he got up, worked out, went to work, joked with friends, sang a little girl to sleep because her mother could not get her to go to bed, sent a text that he was fine to his forever worried mom. Every night, he drank his herbal teas and hoped to stem the tide against him.

Courage is what is needed to live. Courage to continue living fully and well. Blaise showed such courage every day. I am trying to find mine in writing about the son I will forever miss and love.

Thirty

What is Most Real

At first, I could not go back into Blaise's room or even past it without breaking down. Then I remembered his fish. The large tank in my son's room had five fish in it, rather, four fish and an albino frog. Fish and frog had survived for years, growing rather large. Amazingly, those fish lasted through my initial, prolonged period of neglect after Blaise's death. They needed to be fed.

Blaise's jackets hang in a closet downstairs. The idea of clearing away his things is not possible yet. I decide to let someone else makes those decisions. When I pass away, there can be a yard sale with my things and my son's clothes stacked up beside each other.

Dan and I decide not to move anything in his room. We talked about what was expected but come to agreement on what feels right, rather than give all of his things away. I logically knew Blaise was not coming back. Nevertheless, I imagined his spirit would not want his room in tumult, clothes thrown in boxes or tossed. Perhaps at some point in time, Dan and I will be able to return to his room and offer up his clothes and prized possessions to others, but that day is not today or even tomorrow.

In my son's bedroom, I hold the sleeve of one of his sweat shirts too long. I still question whether or not I should be giving items to Goodwill, donating his nice, fairly new clothes, hats, shoes, to someone in need. I am not able to do so. Album covers on his homemade shelf, trophies from sports, posters and pictures, his collection of DVD favorite movies, NBA jerseys, Jordan shoes, all summoning his physical presence in his profound absence. Each item absurdly becomes totem.

I turn to one of my favorite writers, Virginia Woolf.

"Life is but a procession of shadows, and God knows why it is that we embrace them so eagerly, and see them depart with such anguish, being shadows. And why, if this —and much more than this is true — why are we yet surprised in the window corner by a sudden vision that the young man in the chair is of all things in the world the most real, the most solid, the best known to us? Such is the manner of our seeing. Such the conditions of our love."

Virginia Woolf, *Jacob's Room*
***

On my son's bedroom door hangs a poster of a young Frank Sinatra, the singer arrested in 1938 on a morals' charge of seduction. I suppose it appealed to my son's sense of irony, as he was a Sinatra fan. I never thought about Blaise's eclectic tastes in music too much before, but suddenly wondered how he answered his preferences for both Sinatra's velvety crooning "New York, New York" with one of his favorite's, Nasir bin Olu Dara Jones, known as Nas, rapping: "When I think of crime, I'm in a New York State of mind." Blaise was, however, all about the real wherever he found it. What was true and felt true to him was somehow right, regardless of mixing genres and eras.

Real and sometimes reckless. Blaise drove too fast. He lived quietly but often on the edge. During a brief period in his twenties, he racked up a pile of speeding tickets and lost his license. He lost it again later, so that he was forced to ride with his mother until he earned his license back. It did not surprise me that he was drawn to the younger, wilder Frank Sinatra who had been arrested. Both loved women.

Although most of my son's extensive music collection was rap, Blaise would sometimes toss in another song outside of his preferred music genre. He never gave up on trying to convince me of the importance of rap to our culture, but he acknowledged that I would find some aspects of it problematic, in terms of the sexist language.

"Listen to this. You'll love it," he said, putting in a CD as we headed down the road. What began with Jeff Buckley's near whisper and stripped-down guitar arrangement soared in our car until I had to fight back tears, embarrassed at my emotional response to Buckley's version of the Leonard Cohen song "Hallelujah." Blaise proceeded to tell me in precise detail why Buckley's arrangement was the best rendition of Cohen's song. Then we talked about Cohen's recent death at the age of 82. Blaise came back to Buckley, noting the fact that young Buckley walked out into the Mississippi river, turned and floated on his back, singing, before disappearing and drowning at the age of thirty.

"How sad. It's terrible," I said. "I wonder if he killed himself or drowned accidentally?"

"He was singing his heart out," said Blaise, adding, "in the Mississippi at night with his clothes and boots on. He knew he had to go then."

"You mean you think he killed himself because"

"Because it doesn't get any better," my son said quietly. I shot him a glance, wondering, but he had a slight smile on his face. "It was like Cohen wrote the song for Buckley. Cohen had to wait all those years for that younger musician to find his way to it," Blaise said, as we crested a hill. I had no idea that my son even knew who Leonard Cohen was, let alone liked his music. I had played Cohen's albums when I was in college. What drew us both to this poet-songwriter? When we arrived at his AA meeting and Blaise got out, I sat for a few minutes in the car and thought about how our car rides allowed us to talk in a way that we did not at home.

***

Deep breath. On a Sunday in March, Jesse, Blaise's oldest friend from elementary school, stopped by our house. Dan, Jesse, and I talked for a while, then Jesse asked if I had cleaned Blaise's fish tank. I had to nod my head in a bit a shame. "Okay, let's go," he said, getting up and ready to tackle blackened waters.

I had none of the proper aquarium-cleaning equipment, so we improvised. Jesse gave directions, and I gladly followed, grateful to have help in this task. First, Jesse showed me where the temperature gauge was on the tank. I had never noticed it before because it blended so well. "We just have to make sure not to shock the fish with a different temperature," he said as we scooped out pans full of water. I filled other pans with clean water and let them sit.

Placing some of the water in the largest pot, Jesse then took the minnow net, and he scooped out the smaller fish easily. The last one, a 13-inch sailfin Plecostomus or Pleco gave battle. Its twisting and jerking reminded me of a fish on the end of a line before being lifted into a boat. This catfish did not want to leave the tank although it was normally the most docile. After initial efforts, Jesse decided to change tactics.

"We're going to have to nearly empty the tank to get him, and I'll grab him with another pan." I bailed and emptied dirty pots full of water into our toilet in the bathroom as Jesse lifted out artificial plants, tank ornaments, and decorative structures. I cleaned and rinsed each one, drying each before setting it down on a towel at our feet. All around us were pots and pans in various stages of clean and dirty water. Both Jesse and I thought the albino clawed frog would leap out of the little minnow net, but the frog cooperated, perhaps stunned by the commotion. In the tank, the frog had always been the most active.

At one point, we had a dozen or more pans with water or water and fish, stones drying, ornaments drying, and we were both fairly soaked. I started laughing. "Aren't you glad you offered to help me clean the tank?"

Jesse shrugged. "It's a labor of love." Silence. We both knew he meant it, and that the task was all done out of his love for his friend and my love for my son, but we started to laugh hysterically for an instant. Then, Jesse got back to business.

"It worked," Jesse said, as he emptied the pan spilling Pleco into the large pot. Now, there were all the stones to clean and rinse.

After checking water temperature and finding it hit the mark, Jesse returned the fish and frog to their tank. All settled in surprisingly quickly. All survived our cleaning their house.

"A labor of love." I thought about Jesse's remark after he left. I knew how much Blaise would have laughed with us and how touched he would have been to see us working so hard, if inefficiently, to preserve something of his, the fish in his tank that he watched every night before falling asleep.

Another long-time friend of my son's wrote and directed an indie movie in which Blaise had a bit part. Initially, Vin Turturro asked Blaise to help out behind the scenes on his movie being shot in New York City. At some point, Vin gave his friend a line, then another and another. Blaise would have done anything to help Vin be successful in the entertainment industry. Blaise would drive to NYC on a weekend, pick up things for the movie production, then drive home to return to work. Blaise was humble about his lines in the movie, but he did tell us about the fact; something that was unusual for him.

"I've got a few lines," he said grinning, then shrugged. "It's no big deal," but it was. It was a very big deal to him. I never thanked Vin, but he must know.

After Blaise died, Nick Caruso, Blaise's great buddy, sent us a picture of Blaise going over his lines on a New York City street, outside the building in which they were shooting the movie. Nick and Vin are cousins, so Nick had access to Vin's film that most did not have. My son is shown in the photo concentrating, but he also looks relaxed. Something about the way he holds his head suggests he is a little nervous, not exactly feeling stage fright, but he wanted to get it right. We asked Nick if there was any video of the film we could see.

A few days later, Nick sent a video clip from Vin's movie in which Blaise appears. We opened the video on Dan's phone. Instantly startling, the video was also mesmerizing. Hardware shop clerk as character, our son tells the other actor about various locks he might purchase. The other actor is asking about a lock to keep someone from getting away, and the scene is strange and funny, Blaise's matter-of-fact salesman voice adding to the black humor.

Watching Blaise in the movie, speaking and sounding just like himself, we were struck by how natural he was in this unnatural art, how present and fully alive. How could he be gone and speaking in this film? We expected him to walk through the front door again, make a fuss over Bogie, kick off his size 14 athletic shoes, and tell us about his day. Viewing the film knocked my husband and me to the floor. It took several minutes for both of us to stop crying.

***

Empathy

Knowing a Congressman's son,
a brightest light, a young man
with sharpened mind and promise,
would close all the doors and windows
of his life while you watch him
helplessly, just as someone's daughter
catches your attention and eye,
beautiful girl momentarily distracted,
losing control of her car as she flies
through the windshield
only to come back broken.
Empathy lays you out, still breathing.

***

Although my attention span was greatly shortened for an extended period of time after Blaise's death, gradually, I returned to reading. Yet, after reading a few pages, I felt spent. I thought about students in school who could not sustain the attention needed to finish a book. I thought of the various incidences in my life that affected reading retention and knew that an empathic understanding of difficulties others faced outside the norm made me a better teacher.

After a while, I was able to return to literature for shorter periods, however. Reading Shelly, I slowed myself and reread his lines in *Prometheus Unbound*: "To love, and bear; to hope 'til Hope creates/ From its own wreck the thing it contemplates." I longed to create from the wreck of my hope, the image of my son, the very real Blaise.

All of the words in all of literature, however, won't bring Blaise back, but I continue to fill vessels with contemplation. Pouring them out on dry ground, I think, perhaps something will yet grow.

What is most real are the ways in which Blaise's friends have helped me and each other deal with the loss of him. Jesse and Nick, Alena and Vin, Trio and Ben, Shane and Toby, Kevin and Ryan, Rachel, Chelsea, Alexis, Taylor, and a many other young men and women with whom Blaise was friends. These young people, as well as my own friends and family, have reached out, shared stories about Blaise, entered grief with each other, making me realize I was never, not for one minute, really alone. Yet, grief continues to make us feel isolated even in the midst of love. But Blaise's friends gave me something they may not know: they have all given this great gift of showing how much Blaise was loved.

Thirty-One

Benevolence of Blaise

I knew my son well, and still, Blaise remains a mystery. I have, however, discovered a number of surprising things about him in the awful wake of his death. The first is that the revelations are not mine alone. My daughter Colette shared an anecdote about her two-year-old son, my youngest grandson, Luca. Waking one morning early as he always does, Luca popped up and said, "I was playing baseball with Blaise and Miah and Enzo on my team." The clarity with which her little son saw his dream as real rather than imagined was startling. The fact that he had such strong connections to his uncle whom Luca had known for such a short time was rather amazing.

When he was 32, Daniel, Blaise's dad was the father of two daughters and working long hours, often away from home for weeks. By the time my father, Blaise's grandfather, Emerson, Sr. was 32, he was a father to five children, had been in combat in World War II and returned to a changed America, had started a law practice, and was earning his way in a community that was new to him. Blaise felt the burden of that history and accomplishment. His older sisters were also remarkably accomplished.

Yet, my son persevered. Working his way back from addiction is no small feat. Life was changing in America in myriad ways, many of which were not positive, and males in particular were finding their way more difficult to define.

Almost 21 million Americans suffer from an addiction, according to the Addiction Center. Their statistics show that since 1990, drug overdoses have tripled. Many addicts who go through a rehab program must go through again and still return to drug or alcohol abuse. The cycle is very difficult to break. Blaise did not give up his addiction easily either. It is not as if his friends and family did not want him to succeed, but love is not enough. Quitting drugs is not simply about will power either. Quitting a serious drug without help, without a step-down program of some kind, can be fatal.

Yet, Blaise was ultimately successful in leaving his addiction behind. He wrote about that hard journey and finally was proud of how he had turned a corner. That sense of what he considered a small accomplishment, nevertheless, changed him. He was always a sweetheart, but his kindness to others started to spread in the last few years of his life. He got up every day and determined to help other people in myriad small ways, even with a failing body.

A long conflict with unseen physical issues, with drugs, had stifled Blaise's emotional development in some ways, but in others, he had become a wise young man. In some aspects, he was more like a thoughtful 22-year-old at his death than 32 years old. After he had gone through rehab successfully, he started waking to the world around him. This rebirth came with a different level of empathy for others. Animals molting out of their skin, a crab climbing out of its shell, a butterfly emerging from a cocoon: evidence of resurrections.

Only six months after his death did I find that Blaise was asked to help out a young mother who had trouble putting her toddler to bed. Delivering pizzas at the time, Blaise dropped off his deliveries then drove over to his friend's place and sang the little child to sleep. The toddler drifted off, and Blaise headed out to continue making pizza deliveries. When his friend told me this anecdote, I tried to imagine my son singing to this little girl. He had a nice voice, but mostly sang in the shower, not in public. When someone asked for help, he never hesitated those last couple of years.

Only after his death did I discover the hundreds of ways in which Blaise was engaged in daily acts of kindness. He moved people's lives from apartment to apartment and from one threshold to another. Big and strong, he could move furnishings of an entire apartment by himself in no time, without pay, without asking for anything in return. In small gestures and large ones, Blaise made a difference to so many for no other reason than he could: the most generous of acts. It was courageous in that he went about his day fearlessly, without regard for how it would affect him.

Notes from strangers to me, following my son's death, were the beginning of my discoveries and a powerful comfort:

"My 16-year-old has cancer and your son delivered him pizzas, calzones, anything he wanted or craved…cuz he was a good boy, and I want to thank you."

Blaise was giving pizzas to a boy with cancer? How did he never mention this kindness on his part? He never looked for praise.

Facebook messages from people I did not know, but my son did, were a lifeline for me as one stranger after another revealed kindnesses Blaise showed them without telling anyone in his family.

Another message arrived from a young woman I did not know then: "I know that in life, Blaise was a giver. I will never forget his kindnesses."

And another: "You know him best, and you know how he just had a knack for people. He was a man's man but so kind." That comment made me smile because so many young women told us Blaise was their best friend.

Another: "His gentleness within his manliness was because he was raised by a good woman and, of course, a good man."

Over and over, people wrote about my son's gentle nature, a striking quality in such a large man.

Blaise inspired his friends in ways I could not have imagined: "It was almost like his spirit was trying to encourage me to live my best life because then no matter what happens, I'll be fine."

"He had this beautiful aura about him."

The next message from someone I did not know, gave me pause:

"He never tried to guilt you when you f…ed up. He just helped you move on."

"Blaise was such a kind human being. He went out of his way to help me so many times."

"Blaise moved everything in my apartment for me when I was sick."

Cards came from college friends of his I never knew: "Blaise and I were teammates in college. I have so many good memories of us playing games together and shooting after practice. He brought a ton of laughter to his friends and was always there to pick you up if you were down on yourself. He definitely made me a better player, but our time off the court was just as special. He was a great friend. I am so sorry for your loss, and I will keep my memories of your son and our time together well. He was a wonderful person."

There were messages from those who had journeyed with him through addiction recovery: "Blaise was a big part of my early recovery. As paths often do, ours went our separate ways, but I loved seeing his smile and feeling his spirit. He was an awesome person, and truly (but quietly) proud of his sober journey. He was a bright light for me, for all of us. He made us want to do better."

"He helped me more than the counselors."

Some of these notes were about small acts that resonated: "My husband and I began working out at the same gym as Blaise because he encouraged us. He was so conscientious in trying to be healthy, we wanted to become healthier, too. He always made us laugh."

One young woman wrote that during a difficult time in her life, she worked with Blaise and told him about her economic issues. "He helped me buy diapers and pull ups for my daughter. He was there when I needed him. He wanted nothing in return. I've never met someone like him. He was truly one in a million."

Another message arrived: "He was so well-liked because he had such a large personality. He was a blessing to all of us. There is always the longing for more time. He was very giving in that quiet way of his."

He gave rides for people caught in sudden metaphorical and physical storms without asking for anything in return. A young woman I did not know well at the time, but have since become friendly with, told me Blaise gave her a ride in a lightning storm. Chelsea told me Blaise offered up his brand-new sweatshirt to keep her warm as her own had become soaked in the storm when she was walking. She contacted me after his death to see if she should return the sweatshirt. "Of course, not," I said. "It was his gift to you." Chelsea became his friend through his simple acts of kindness, telling me even her little son and daughter looked up to

Blaise, literally and figuratively. They have drawn pictures for him and left those illustrations with us.

People whom Blaise helped in ways I am still not aware of brought us little gifts and left them on our porch or in our mailbox.

News of my son's death from complications of having had MFS spread on Facebook, and I began receiving messages from strangers with questions about this little-known syndrome:

"My son, too, has physical signs, i.e., stretch marks, flat long feet. All things you could think are no big deal. I asked his doctor, and he didn't seem concerned. His doctor said most people with MFS live just fine [totally inaccurate and bordering on malpractice]. My question to you, if it's not too much to ask, is what were your son's signs and symptoms? I hope in sharing your story, it will help others."

There were a number of messages in a similar vein, and I began to think about the need for more information about Marfan's syndrome. If one thing could come of the terrible loss of my son, it would be to help someone else. I know, particularly after finding out about all of the people he was helping, Blaise would have wanted me to try to help, as well. These people who reached out to me after my son's death are a part of the reason I decided to write this book.

I came to recognize the terrible loss of my son was not mine and my family's alone. Blaise was important to so many other lives. Grief does not belong to any one person. It is not something that is ours, though we permit it to inhabit every fiber of our being. Everyone will experience terrible grief at some point in his or her life if the person lives long enough.

I should want to be done with grief. Instead, I hold it close because the emotional state is also where I am closest to my lost son.

My daughters have been my hope and show the way forward. Blaise's sisters, Nicole and Colette, wrote something for their brother's funeral. I asked if I could share their words again.

***

Nicole's words to her brother:

"My family is thoroughly heartbroken. But seeing all the faces of the people who loved him, people who travelled to be here, people who moved mountains to support us, family and friends who brought us food, babysat our children, held our hands, and momentarily held our grief, are the only reprieve in this waking nightmare. So, thank you. And know that Blaise would be so moved by your display of love and goodness, just as we are.

"One of my earliest memories is the day I first met my baby brother, Blazer. I was five years old, and my parents let me hold him (so long as I was sitting on the couch). I distinctly remember thinking: 'I'm going to dress this baby up so much.' But then I sensed something that has stayed with me for 32 years, something I've only felt again when my own sons were born. I felt that I both loved him fiercely, and I desperately wanted to protect him.

"Rivaled in male beauty for me only by his father and beloved nephews, Truman, Enzo, Owen and Luca, Blaise was the cutest little boy. But after a few years of treating him like a doll, I realized he had turned into a formidable playmate and my absolute best friend. We were inseparable for the next decade, playing every imaginative game we could think of: we were ghostbusters with cardboard proton packs; we were American gladiators setting up couch cushion obstacle courses; and we were Batman and Robin. It will surprise none of you that Blaise loved his pop culture references even when he was four-years-old.

"We were best friends, and we were each other's confidantes. As a child, Blaise was tremendously empathetic, a quality that he took with him into adulthood. It was as if he could

253

absorb your pain through osmosis, but without any of his own armor to guard his big, beautiful time-bomb of a heart.

"And he was giving. It's hard for most kids to be giving but not Blaise. He was always willing to play sidekick or lead, whichever I needed. Although it was almost always as sidekick because I was already playing sidekick to Coco's lead.

"And Blaise never, never tattled on me. Even when we played basketball indoors, and I shoved him and split his little forehead open by accident. My parents were furious with me, and he pleaded, telling them it wasn't my fault. He was six, begging our parents to forgive his much older sister, who certainly knew better. I remember thinking some version of, 'wow, this kid is solid gold.' And I have been resolute in that belief to this day.

"I heard many similar stories of Blaise's character. Stories where perhaps you made a mistake, or you were feeling lost, helpless or hopeless, and he had your back. Blaise always had my back. And sometimes, I had to have his back, too.

"But mostly, we just laughed together from babies to adults. We laughed so much and so hard. You know that funny, unique laughter of his. I was always trying get him to do that high-pitched, slightly embarrassing one.

"As we got older, Blaise was undeniably cool. Sometimes I felt acutely aware of my lack of coolness next to him. Maybe I always tried to make him laugh so hard to make him my little sidekick again. And then for a second, I could be Batman, and he could be Robin.

"What I didn't know when I first met my baby brother, but that I know now, was that Blaise was easy to love, but he was not so easy to protect. It didn't stop me, or my sister, or our parents, or many of you in this room, from trying. And he never, never stopped trying. I want everyone to know how hard he tried; how much he wanted to live and be happy, to give love and to be loved.

"And that when we surrounded him, as my brother left this world, that he was out on a boat on Little York Lake, under a hot sun, sailing on cool waters, and he was happy, and he was weightless, and he was free."
Nicole Dafoe

***

Colette's Words to Her Brother

"So many people require something of you: your attention, your affirmations, your time, not my brother Blaise. There were no conditions or unmet expectations. There was no judgement. He knew who he loved, and he loved them unconditionally with unmatched loyalty. He loved his family, and he loved his friends like family. I don't want to give away his secrets, and I can't tell you how many of you I've heard from that felt you had a 'special relationship' with him or that he was your 'best friend.'

"Blaise also loved traditions. I thought the three of us together with his brothers-in-law Dave and Adam and four nephews, and maybe his future wife and children, too, might be sitting at the top of the stairs together at 1829 Mountainview Drive waiting for permission to come down to open Christmas presents until we were 80 years old. Blaise lavished all of us with the most generous and carefully planned gifts, his latest hip hop mixes a favorite gift for his sisters every year, always an education for me but also his way of sharing something he loved because of the way it made him feel: the beat and authenticity.

"I thought that we would all judge the 4th of July fireworks over Little York Lake for the next 50 years and confidently agree that the current year's display was always better.

"Some of my favorite moments with my little brother have always been just lounging on the couch watching Seinfeld reruns or some late-night TV, learning what new show I should be watching from the only television critic I truly trusted. It didn't matter what was on though. Just being in the room with him was always enough. He didn't have to say anything and didn't expect me to fill the air. We could just be.

"I always knew what a big presence he held for me, not just his size or his giant sneakers
seemingly everywhere, but just his state of being. Blaise was always magnetic.

"I've been made acutely aware of his absence a thousand times since his death. Every time the door opens, I look up, waiting for him to almost duck as he walks in the room.

"I'm so sorry, Blaise. I was one of those people who demanded something of you. 'When are you coming to visit? When are you going to move to D.C. with us? What time are you coming home? Can you get off work early, so we can steal time with you? Can you come back out on the boat with us, even though you just got off and are headed inside? Can you come on vacation with us, maybe just for a couple of days? Can you stay out of trouble, Blaise? Can we wake you up before 6 a.m. to give you hugs and say goodbye before we hit the road?'

"It was always about stealing more time with him. I have always wanted more, and I always will."
Colette Dafoe

***

There is nothing fair or right about my son's untimely death. There is no poetic justice or balance. But I try to remind myself, my son's death was mercifully quick. He was not out driving when his heart split. He did not crash a car into another car while having a heart attack, taking away other lives in the process of losing his own. He was not at the family table eating dinner. He did not scream or cry out in agony, pleading with us to save him.

Leaving this life is never really peaceful or easy, but my son's death was quiet, like him.

Thirty-Two

Last Words

Before the rest of our household was awake, Blaise would shower, dress, pop in a capsule, and drink his Nespresso while smoking a cigarette on the front porch. I used to nag him about quitting smoking, sometimes rapping on a kitchen window with my disapproving look. He would look up, wryly smile at my persistence but never argue. There was something more he wanted to say, yet he always let that potential conflict go. No use getting into it with your mother over a cigarette.

I know he was thinking, "come on, Mom. I left the drugs and alcohol. Let me smoke a cigarette now and then."

A short time ago, I came out of a restaurant with my friend Judy McGinn when I nearly collided with a young man smoking near the entrance. A whiff of tobacco that I had always hated floated around me, and I welcomed it. I wanted to linger on the steps near the young man bathed in smoke and breathe in odors of those aged leaves.

More than that: I want to go back in time and light up a cigarette. I had never smoked in my entire life, but I wished to just stand on our front porch with my son, having a smoke together, quietly listening to the morning.

In these lines about my loss and love for my son, I recognize that memory is inherently unreliable. Even if every last detail, smoke curling around a young man on open porch, is unfailingly honest, it is in the details I have chosen that bias remains, my perspective alone. What I chose to ignore as well as what I chose to include are all part of life's story that leaves us with amorphous mysteries. Yet the duty of the memoirist is to state with as much honesty as possible what she set out to do: how my son grew from sweet little boy to quiet, reckless, and restless young man who was lost for a while. Then he became master of the direction of his life again, generously giving to others, turning into a gentle adult, a life arc of transformation, and finally, transcendence. Telling that complex story is, to say the least, daunting.

Recalling my son's last days when no one knew they would be, I caught Blaise at his dresser, getting his wallet and keys, turning to give me that half smile before heading out for the day. He was always leaving, busy. I had no idea at the time that he was driving a neighbor woman to work before he went to work himself. That he was buying diapers for a single mother; that he was dropping off a concerned mother at the hospital where her son had been admitted, that he was picking up a friend who had too much to drink and needed a ride home, and so much more. Then there would be his texts to me. Careless with his offhand, shorthand, but I wish I had held onto every single meaningless SMS bit of his language, now imbued with portent.

Filing papers in our library, I find Blaise's fifth grade report on his shoebox project. Topic: his favorite room. He wrote, "I selected my bedroom because I can go to sleep there and dream." I used to think he slept too much. With wisdom comes understanding. I now know that his predilection for sleep was likely symptomatic of his failing heart. I have given my wish for myself already: to be with him one last day. My only possible wish for him now is the long sleep of infinitely beautiful dreaming.

After the death of my son, I find I am attuned to the natural world around me from a different perspective. I am more cognizant of what is going on in nature. It is as if I can make myself very small and hear things I did not hear before. I watch birds, listen to their variety of songs in the morning, only recently learning to recognize different bird calls and what they may mean. Distinguishing between the blue jay's rough screech and the belted kingfisher's chittering rattle before flight. From a distance and to the less observant, those two very distinct birds look similar. The eagle's high-pitched call instantly silences cacophony of other birds when he flies overhead.

I am not constantly in mourning but always aware of loss in entirely new ways, as if grief had been waiting for me to assess life anew.

***

Sometimes Loss Weighs Lightly

Absence
of hummingbird nest from thinnest
of pine branches overhanging the porch
where, if I sat quietly,
she would seem to spontaneously appear,
hover near my face, dart sideways,
then settle onto lichen and spider silk nest.

Two chicks' spiked bills straight up,
like blackened toothpicks
jabbing air
until she arrived and offered bounty.

Absence

nothing at all like the time I gathered photographs
of my father who lay in his coffin,
congratulating myself on how I'd held it together
until I picked up his Syracuse cap.

Nothing at all like my brother's deepest dive,
or the way I felt when the Sherriff had to break
windows in my aunt's house to find her body,
or my mother mouthing words no longer hers.

Absence
nothing like the moment my son did not wake;
nothing whatsoever like seeing his shoes in the entrance
he would never walk through again.

Two summers the hummingbird had come
and made her nest in my tree,
but I haven't seen her since.

Even if I waited patiently all day and night—
sometimes loss weighs lightly,
but it always weighs.
  Yes, aware of loss but also keenly aware of how precious
life is.

***

  Drizzling rain dropping with temperatures, that kind of
weather seeping into everything. Time to take boats out of the
water; our big pontoon boat having seen better days, and our little
rowboat for fishing needs to be winterized. The county will be
lowering lake levels in a few days, and we don't want to find our
boats stuck in muck the way we did last year at this time. End of
season. They release valves in dam conduits, and down goes the
water.

Late getting our boats out of the lake last year, the two were sucked into mud more like thick syrup, and it took a small team of volunteers to help us lift them, float boats north to natural incline that serves as ramp in the Cortland County park at the other end of the lake. One year ago. One year before the day we easily removed our boats from the water, we were driving home from a hospital, leaving the body of our son.

Steering while crying, my husband glanced to his left as we crossed over the narrow bridge to our home.

"They lowered the lake," he said between stifled sobs. Still trying to locate speech, I could not quite comprehend. When we pulled up to our house, we could see our boats below dock level, not settled but sinking. Muck on the south end of the lake is feet, not inches, deep. What did it matter? Our 6-foot five-inch son's body lay on a hospital bed too short for him awaiting the medical examiner's arrival and autopsy. Blaise was gone, but all I wanted was to bring him with us for this seemingly impossible journey or to go with him myself.

When we arrived home, there was food waiting on the porch. It was raining then, too. Assembling a group, my husband was able to get our boats out, and we settled into internal muck, unable to think, only to descend. Even when we tried climbing out, grief has a way of sticking to you, pulling you back when you are managing otherwise herculean feats.

A year has come and gone, but cold drizzle outside belies the idea of change even if it is slowly insinuating itself. Still, we are not paralyzed, not as continually wracked with horror, just immeasurably sad, just aware of, living with, bottomless loss.

The country, too, has seen endings as a worldwide pandemic crossed boundaries into nearly everyone's lives, breaking ties, bodies, routines, concepts of normal, whole economies. There will, perhaps, someday be an end of COVID-19's daily presence in all of our lives. The dead from COVID-19 worldwide is nearly three million, well over 500,000 of them Americans, as the number of infected continues to rise, reaching millions upon millions in the world. As this strand of the novel coronavirus seems to be mutating, human life on the planet is changing, too. An end to "normalcy," whatever that means in our ever-changing world, certainly has meaning for Americans who are suddenly without work, without security, without means to provide for basic necessities of life. Life as we knew it. End stop.

With the onset of COVID-19, the world, our country began experiencing a metaphorical hailstorm: common decency in public discourse disappearing, empathy too often gone, even the pretense of sympathy for those less fortunate. There was a striking down of laws and regulations designed to protect air and water; disappearance of laws and regulations designed to prevent the millionaire class from permanently subjugating everyone else. Legislation designed to ensure healthcare was chipped away; legislation designed to ensure voting rights for people of color gutted, for starters. Over the last few years, attacks on voting rights and belief in science remain baffling. End of a belief in justice, however flawed, for far too many. End of any pretense of American exceptionalism. Seeming fractures of our European alliances and friendships, or at least recognizing the severe damage they have sustained. End of trust in institutions that protect a fragile "democracy." All democracies fragile, suddenly transparent.

End of an era in which racism and white supremacy were viewed as wrongs to be righted. Fracture to participation in the Paris Climate Accord. Fracture of participation in the UN Population Fund. End of trust in media reporting news, and the end of believing the facts before our eyes and those heard with our own ears. End of America's Century with a backward look. End of world respect. End of life for thousands of other species on the planet. End of some semblance of universally accepted reality and truth. End of United States citizens viewing one another as countrymen/women. End of the myths of capitalism. End of American idealism myths. Yet, for all of this loss, it is important to state, we can still be better.

End of the season. End of a way of life. And all of it, while national in scope, felt like an extension of the loss of our son. I could feel national pain through both my exterior and interior lenes.

Blaise made himself a better man the last few years of his life, an extraordinarily giving and kinder man. I thought I might try to be a better human being in the few years remaining of my own life. All of us might try to be better than we currently are.

***

After Lightning, Before Thunder

In absence, there is expanse.
I have lost time, not in a sense, as in,
"It's two o'clock already?"

I have lost progression,
timelines and while—
tempo and duration.

Winds beat my doors and windows
and compass can no longer
find true north.

As Emily Dickinson said,
"When everything that ticked
—has stopped—"

After the death of my father,
I thought it was a Tuesday
when Monday entered.

After the death of my mother,
I stepped outside and stared
at setting sun until dawn.

After the death of my brother,
I bent to pick up a small stone
and knew not where I was.

After the death of my son,
I dropped a glass, shattering,
and broke open the immeasurable.

***

With every great and terrible loss, there is also an opening in which something may change for the better or for the worse. But the possibility for better still exists.

Periodically, I erase text threads on my cellphone in clumps, destroying 50 or more at once. Every memory brought up by those old phone messages from my son now carries additional weight, foreshadowing not intended, but now read as such. So many messages running back and forth between us because Blaise liked to text. Wanting every last note from him back, I was grateful I still had at least a handful.

Our text messages were mostly about food: "Bring home Bob's Barbeque ribs with coleslaw and mac salad; don't forget carrot cake if they have it." Several texts in response to my warnings about avoiding police speed traps on certain roads, or requests for items to be picked up from the grocery store on the way home. Questions about what time he would get in. His gentle reminders to allay my ever-present fears: "You don't need to worry about me anymore, mom. I'm good." Reminders, an endless string of reminders from me to my son who no longer needed them. I would rather write that our last messages to one another involved a pithy dialogue, but that would be false. Yet, our abbreviated notes back and forth on a daily basis are exactly the stuff of life: food, warnings, reminders, fears, and unstated love.

I was about to clear away the last text messages from him, once believing there would be so many more to come. Yet these simple notes of seemingly insignificant bits of language had absurdly become critically important after his death.

Blaise's sister Colette called me this afternoon in the middle of her work day. She told me she was having a moment, a little panic attack over the loss of her brother, and she indulged her wishful thinking, deciding to text him because the act felt right: "I love you. I miss you so much. I hope you are all right." She hesitated in a moment of clarity before sending it into the ether anyway. There could not possibly be a response.

We closed out Blaise's phone number shortly after his death. Of course, the phone company reassigns numbers. Believing she was sending her message to Blaise into nothingness, Colette said she was stunned when someone texted back, "I'm okay. How are you?"

My daughter returned a text to the person answering and discovered that Blaise's old phone number had been given out to someone who knew him. The woman, another mother of a son, was gracious in answering my daughter's question, and wrote, "You can text Blaise/me anytime you want." What a kindness. We seldom realize how much goodness we can offer in small acts. Blaise certainly came to know and appreciate that fact.

***

Months after Blaise's death, a package arrived for me. I had no idea what was in the padded envelop and unwrapped it with perplexity. After layers of unwrapping, I found a metal bar attached to a silver necklace. The small silver bar had markings on it. I realized those indentations looked like voice images. A note in the package informed me of the impossible: "This necklace holds an image of a voice recording of your son Blaise's laugh. I hope you like it. Liv."

My former student and friend Olivia McKelvey had taken a video recording of Blaise laughing from his Facebook page. She had it made into a voice image. I played the video recording from his Facebook page, bursting into tears as he sprang back to life before me. Played it again and finally smiled rather than cried upon subsequent repetitions. Blaise was right with me, happy, enjoying life. Of all the many kindnesses I received after my son's death, this one holds prominence. It was a gesture of beneficence I will never forget. I put the chain around my neck and repeatedly touch the silver bar, hearing my son in my head again.

I want to text him about the necklace. During the last month of his life, I retained that small cadre of more recent messages from Blaise. I look at those texts now and think, he had fourteen days left to live. On this date, he had ten days left to live. He had four days left of his life. His tragic death elevated those trivial notes to ones of gravity, of consequence and value.

There were few last words from him still preserved in his text messages to me: "love you too. What are you making for dinner? Pizza and More? Happy Bday btw! Alls good. Got you something. Picked it out, no help. Haha. All's well. Have an awesome time. AC on for ya. Good to have ya back. Don't worry. I'm fine. Bogie's good. Mom, I got this."

When our front door opens and closes late at night, for half an instant, I sense my son coming in the house. Even when my logic tells me my husband is downstairs putting out the garbage for morning pickup. For those few moments, I hear my son returning with the click of that latch.

Mystery of our temporality, and the questions of how to mark "we were here," remain. This import is why we suffer over wording on gravestones, fantasize about our legacies. Blaise moved through his part of the world quietly, yet dynamically, and with uncommon grace in every sense of the word, and at the end, extended extraordinary kindness in trying to help others.

I am stopped when coming across 17th Century poet Andrew Marvell's quotation in Wendell Berry's novel *Jayber Crow*: "Magnanimous Despair alone/ Could show me so divine a thing." There is something of divinity in absolute love and loss.

Struggling over what to have incised on his black marble gravestone, we came to accept his sister Nicole's suggestion for the words for her brother because each phrase rang true to the once boy and man he became:

***

Ever Cool

Ever Kind

Ever Thoughtful

Ever Young

***

That last phrase still makes me break down each time I read or see it. Blaise will be forever young to those of us who continue to age until our own ends. He will be no older than the last time we saw him. I miss him terribly. I am at moments desolate but not every second of the day and night. At our end, life itself is both illusory and real. Desolation comes and goes. It is not with me in the way in which love is constant.

Indeed, I am fortunate in that I continue to experience love from others: the great and lasting love of my wonderful husband Daniel and generous love from my beautiful daughters, and my four little grandsons. The love from my friends. I remember the love from my son and the love I forever hold for him. I am also daily reminded of the many individuals who loved Blaise, his friends and fellow travelers through this world.

I knew my son. He lived with his father and me at the beginning and at the end. We did not know about the rare genetic syndrome that led to his death. Neither did his doctors detect it.

All would have remained secret but for an extraordinary medical examiner. His death was sudden and ultimately a conundrum. Yes, we knew Blaise, likely better than anyone, yet he remains a mystery to me, an incredible, beautiful mystery, as is life itself.

"If the past, present and future come together, as we sense they must, then death is a process of becoming," wrote Dr. BJ Miller in his essay "What is death?" that appeared in the December 18, 2020 issue of *The New York Times*. Yes, we ask that question again and again.

If I could give Blaise one last note, it would be: "My son, your life was over far too soon for all those who loved you, but your journey to find yourself, to be fully you, to give to others and forgive yourself, was complete." He must have known this, too.

The last text Blaise ever sent me, the night before his unexpected death, the text that is first and forever on my phone message wall is simply, "Heading home."

Index of Poetry by the Author

Index of Writer References

About the Author

Author and educator Nancy Avery Dafoe writes across genres and has won multiple awards for her work, including the William Faulkner/William Wisdom creative writing competition in poetry (2016). She won the international short story competition from New Century Writers and first prize in prose poetry from the Soul-Making Literary competition, among other awards. Dafoe has twelve published books.

In addition to her memoir *Unstuck in Time* (Pen Women Press), Dafoe wrote about her mother's Alzheimer's and its effect on the family in her memoir *An Iceberg in Paradise: A Passage Through Alzheimer's* (SUNY Press). Her novella *Naimah and Ajmal on Newton's Mountain* (FLP) joins her other fiction work: three mystery novels, *You Enter a Room, Both End in Speculation,* and *Murder on Ponte Vecchio* (RPP). Her poetry books include *The House Was Quiet, But the Mind Was Anxious; Innermost Sea;* and *Poets Diving in the Night* (FLP). In addition, Dafoe has books on educational policy and teaching writing published through Rowman & Littlefield Education: *Breaking Open the Box, The Misdirection of Education Policy,* and *Writing Creatively.*

Her fiction, poetry, and nonfiction appear in several anthologies, including *Lost Orchard* (SUNY Press) and *Lost Orchard II* (PWP); *NY Votes for Women: A Suffrage Centennial Anthology* (Cayuga Lake Books); and in literary journals and magazines.

Dafoe has taught English and writing in a variety of settings, including high school, community college, and workshops. She is a member of the NLAPW and former Central New York (CNY) Branch president and NLAPW Letters Chair. She lives with her husband Daniel in Homer, New York.